POVERTY OF GANDHIAN PHILOSOPHY

GANDHIAN STUDIES AND PEACE RESEARCH SERIES (GSPRS)

1. Gandhian Model of Development and World Peace, **R.P. Misra**
2. Conflict Resolution Through Non-Violence : Role of the Universities, Vol. I : Science and Ethics, **K.D. Gangrade** and **R.P. Misra**
3. Conflict Resolution Through Non-Violence : Role of the Universities, Vol. II : Development without Destruction, **K.D. Gangrade** and **R.P. Misra**
4. The Social Philosophy of Mahatma Gandhi, **K.S. Bharathi**
5. Gandhian Humanism, **Mohit Chakrabarty**
6. Gandhian Holistic Economics, **Shashi Prabha Sharma**
7. Gandhian Spiritualism : A Quest for the Essence of Excellence, **Mohit Chakrabarty**
8. Gandhian Perspective on Population and Development, **A.K. Sharma**
9. Thoughts of Gandhi and Vinoba : A Comparative Study, **K.S. Bharathi**
10. Economic Philosophy of Mahatma Gandhi, **Shanti Swarup Gupta**
11. The Political Thoughts of Mahatma Gandhi, **K.S. Bharathi**
12. Gandhi and 21st Century, **Janardan Pandey** (Ed.)
13. Gandhian Philosophy of the Spinning Wheel, **Mohit Chakrabarty**
14. Gandhian Satyagraha : An Analytical and Critical Approach, **Ajay Shankar Rai**
15. Gandhi and His Religion, **P.A. Raju**
16. महात्मा गाँधी —विचार वीथिका, **एस॰पी॰ अग्रवाल**

About the Author

Dr. Himansu Roy was former Principal of Ananda Mohan College, Calcutta. He was also a member of the Undergraduate Council of Calcutta University and a Calcutta University Nominee on the West Bengal College Service Commission.

Dr. Roy is the founder-editor of Economic Affairs, an internationally accepted research journal, since 1956.

Dr. Roy is a constructive analyst and critic. His Tea Price Stabilization – The India Case stirred the tea world in sixties. *The Economic Times* writes in its review column : "it has become difficult to raise fresh funds to develop the tea industry. Had Prof. Roy's ideas been accepted... such a situation could have been avoided". V.D. Wickizer from Standford conveyed congratulations: "for the successful development of your ideas and plans for India".

Dr. Roy was invited as a guest in seminar organized by the Tea Board. He had also participated in the seminar organized by Merchants' Chamber of Commerce, Calcutta on "Impact of Fiscal Policy on National Economy", contributing a paper 'Taxation Policy and the Corporate Sector'. Dr. Roy's latest book is 'Critique of Leninism', 1994.

Gandhian Studies and Peace Research Series–17

POVERTY OF GANDHIAN PHILOSOPHY

HIMANSU ROY

CONCEPT PUBLISHING COMPANY, NEW DELHI - 110059

ISBN 81-7022-902–2

First Published 2001

Published and Printed by

Ashok Kumar Mittal
Concept Publishing Company
A/15-16, Commercial Block, Mohan Garden,
NEW DELHI -110059 (India)

Phones : 5648039, 5649024
Fax : 091-11-5648053
Email : *publishing@conceptpub.com*

IN
MEMORY
OF
BELOVED
UMA ROY

PREFACE

M.K. Gandhi was a social being, noble in character, modest in ambition. He left India for South Africa to earn bread by labour. There suddenly came a turn in his life. He was the victim of racism of the Whites. His experiences made him realize that an unarmed man must have arms and men to win the might of the mightiest. But that arms are the soul-force and the men are purified hearts. For only the soul-force of the purified hearts can win the sword-force, however mighty may it be. Sword to sword leads to incessant violence and anarchy while conversion of hearts will lead to eternal peace. And in and through the very process of conversion the truth will be realized. Thus, to Gandhi's thought non-violence is the only means of redress and realization of truth. Man is born grand, shows devilism under pressure of circumstances. The devilry is an outward phenomenon. It should be distanced through non-cooperation. This is what non-violent non-cooperation is. In order to redress the problems and realize the truth experience and experiment is needed and through experimentations perfection will come in. Thus, Gandhi emerged as an astute experimentalist.

Gandhi came back to India to experiment his philosophy on Indian soil. He entered into Congress not to be a politician to make politics his profession but to make politics the instrument of his experiment. To him politics is not untouchable to religion. Life is inseparable from politics and politics is full of problems. And Gandhi's experiment was to redress all the problems by means of compromise and conversion following the means of non-violent non-cooperation. Secularism does not mean exclusion of religion from politics. It means insertion of 'dharma' in politics with wide spiritual sense of 'tolerance'.

However, he took up the helm of the Congress which was then the only national organization; under its leadership the people were struggling for freedom. Then from 1920 onwards the people were under the one-man leadership of Gandhi. The result was such that India was divided into two and freedom was won over the flow of blood of people and agony and anger of millions of refugees who were hovering round for life and living. All this reveals the poverty of Gandhian philosophy.

But that does not mean that the poverty is absolute. There is plenty of truth and reality in it. A glimpse of the world today will show how the world is passing through incessant courses of experience and experiment to catch up the means of non-violent non-cooperation. The globalization, environmental pollution, non-proliferation on the one side and inequality, poverty and domination of a new class of capitalist power on the other are well written in Gandhi's thought and as a positivist he has also made tract for redress. And as a man professed by truth his journey was for eternal truth. Man is world, the world is the manifestation of truth. The journey of the world must be for eternity. Here lies the essence of Gandhian philosophy.

The purpose of the present labour is to highlight the poverty in plenty of Gandhi's philosophy to build up his image clean of myths surrounding him.

HIMANSU ROY

CONTENTS

1

PHILOSOPHY

In Search of Truth

Introduction

Mohan Das Karamchand Gandhi (Gandhi) was born at Porbandar (Sudamapuri) in Gujarat on 2nd October 1869. He belonged to a *banian* (trading) caste. His father Karamchand Gandhi was for some time the Prime Minister in Rajkot and then in Vankaner. The family was *vaishnava* by sect and highly religious and conservative in outlook. Gandhi's mother would not take meals without performing her daily prayers. His father had no education, save that of experience. He too in his last days used to read the *Bhagavad Gita* and repeat aloud some verses everday at the time of worship. Gandhi himself inculcated religious spirit. His mother impressed him most : "The outstanding impression my mother has left on my memory is that of saintliness."[1] At that stage his spiritual philosopher was a nurse, an old maidservant of the family, named Rambha. It was Rambha who advised Gandhi, who was by nature timid and fearful of thieves, ghosts and serpents, to repeat '*Ramanama*' to overcome all fearness. Gandhi followed her advice upto the last. He writes : "I think it is due to the seed sown by that good woman Rambha that today *Ramanama* is an infallible remedy for me."[2] Throughout his life he chanted 'Ram'; even he breathed his last saying : 'Hey Ram'

Towards Truth

The *Ramayana* and the *Bhagavad Gita* ever evoked religious fervour in the gracious heart of Gandhi. He was a sanatan Hindu and was ever proud to say that he was a Hindu himself and that he was a sanatan Hindu. Gandhi, however, ever showed tolerance to all branches of Hinduism and the sister religions. The Gandhis by tradition had inter-cultural relations with the Jain monks and also friendly relations with the Muslims and Parsis. At one stage Gandhi took interest in the *Manusmriti* but in the laws of Manu he could not trace *ahimsa* (non-violence). However, contrary, the *Manusmriti* impressed him : "But one thing took deep root in me – the conviction that morality is the basis of things, and that truth is the substance of all morality. Truth became my sole objective. It began to grow in magnitude every day, and my definition of it also has been ever widening."[3]

What is Truth?

To Gandhi 'Truth is God'. But what is God? To him : "God is not a person, but an immutable law." In this case the Law and the Maker are one. Gandhi's expression : "In ordinary expression the word 'law' means books of law, but here when I speak of law, I mean the living law. That is what God is. And this law does not change; it is eternal. It is not a personal God who changes with changing circumstances. God is an eternal principle, and that is why I have said that Truth is God."[4]

Truth and Love

Gandhi was accosted with : "Why Truth is God and not Love is God? Gandhi says : "I too say God is love. But in my heart I thought that though God may be love, God is above all, Truth."[5] Gandhi's apathy to Love lies in some sort of sense of passion in it. Besides, it bears many meanings. But Truth has no double meaning. His adherence to Truth has another essence, that is to cover up the atheists : "In their passion to discover truth, the atheists have not hesitated to deny the existence of God, *and from their point of view they are right*. It is because of this reasoning that I decided that rather than anything 'God is Truth'. I should say 'Truth is God'.[6]

Incidentally, to Swami Vivekananda, an Advaitist : 'God, the Truth, the *Atman*'. About the agnostics and atheists his saying: "the agnosticism of Buddhists and the atheism of Jains, each and all have a place in the Hindu religion."[7] Gandhi's compromising spirit of making Love is God is to make Love as the means and God as the end, that is, to make 'means' and 'end' inseparable in substance. Thus : "when you want to find the Truth which is God, the only infallible way to it is by Love, which means non-violence. And since I believe in the last analysis the end and the means are interchangeable terms, I have no hesitation in saying that God is Love."[8] In short, non-violence is the only means to realize the object, be it freedom, Truth or God.

Inner Voice

Gandhi has another vision of Truth which is absolutely a subjective and self centric concept : "I have solved it for myself by saying that it is what the 'inner voice' tells me."[9] The 'inner voice' is nothing else than the voice of God inside the man. It is the voice of his master who prompts, it is the voice which works – man being a dummy functionary. This does not mean that man has no consciousness, intuition, intelligence or reasonings. He has the possession but above all he is possessed by Truth.

The 'inner voice' in each may voice differently or may be conceived differently by different persons at the same time. Then, whose understanding will prevail? Gandhi says : "It follows that what may be truth for one man is non-truth for another. Those who seek truth in this way have come to the conclusion that certain conditions must first be observed. In the same way that there are indispensable courses of scientific instruction to be undergone before anyone can carry out scientific experiments, a strict preliminary discipline is necessary before a person can be qualified to make experiments in the spiritual domain."[10]

Gandhi 'qualified' himself to carry out scientific experiments getting through the indispensable courses : Chastity (*Brahmacharya*), Non-violence, Poverty, Non-possession. He expressed categorically that "it is not fitting for everyone to claim that he hears the voice of conscience. [11] He then added: "And since now-a-days everyone demands the right to speak of his conscience without having undergone any kind of discipline at all, and since there are so many non-truths in this disoriented world, all I can say to you in all true humility is that *truth cannot be found by anyone who has not achieved an abundant sense of humility*. If you want to swim in the bosom of ocean of Truth, you must reduce yourself to zero."[12]

It follows that 'democracy' was a mockery to Gandhi. For only that man has the right to lead the country who has qualified to hear the 'inner voice', that is, the 'voice of conscience'. And it was only Gandhi himself, qualified as such, who had the right to lead the country. Possibly this enthused Gandhi mentally to play the role of the dictator in Congress politics with profound interest to become the 'world teacher' of non-violence and truth at the same time.

Means and End

To Gandhi means is not mere means, means is after all everything. He says : "For me it is enough to know the means. Means and end are convertible terms in my philosophy of life."[13] He proceeds : "There is no wall of separation between means and end. Indeed, the Creator has given us control (and that too very limited) over means, none over the end. Realization of the goal is in exact proportion to that of means. This is a proposition that admits of no exception. Holding such belief, I have been endeavouring to keep the country to means that are purely 'peaceful and legitimate'."[14]

Thus, in the domain of Gandhi there had been no place of compromise with violent revolution : "Violent means will give violent *swaraj*. That would be a mennace to the world and to

India herself."[15] His assertion was that let there be no *swaraj* than *swaraj* by means of violence. His emotional expression : "When India accepts the supremacy of brute force, I should no longer be happy to call her my motherland."[16] So affirmative was he that he did not hesitate to say that a revolutionary "does the evil and dies."

Was Gandhi himself a brave non-violent soldier? No, and that was his own admission : "There is lot of cowardice in me." In facing a communal riot his heart 'trembled' : "I do not know how high the blood-pressure rose." If that be the condition of the supremo of the non-violent revolutionists then what could be expected under his leadership? Does it carry any moral or practical value when shivering Gandhi says that the *satyagrahi* should go and get killed but not in anger but out of love? Once being confounded he said : "I found that there were many hurdles in our way, if you ask me how we can overcome all these, I can give neither you nor myself a satisfactory answer. I would only say that if you believe in these principles you too should experiment with me. In that case, we shall certainly find the way."[17] That is, let the people of India go on experimenting with him the doctrine of *ahimsa* and then let them see when and what becomes the result. But what dared Gandhi to call the people to experiment with him when he himself was coward and imperfect in practice of non-violence? Perhaps that was his understanding with the 'inner voice'.

Double Object : Principle

The Gandhian philosophy has double object : Principle and Policy. The idea of principle is to realize the 'end', the 'truth'; and the idea of policy is the 'means' of redressment for realization of truth. Gandhi was a 'practical idealist' as well. His policy was to objectify the means of non-violence for redressment of the problems of everyday life : "But after all my non-violence cannot deviate from what is practical. I wish to work through non-violence while yet solving the problems of everyday life."[18] Sometimes he became so emotional that he did not hesitate to contradict himself : "If while I am a Minister Hindus and Muslims start fighting amongst themselves, and if I realize that I can stop this violence and bloodshed by calling in the army and having a handful of men shot, I would have to resort to this course for the sake of restoring order. I will have to give orders to stop the massacre with the least violence."[19] It is nonetheless the 'truthful means'.

Gandhi was ever aware that man is born violent. Yet to him man is by nature non-violent. In order to spiritualize the concept of non-violence he says : "We fulfil our human life when we see the *atman*, and when we do so we pass the test."[20] Realization of God means seeing Him in all things, that is, we should learn to become one with every creature. And this is the privilege of man that distinguishes him from the beasts. For Gandhi non-violence is a matter of faith and devotion. He who has no faith in the *atman*, or in God and prayer, non-violence is not going to prove useful to him. That is, non-violence has no purpose to the non-believer in God and prayer.

But what about the natural law that 'life lives on life'? Gandhi attempts to resolve this by classifying 'violence' as outward and inward. He says : "Man cannot for a moment live without consciously or unconsciously committing outward *himsa*. The very fact of his living – eating, drinking and moving about – necessarily involves some *himsa*, destruction of life, be it ever so minute... he can never become entirely free from outward *himsa*.[21] Thus, man is outwardly violent but inwardly pure, which calls for further purification and that is the function of non-violence, the soul-force. If so, can it be said that a militant revolutionist transgresses Gandhian concept of outward violence and inward purity? A man cannot sacrifice his noble life without inward purification. On that score Gandhi's explanation is a bit compromising as he holds that a militant revolutionist is 'misguided and doomed to fail'. Such contradictions are not uncommon in Gandhi's character. Whenever, he is trapped with contradictions he manages to distance himself : "As for my own attitude whilst my faith would not permit me to invite or encourage a war of violence, I do contemplate with equanimity a state of war in preference to the present state of effeminate peace imposed by force of arms."[22]

Policy

The object of Gandhian policy was to politicize *ahimsa* as the means to win freedom for India and transform the world as a whole from violence to non-violence. Intuitively, the policy was to convert the brutes to grands by means of non-violence. For Gandhi it would be a hard task but not absurd. He traced sleeping grands in the hearts of devils. For in all beings there exists the spirit of God. These devilish hearts could be won by 'love for enemies', that is, by non-violent means and by non-cooperation with the evil spirit of the being. For Gandhi non-cooperation is not an act of violence nor is it enmity towards the wrong-doer. He is only deprived of his doing wrong. But to inflict punishment on the wrong-doer is violence. Gandhi illustrates : "If a man kills a little child and robs it of its ornament and if I deprive him of the liberty to repeat the performance, I would not call my act violence. It would be violence, if my act was meant to be punishment."[23] That is, deprivation of wrong-doing is not an act of punishment nor violence; it is the means of 'conversion'. According to Gandhi to realize God or any object one should shun voluntarily all physical force and develop the consciousness of non-violence as the true force which is latent in every one of us and this will come out only of strength. He also says that non-violence is not a 'direct action' but a 'direct active expression'. And it is "the greatest and activest force in the world. One cannot be passively non-violent. . . one person who can express *ahimsa* in life exercises a force superior to all the forces of brutality."[24] Gandhi had aversion to the expression of non-violence as 'passive resistance'.

Gandhi pitied the weak and helpless because of their duality: "The weak and helpless are non-violent in action, because they must be. But in reality, they harbour violence in their hearts and simply avail of an opportunity for its display."[25] He however, overlooked another class whose faith in non-violence was simply to avail of an opportunity to display its violent character to wield power which was a danger to nation. However, what Gandhi asserted was that 'non-cooperation' and 'non-violence' were not a contradiction in terms. And as such non-violent non-cooperation became the instrument of Gandhi's movement for freedom.

Gandhi was an astute politician. His adoption of non-violent non-cooperation policy was to convince the people of the superior force of non-violence. He marked out the contrast between the two opposite forces : Violence, the 'sword-force', and, non-violence, the 'soul-force'. He said that Hitler and Mussolini on the one hand and Stalin on the other were able to show immediate effectiveness of violence. But that would be transitory as that of Jhenghis slaughter. Whereas "the effects of Buddha's non-violent action persist and are likely to grow with age. And the more it is practised, the more effective and inexhaustible it becomes, and ultimately the whole mankind stands agape and exclaims, 'a miracle has happened'. All miracles are due to the silent and effective working of invisible forces. Non-violence is the most invisible and most effective."[26] Gandhi unfortunately reduced the existence of the 'third force', which was superior force – the force of sword in the hands of the supreme force of soul.

Gandhi ventured to create around himself a holy spectre to explain : 'a miracle has happened'. But in the world to date no 'miracle' has happened due to the effects of 'invisible force'. Whatever 'miracle' has happened it is the effect of violence – mental or physical – in the forms of : science and war, war and science; peace and war, war and peace. And then in course of progression of violence the greater urge of mind is to realize the Absolute. About the 'invisible force' : Where are Buddha, Jesus, Ram and Rahim? Is it not that time has confined them in temples? Is it not that the process of 'conversion' is the aggression of 'sword-force'? Can it be denied that the Buddha's non-violent action is the major cause of the poor quantitative result of Buddhism?[26a] What does it indicate when Gandhi says : "Indeed most of the scriptures of the world seem even to go beyond non-cooperation and prefer violence to effeminate submission to a wrong."[27] Thus, be it in religion or in politics violence did play a vital role in determining the man. This hard truth cannot be jumped over by any 'Mahatma', however great he may be. Life is transitory. It needs immediate effect – the ultimate or eternity is simply relaxation in worldly life and thought. Revolution against 'accumulation' is nothing but a radical turn in the process of evolution for realization of 'self-consciousness'. Gandhi had conceded that "A violent and bloody revolution is a certainty one day unless there is a voluntary abdication of riches and the power that riches give and sharing them for the common good."[28] Gandhi time and again dallied with 'miracle' as the blessing of the 'invisible force'. But the world needs some visible force to deal straightway with the visible evils all around at right time with right measures. God may be Law, unchangeable. But the 'lips' and 'scriptures' are not necessarily unchangeable or cannot be reinterpreted. For they are the makings of 'prophets', born with flesh and blood. That is, what is determined today is undetermined tomorrow. Thus the 'miracle' is a false objectification of 'idea' as fantastic as dependence on the pleasure of 'invisible force'.

To conclude, Gandhi's policy of 'redress' and principle of 'truth' bear both political and spiritual strategy to display simultaneously the miracle of invisible force. As a practical idealist Gandhi came down to the people, religiously cultured and economically poor and depressed, to convince them that the 'soul-force' was the only means to win freedom and salvation. He demonstrated it in politics with surprising success chanting all through *Ramanama*.

His political demonstration was so great a success that the people really stood up agape and exclaimed 'a miracle has happened'. But his persistence in 'truth' distanced himself from the people, particularly of the other communities. The people might be convinced about *ahimsa* as the means of winning freedom. But Gandhi himself remained unconvinced : "I know that non-cooperation was a dangerous experiment, non-cooperation in itself is unnatural, vicious and sinful. But non-violent non-cooperation, I am convinced, is a sacred duty at times... Non-violent non-cooperation was the only alternative to anarchy and worse."[29] It is clear that Gandhi constructed his policy of non-violent non-cooperation to thwart the violent revolution to win freedom. This is further exposed in his words : "I dispute the claim that the revolutionaries are succeeding with the villagers. But if they are, I am sorry, I shall spare no pains to frustrate their effort."[30] This makes the observation of Romain Rolland highly significant : "However pure this may be, it hinders the freedom of his vision. The social experiment is always open, always in progress. It cannot be subordinated to any sentimental preference or to any creed. If Gandhi does not succeed in breaking away from the hold of the past which is delaying his march forward, he is bound to lose control of the great Indian movement, which is already beginning to go beyond him."[31] This prediction was not prophetic but analytical that Gandhi had to admit murmuringly at the edge of his life.

The Man

Gandhi was not a philosopher nor a politician. He was explicit in saying that he had not originated any new principle nor any doctrine neither in philosophy nor in social science. In his words : "There is no such thing as 'Gandhism', and I do not want to leave any sect after me. I do not claim to have originated any new principle or doctrine. I have simply tried in my way to apply the external truths to our daily life and problems... The opinions I have formed and the conclusions I have arrived at are not final; I may change them tomorrow. I have nothing new to teach the world. Truth and non-violence are as old as the hills. All I have done is to try experiments in both on as vast a scale as I could do."[32] In short, Gandhi was an applied scientist – a tryst with destiny "to convert every Indian, even Englishmen and finally the world to non-violence."[33] He aspired not to be a Buddha or Jesus, who were teachers and preachers with prophetic character, but to usher in a new era in the world history demonstrating personally how to convert by means of *ahimsa* the devils into grands, wipe out the weeds of *himsa* (violence) from the soil of earth to make the livings peaceful for self-realization of the Absolute.

This tall idea of Mahatma was unimpressive to reality of that era. The people of India welcomed him as a political hero and not as the maker of *ahimsa* era. For to them freedom was their only consideration. And to the intellectuals of the world *ahimsa* has no role to play in social science. The social science is concerned with 'system' which has taken the turn of 'modern civilization' due to the contributions of the capitalist system. The 'grands' have been reduced to 'devils' because of this system. So long as the capitalist system prevails and nature provides unending sources of material pleasure the Gandhi's 'inward purity' will remain dormant. Gandhi's focal point was not the 'system' but the applicability of *ahimsa* in daily life. The Indians at the time of Gandhi were undergoing the experience of the devilish character of the colonial rule. They wanted to get rid of the yoke of slavery by any means. And thereafter to experiment with a new system as an alternative to the capitalist system and its attributes to modern civilization. Gandhi's emotional outburst of 'a miracle has happened' was pleasing but unproductive to history. Of course, Gandhi had little regard for history : "Whatever conclusions I may have come to in my life, I have not drawn them from history, which played a very small part in my education. My method is empirical; all my conclusions are based on my personal experience."[34] His reality : get killed but don't kill; it is not submission, it is 'redemption'. The people's inner urge: 'freedom' without submission, and then contemplation of 'redemption'; don't hit, but hit back; don't beg, but assert; their call 'Quit India or feel the dire consequences'. Gandhi might be horrified. But that was the actual passion of the Indians at that time. The world history would boast had that passion been experimented with by Gandhi.

Instead Gandhi's *ahimsa* as the sole means of liberation inducted religiosity into Indian politics. But Gandhi was not least worried about that. For "Politics bereft of religion are the death trap because they kill the soul."[35] Further : "For me there is no distinction between politics and religion."[36] But in reality religion in politics developed more distrust and disunity. His recurring observations : "Islam is said openly to preach violence to the wrong-doer... The so-called votaries of Christianity justify organized warfare for the removal of wrongs, fancied or real."[37] Whatever, may be the nobility of purpose, it could not be expected that it would be taken with the idea of tolerance by the fundamentalists and their associate politicians. But Gandhi was a man of the external world. To him *ahimsa* was not for India's freedom, but for 'eternal freedom' : "my patriotism is for me a stage of my journey to the land of eternal freedom and peace."

The 'unity' depends on cementation of common causes to unite the whole without any discrimination for realization of universal eternal freedom and peace. But he had faintly discovered in his means the common causes. What he had discovered was the mandate of the 'inner voice' : conversion by soul-force to gain the 'miracle'. Such obsession was reverse of tolerance to other faiths.

Knowing Gandhi

To know Gandhi was to know beforehand the characteristics of his faith and morality.

1. He was a *vaishnava* with indepth religious temper and tolerance : "One who does not follow truth and has not acquired control over all senses is not a *vaishnava*.[38]
2. To him Hinduism is the most glorious religion : "Hinduism with its message of *ahimsa* is to me the most glorious religion in the world."[39] He was ever proud to say that he was an orthodox Hindu.
3. He was not a saint : "It is too sacred a word." He "claims only to be a humble searcher after truth." Nor was he a politician : "the politician in me has never dominated a single decision of mine."[40]
4. He was scientist experimenting with *ahimsa* in social

science : "like a scientist, is making experiments about some of 'the eternal verities' of life." He sketched his contrast with Christ : "Christ died on the Cross... defying the might of a whole Empire... I raise resistance of a non-violent character."[41]

5. His dependence on mystic 'inner voice' and dogmatic faith in *ahimsa* made him intolerant of *himsa* making him a dictator : "my word will be law."

6. His policy of redress by means of compromise for the sake of his principle of truth made him a 'half-way' leader : "The *hartal* illuminated the whole of India as if by magic on the 6th of April, 1919. And had it not been for the interruption of the 10th of April, brought about by *Satan* whispering fear into the ears of a Government conscious of its own wrong and inciting to anger a people that were prepared for it by utter distrust of the Government, India would have risen to an unimaginable height."[42] Incidentally, the movement was subsequently withdrawn in apprehension of violence.

7. He sought national unity without any common cause. However, he had his own cause much higher than the aspiration of the people : "I would not be tempted to give up my striving after *moksha* even for the sake of *swaraj*."[43]

8. His mission was to be the maker of a new world depending on the voice of *Bhagavad Gita* defying the might of the whole world history. This is well exposed in the genesis of his 'trusteeship' as the higher stage of capitalism : "I understand more clearly in the light of the *Gita* teaching the implication of the word 'trustee'... I discovered in it religion."[44]

Now, to know the voice working in Gandhi it is wise to follow him : "I am a person with an inquiring mind. With great patience I am discovering and developing the science of *satyagraha*. In the course of this search I am acquiring new knowledge and new light every day."[45] Thus, Gandhi was a discoverer and developer acquiring new knowledge and new light every day to search out the 'truth'. Freedom of India was a part of his effort for *moksha*. He was performing *tapascharya* for *moksha*. He entered into Congress with the sole purpose of attaining *moksha*. His discovery was a 'novel policy' – non-violence. He had to test it. And the ground was there where violence prevailed, that is, in politics and power, and that caused him to enter into Congress politics. He said: "My non-violence is tested in the Congress where I am opposed, censured and criticised... There I grow."[46] There he developed his policy of non-cooperation to make non-violence active : "The method of non-violence implies that when we do not have the capacity to undo an evil, we should keep away from it. This is non-cooperation. I have placed before India the great principle of non-cooperation. I am applying that very principle here."[47]

All this indicates that Gandhi was not a great national freedom fighter. He was an experimentalist with non-violent non-cooperation with the yearning for *moksha*. That is, self-salvation, making all other objects secondary.

If the 'experiment' fails? The implied answer is let the people suffer and let the nation be torn into pieces. Any experiment may fail so Gandhi bears no responsibility. He said again and again that he was an experimentalist in quest of Truth, might be a 'Mahatma' but was not a saint nor a politician.

NOTES AND REFERENCES

1. M.K.Gandhi, *An Autobiography*, Navajivan Publishing House, Ahmedabad, 1988. p. 4.
2. *Ibid.*, p. 36.
3. *Ibid.*, p. 39.
4. Romain Rolland, *Diary*, Dec. 1921 in Romain Rolland and Gandhian Correspondence, Publications Division, GOI, New Delhi, 1976, p. 188.
5. *Ibid.*
6. *Ibid.*

7. Selections from Swami Vivekananda, *Advaita Ashram*, Calcutta, 1981, p. 3.
8. Romain Rolland, *op. cit.*, p. 189.
9. *Ibid.*
10. *Ibid.*, pp. 189-90.
11. *Ibid.*, p. 190.
12. *Ibid.*
13. *Ibid.*
14. Collected Works of Mahatma Gandhi, *op. cit.*, Vol. 24, p. 398.
15. *Ibid.*
16. *Ibid.*, Vol. 18, p. 158.
17. *Ibid.*, Vol. 66, p. 434.
18. *Ibid.*, p. 438.
19. *Ibid.*
20. *Ibid.*, Vol. 66, p. 421.
21. *Autobiography*, *op. cit.*, pp. 407-08.
22. Collected Works, Vol. 19, p. 560.
23. Tendulkar, Vol. 4, p. 316.
24. *Ibid.*, p. 49.
25. *Harijan*, March 26, 1938.
26. Tendulkar, *Mahatma*, Vol. 4, pp. 141-142.

26a. Because of non-aggressive character of Hinduism and Buddhism they are quantitatively poor: Hinduism (C 1500 BC) : 764,000,000 ; Buddhism (C 500 BC): 338,621,000; Christianity (1st C AD) : 1,900,174,000; Islam (7th C AD): 1,033,453,000. *Source* : World Almanac of Facts, *The Statesman*, Calcutta, 4-9-96.

27. Collected Works of Mahatma Gandhi, Vol. 18, p. 116.
28. Tendulkar, Vol. 6, pp. 26-27.
29. Collected Works of Mahatma Gandhi, Vol. 25, p. 199 : While on fast on September 22, 1924.
30. *Ibid.*, Vol. 26, p. 49.
31. Romain Rolland, *Diary*, April 1935.
32. Tendulkar, Vol. 4, p. 54.
33. *Harijan*, January 13, 1940.
34. Romain Rolland, *Diary*, December 1931.

35. Tendulkar *et at, Gandhi – His Life and Works*, 1945.
36. Collected Works of Mahatma Gandhi, Vol. 22, p. 404.
37. *Ibid.*, Vol. 18, p. 219.
38. *Nabajiban*, Dec. 5, 1920.
39. *Young India*, Jan. 19, 1928.
40. *Ibid.*, May 12, 1920.
41. *Ibid.*
42. Tendulkar, *op. cit.*, Vol. 5, p. 262.
43. *Young India*, May 12, 1920.
44. *Autobiography, op. cit.*, pp. 305-306.
45. Letter to Mathuradas Trikunsji, Nov. 1, 1921.
46. Speech at Gandhi Seva Sangha, Feb. 21, 1940.
47. *Ibid.*

2

A TURN IN LIFE

Experience and Experiment

Gandhi belonged to a middle class family. He had to have his bread by labour. He passed the matriculation examination in 1887. He could not stick to college because of his rawness : "I was so raw. At the end of the first term, I returned home".[1] To become graduate was an impossible task for him. His guardians decided that he should be sent to England to become a member of Bar-at-Law, which was a short and easier course to make a career. Gandhi's mother initially did not agree to allow her son to cross the sea. However, she agreed when Gandhi vowed that he would not touch wine and women there and would also not take meat. Gandhi married Kasturba when he was only thirteen years old. His wife was also almost of same age.

In June 1891 Gandhi was called to the bar (humorously known as 'dinner barristers') and then sailed for home. He was aware of his deficiencies as a lawyer so much so that he did not think himself qualified to practise law. In fact, he proved himself a briefless barrister in Bombay where he began his practice. Growing restless to make a career he left for South Africa on a short period assignment offered by Dada Abdulla & Company. To Gandhi it was not that he was going there as a barrister but as a 'servant of the firm'. However, what he did want was to leave India for earning and touring a new country.

A Turn in Life

Experience

In South Africa racial hatred at that time was beyond limitation. Gandhi's first such experience was in the Durban Court which he attended on second or third day of his arrival in that country. The Magistrate asked him to take off his turban. But Gandhi refused to oblige and ultimately had to leave the Court. He became socially conscious and shortly marked that there in South Africa the Indians were divided into different groups – Muslims, Hindus and Parsis. The Muslims were by and large merchants and called themselves not Indians but Arabians. The Hindus and Parsis were by profession mostly clerks and were employed in the firms of the Muslim merchants. The largest component of Indians consisted of Tamil, Telugu and inhabitants of Northern India who were employed as indentured and freed labourers. The Englishmen called them as well as all the Indians '*coolies*' or '*sami*'. Gandhi himself was known as a '*coolie barrister*'. In the meantime Gandhi did one thing. He addressed the press about the incidence of wearing turban in the court. This gave him publicity; some supporting him and some others seriously criticising his tenacity. He was described by the press as an 'unwelcome visitor'. Here Gandhi learnt one thing that to go to press or proper authorities with a cause would yield value. Possibly, this made him a future 'petitionist' in public activities.

Gandhi had had enough experience of such racial discrimination. Thus, he wrote in his Autobiography that on the seventh or eighth day of his arrival in South Africa he left for Durban. A first class seat was booked for him. The train reached Maritzburgh, the capital of Natal. An official came to him and told to go to the van compartment. Gandhi said he had a first class ticket. He was rebuffed : "That doesn't matter, I tell you, you must go to the van compartment".[2] Gandhi refused to get out voluntarily when he was threatened with physical force. Then a police constable came, took Gandhi by the hand and pushed him out. His luggage was taken out and the train steamed away.

It was winter then. Gandhi remained sitting in the waiting room and shivered throughout. There he made up his mind that it would be cowardice to run back to India. The hardship which he had suffered was superfluous to him. Instead this deep disease of colour prejudice must have to be fought out. He despatched a letter to the General Manager of the Railway who instead justified the conduct of the railway authorities and the railwayman. The Muslim merchants tried to pacify him stating that what had occurred to him was nothing unusual.

On another occasion, worse than that have been mentioned above, Gandhi was physically assaulted for his refusal to sit at the feet of the 'leader', the White man in charge of the coach in which he was travelling. His only fault or lapse was that he forget that he was a *coolie* and the 'leader' wanted to smoke comfortably occupying his seat, having fresh air. When Gandhi refused the man came down upon him and began to box his ears heavily. He did not box back. Possibly because the 'leader' had greater show of physical strength. Gandhi's passive reaction: 'Prayed to God to help me'. Thus developed his passion for 'passive resistance'.

Experiment

Gandhi sought redress of racial injustice in South Africa. He met the Indians there. In Pretoria in the house of Sheth Haji Muhammad Haji Joosab a meeting was held, which was attended mostly by the merchant class. Gandhi addressed the audience. It was his first public speech. He emphasized on truthfulness and unity among Muslims, Hindus, Parsis, Christians and others of Indian origin. In conclusion he suggested that an association should be formed to communicate with the authorities in power. The association under the leadership of Gandhi worked well. This made Gandhi widely known in Pretoria and his communication skill with the authorities about injustice to Indians also evoked positive response. Then Gandhi's area of activities spread over Transval and the Orange Fee State. More he saw and experienced and more he studied he became convinced that

South Africa was not a country for the Indians to live with self-respect. What haunted him was how to improve their self-respect.

Gandhi made his mind to defer his sail to India in order to fight for the cause of the Indians in South Africa, who were not only divided but also had no means to fight out justice for them. South Africa was then a British colony. There he organized a number of forums and launched movements to fight out justice by means of non-violence for the lame, unlettered South African Indians who had been going through deprivation for decades past. This means of non-violence was his policy as well as principle. He through his notion-oriented non-violent movements realized the immense practical value of non-violence and compromise in restoring self-respect and realizing truth. He writes: "But all my life through, the very insistence on truth has taught me to appreciate the beauty of compromise. I saw in later life that this spirit was an essential part of *satyagraha*. It has often meant endangering my life and incurring the displeasure of friends. But truth is hard as adamant and tender as a blossom."[3] Thus, Gandhi emerged as a man possessed with the idea of conversion of the opposite by means of compromise and non-violence. This made him a hard-core British loyalist as well.

However, a great turn came in the life of Gandhi : "Thus God laid the foundation of my life in South Africa and sowed the seed of the fight for national self-respect".[4]

NOTES AND REFERENCES

1. M.K. Gandhi, *Autobiography*, Navajivan Publishing House, 1988, p. 41.
2. *Ibid.*, p. 128.
3. *Ibid.*, p. 169.
4. *Ibid.*, p. 160.

3

INTO THE CONGRESS
Turned Political Hero, A Mahatma

Gandhi came back to India in 1914. Gopal Krishna Gokhale, an eminent moderate leader of Congress, organized a public reception for Gandhi in which many other eminent leaders, including M.A. Jinnah, were present. Gokhale cautioned Gandhi not to open his mouth on Congress politics but only to observe for one year. Gandhi did abide by his advice. He started studying with keen open eyes and analytical mind what was and what was not the Congress. Congress was then suffering from division into 'moderates' and 'extremists'. It had no policy, no principle, no grass-roots, no unity between Hindus and Muslims. The young generation was revolutionary in outlook and violent-minded. Gandhi as an astute politician with high ambition and having some firsthand experience in *satyagraha* in South Africa felt that the Congress was in need of a new leadership with innovative means and end matching with the souls of the sons of the soil. He found within himself that spirit of leadership and discoveries. He was determined to advance to hold the helm of the Congress. His spiritual feelings in search of Truth in life and politics were working in his mind. He entered into politics as a shrewd politician, inwardly as tryst with Truth.

Gandhi turned himself as a dedicated whole-time worker of the Congress. He toured the whole country and met the Congress stalwarts. His self-publicity began with his publication of *Green Pamphlet* in which he highlighted the conditions of Indians in

South Africa and his contributions there to struggle for social justice by means of non-violence with success. He gave wide publicity to his publication. His non-violent operation in politics under the mighty British rule and its success naturally attracted the attention of the Congress leaders. Gokhale stepped forward to bring in Gandhi to the Congress dais by arranging to permit him to move a resolution on South Africa at the Calcutta session of the Congress. However, that was only for five minutes.

The real initiation of Gandhi into the Congress took place at Amritsar session of the Congress. At that time Congress had no Constitution save that of the 'Gokhale Legacy'. The responsibility of framing the new Constitution was assigned to him and thus he became the maker of the Constitution of Congress, a historical event in his life : "With the assumption of this responsibility I may be said to have made my real entrance into the Congress politics."[1]

Congress in Stagnation

The All India National Congress (1885) was formed almost over a cup of tea, so to say, without any ideology or plan and programme. It was an organization of an elite class representing mostly affluent lawyers knowing constitutional means of reforms and the bureaucrats knowing the fine way to beg the authorities to gain some benefits. Among the organizers of the Congress the names of Surendranath Banerjee, Allan Octavian Hume and Sir William Wedderburn come to the frontline. Surendranath Benerjee was in Indian Civil Service and Hume was also a retired civilian. The Governor-General Lord Duffrin and Viceroy Lord Lyttons, among others, welcomed the Congress. The British Government was in need of an all-India organization to act as a 'buffer' to the revolutionary spirit among the people for the liberation of the country. Thus, the Congress emerged as the 'buffer force', a 'safety valve' of the British Empire.

However, the perspective was changing. The victory of Japan over Russia in 1905 and the nationwide stir against the Bengal partition in 1905 roused the national spirit among the people. The moderates, which included Gokhale, the political *guru* (mentor) of Gandhi, were challenged by such extremists like Bal Gangadhar Tilak, Bipin Chandra Pal, Lala Lajpat Rai, Aurobindo Ghosh. They designated the Congress as the 'begging institution'. Tilak raised the slogan: "Freedom is our birth right." He developed religious means to awaken the patriotic feelings among the people and launched 'no-revenue' and 'boycott' movement during 1896-1897, long before the entry of Gandhi into the Congress.

The division of the Congress into 'moderates' and 'extremists' surfaced in the Surat session of the Congress (1906-1907). Side by side the revolutionary groups in Bengal and Punjab became active. So much so that during the First World War (1914-1918) a revolutionary group under the leadership of Jatindra Nath Mukherjee ('Tiger Jatin') organized an armed upsurge; however betrayed and failed. The Congress was even then a loyal subject of the British. In December 1914 at Madras the Congress expressed : "its profound devotion to the throne, its unswerving allegiance to the British connection and its firm resolve to stand by the Empire at all hazards and at all costs."[2] The British Government was delighted at the slavish mentality of the Congress. Thus, it became open that neither the moderates nor the extremists nor the revolutionaries were strong enough to lead the country to win freedom. The moderates were mere 'petitionists' and 'constitutionalists'; the extremists were one step up than the moderates; and the revolutionaries were too immature and adventurists. They had no resources, no training, no mass awakening nor any touch with the Indian soldiers. So there existed a vacuum for new leadership with innovative means and end.

A Breakthrough : Non-Violent Non-Cooperation

The history had kept the Indian political gate wide open for the entry of Gandhi and to hold the helm of national leadership. He stepped in at the right time. He might be a new-comer in Indian politics but he was a man possessed by the idea of 'means and end'. He was shrewd politician as well. His 'inner voice' was his guide, friend and philosopher. He well studied the sons and soil of India and also the might and character of the ruling British power. His analysis was that the soil of India was religious and half of the people of India were too weak to offer violent resistance and the other half were unwilling to do so and further that no power could rule without the cooperation of the people, which would be more impressive if it was peaceful. Gandhi perhaps could not exactly follow the policy of divide and rule of the ruling power, which was equally peaceful and legitimate action to rule and then leave dividing the colony into pieces. All aside, Gandhi's non-violent revolution had no support in world history. During his lifetime the most illustrative one was the Russian Revolution (1917) – a violent revolution organized by a group of intellectuals on the basis of an ideology against the powerful monarchy. However, Gandhi was in search of the quickest method to win over the people and his finding was the non-violent non-cooperation : "The way of peace and suffering is the quickest method of cultivating public opinion, and therefore, when victory is attained, it is for what the world regards as Truth."[3]

The death of Lokamanya Tilak (1856-1920), Lala Lajpat Rai (1865-1928) and Chittaranjan Das (1870-1925) cleared off the stuffs from the path of the eternal journey of Gandhi. Tilak was a national leader with pragmatic stand and innovative outlook. Had he lived longer India might have been something different. Romain Rolland, who had enough softness for Gandhi, wrote : "If Tilak had lived Gandhi... would no doubt have remained religious leader of the movement."[4]

Lokamanya Tilak was a man of action and to him saint had no place in politics : "Politics is a game of worldly people and not of *sadhus*.[5] However, showy, Gandhi had to utter, echoing Tilak : "Freedom is our birth right." Of course, it was after the death of Lokamanya Tilak.

Gandhi was shrewd enough. He avoided all likely confrontations and proceeded in his own way with a handful of followers to establish the real value of his means of non-violence.

Thus, bypassing the stalwarts Gandhi started his experiment with Hindu-Muslim unity. At that time Khilafat agitation was in full progress. Gandhi by then had developed his idea of 'non-violence'. He had a long discussion with Maulana Abdul Bari and other *Ulemas* about the Islam's acceptance of the rule of non-violence. They assured him that it would not be unIslamic and also pledged to his policy of non-violence. Gandhi was emboldened about the prospect of the Hindu-Muslim unity. At the Khilafat Conference which was held at Delhi he moved the non-violence resolution. Having 'won' the hearts of the Muslim fundamentalists he then advanced to his home province, Gujarat, to organize a base there. At the Gujarat Political Conference the non-cooperation resolution was moved by Gandhi. The opposition raised the point of order whether a provincial conference could adopt a resolution in advance of the Congress. The determinist character of Gandhi was exposed there : "I suggested that the restriction could apply only to a backward movement; but as for going forward, the subordinate organizations were not only fully competent, but were in duty bound to do so, if they had in them the necessary grit and confidence."[6] The resolution was finally adopted.

Then Gandhi moved to Congress to convert it into his creed of non-violence. At the special session of Congress at Calcutta in September 1920 he was scheduled to move the non-violent non-cooperation resolution. He, however, 'forgot' to include the word 'non-violent' in the resolution. Possibly because prior to that he "only saw an imposing phalanx of veteran warriors assembled for the frey at Calcutta."[7] Even in the resolution 'non-cooperation' was postulated only with a view to obtaining redress of the Punjab and the Khilafat wrongs. Gandhi was clever enough not to jump with his creed but to advance step by step. Lala Lajpat Rai, who presided over the meeting, and Chittaranjan Das had reservations about the resolution. However, at the Nagpur annual session, after some amendments and understandings, the resolution was passed unanimously. Thus, Gandhi turned the wheel of the Congress to his creed and leadership and became the 'maker' of Congress in 1920. Then within some few years demonstrating the success of his means of non-violent non-cooperation emerged Gandhi as the political hero and Mahatma at the same time.

NOTES AND REFERENCES

1. *Autobiography*, p. 566.
2. B.R Nanda, *Gokhale*, Oxford Press, Delhi, 1977, p. 448.
3. Collected Works of Mahatma Gandhi, GOI, 1965, Vol. 22, p. 29.
4. Romain Rolland, Mahatma Gandhi, GOI, 1975, p. 15. In 1917 Edwin Montagu said about Tilak : "at the moment probably the most powerful man in India." And about Gandhi : "a social reformer... He dresses like a coolie, forswears all personal advancement, lives practically on the air and is a visionary." Nanda, B.R., *op. cit.* p. 153.
5. Tilak's letter to Gandhi on January 18, 1920.
6. *Autobiography*, p. 577.
7. *Ibid.*, p. 578.

4

MOVEMENTS

One Step Forward Two Steps Back

Gandhi after coming back from South Africa opened an 'Ashram' at Sabarmati, near Ahmedabad, Gujarat, and then for the first time took the initiative to undertake a campaign at Champaran, Bihar, in 1917 for the cause of oppressed indigo peasants against the landlords. He gained some success and came to the limelight of the Congress leaders and the British Government.

Then came 1919, a landmark in Indian politics. The Rowlatt Bill was placed before the Central Legislature, which was passed but hailed by the people of India as the 'Black Act'. The Act made provisions for imprisonment without trial. Thus it robbed the fundamental rights of the people. Gandhi was seemingly shocked.

However, the Rowlatt Act enlightened Gandhi about the reality. He felt that no one having self-respect could submit to the recommendations of the Rowlatt Committee and something must have to be done as a measure of protest. He had also felt the pulse of the people. He told Vallabhbhai Patel : "I should give battle against it alone."[1] A meeting was convened at Sabarmati Ashram where hardly a score of persons were invited. The *satyagrahaha* pledge was drafted at the meeting but as it seemed to be in vain Gandhi then organized a separate body – *Satayagraha Sabha.* He became the President of the Sabha but soon after most of the members left the Sabha as they could not put up with the 'idiosyncrasies' of Gandhi. Gandhi realized that his "emphasis on truth and *Ahimsa* had begun to be disliked by some of its members."[2]

Then Gandhi advanced to the authorities with his characteristic communicative skill and loyalty. He wrote open and private letters to the Viceroy for kind redress. He also threatened the Government to use non-violent *satyagraha* but all this failed to wake the Government which was merely pretending sleep. For the Government's assessment was that the Gandhian agitation would be at best a spark for the moment. But the anger of the people was growing in volume and intensity. Gandhi asked himself : How he could civilly disobey the Act; could he civilly disobey other laws? And also : What would be the dead-line? Then what? His 'inner voice' sparked inside and dictated : *Hartal*. He wrote : "The idea came to me last night in a dream that we should call upon the country to observe a general *hartal*."[3]

The call to observe countrywide general *hartal* was to Gandhi his commencement of 'self-purification' for a 'sacred fight' and his call was : "Let all the people of India, therefore, suspend their business on that day and observe the day as one of fasting and prayer."[4] The date of *hartal* was finally fixed April 6, 1919. How far the 'call' was the voice of the 'inner voice' or the voice of the voices of the relentless people was no issue to anybody. The fact was that the whole of India observed a complete *hartal* on that day. It was a most wonderful spectacle indeed. The Muslims also participated in it as one with Hindus and the other communities.

Gandhi flared up, brightened. To him it was a victory of *ahimsa* – a great success of his experiment. His next step was to start a civil disobedience movement. The most interesting as well as tragic event was that in the meeting of taking pledge with regard to *swadeshi* and Hindu-Muslim unity only a handful persons were present. It was not surprising to Gandhi : "for I have noticed this characteristic difference in the popular attitude– partiality for exciting work, dislike for quite constructive effort."[5] That is, Gandhi's '*satyagrahi-hartal*' roused excitement for exciting work, had no urge to self– purification for sacred fight.

Jallianwala Bagh Massacre

The All–India *hartal* was observed on 6th April, 1919. Gandhi was arrested. This caused riots in Punjab. General Dyer arrived in Punjab on 11th April. At Jallianwala Bagh (Amritsar, Punjab) hundreds of people, including women and children, assembled there to observe a Hindu festival day. This was taken as the violation of the Government order of holding public meetings, which was notified in the official paper only. Dyer appeared in the Bagh with his troops and without warnings gunned down hundreds and injured thousands. This was followed by a reign of terror and martial law. Bombs were thrown from aeroplanes on unarmed crowds. The people were flogged publicly and both innocent men and women were forced to crawl along certain streets like worms on their bellies. A man like Gandhi, whose creed was non-violence, was also surprised how Punjabis, violent by nature, could take up all these excesses and humiliation lying low.

Then Gandhi became active to pacify the feelings of the people. The Government appointed a commission to inquire. The Congress boycotted the commission and appointed its own committee for the purpose in November 1919. Gandhi was given the responsibility to organize the work of the five-member committee and draft the report. In the report it was stated : "to what lengths the British Government is capable of going, and what inhumanities and barbarities it is capable of perpetrating in order to maintain its power."[6] Yet the report pleaded with no punishment for Dyer; he should however be recalled. Further, as a loyal subject and in apprehension of further violence Gandhi suspended his movement on 18th April. The people not only felt disappointed but also betrayed.

Khilafat Agitation

Gandhi then entered into communal unity adventurism, known

as Khilafat agitation. He had been looking for an opportunity to put ahimsa to its severest test on Hindu-Muslim unity. He found enough in Khilafat. Khilafat was a fantastic religious issue to the Indian Muslims. Turkey entered the First World War (1914-1918) as an ally of Germany. After the defeat of Germany Turkey took a new turn. The Sultan of Turkey was also the Caliph of Islam or head of the Islamic Church. After defeat the Sultan had lost his Caliph status. This had made the Indian Muslims furious. They demanded restoration of his religious status under threat of agitation. But sooner they had realized that they were too weak to face the British power. To Gandhi it was a golden opportunity to bring in Muslims in his own fold and *ahimsa* creed. So enthused that he said : "that will not come again for hundred years."[7] He stepped forward to take up the Khilafat wrong in political forum of the nation. He pronounced : "If the Government could betray us in a great cause like Khilafat we could not do otherwise than non-cooperation."[8]

Thus, 'Khilafat' was a 'great cause' of nation to Gandhi. The critics of Gandhi's communal politics were vocal. Gandhi was indifferent. He found no harm in his deeds. He said : "those who say that religion has nothing to do with politics do not know what religion means."[9]

Gandhi's shortcoming was that he could not visualize the perverse character of religion in politics. In a sense, he was an idealist visionary. However, he was firm : "In spite of the criticism, I feel that I have no reason to revise it or to regret my cooperation with the Muslims."[10] He was conscious of the history of tyranny of the Mughal Raj in India : "you will find in history cases of injustices done by the Muslims." Then and there he corrected himself : "But their religion is a noble one and Muslims are a noble people."[11] Gandhi as an astute sadhu-cum-politician knew whom to placate how and when.

In November 1919 a Khilafat Conference was held in Delhi under the guidance of Gandhi. In February 1920 at the Khilafat Conference in Calcutta presided over by Abul Kalam Azad the non-cooperation programme of Gandhi was considered and then passed unanimously at the meeting of the Khilafat Committee held on June 9 at Allahabad. In the Khilafat Conference Gandhi proposed and that was for the first time non-cooperation with the Government unless the grievances of the Indian Muslims were redressed. Instantly, the whole Muslim community embraced Gandhi as their own. They were so jubilant that while Gandhi was on tour with the Ali Brothers (Shaukat Ali and his elder brother Maulana Mohammed Ali), the leaders of the Khilafat Committee, they were greeted with: '*Mahatma Gandhi ki Jai*'; '*Ali Bhaio ki Jai*'. Non-Muslims shouted : '*Bandemataram*', while the Muslims shunned it and shouted '*Alla-o-Akbar*'. However, Gandhi found in all this the bright signal of Hindu-Muslim unity.

To any intellect the Khilafat movement was a mere religious spur. The Arab world was almost indifferent about Khilafat. Kamal Ataturk pulled down the Sultan regime in Turkey and forced the Sultan to abdicate. Thus, the Turkish Muslims themselves brought an end of the Sultan, the head of Islamic Church, and consequently the *Khilafat agitation* in India lost all its lusture. The Muslim agitationists left Gandhi and slipped into the Muslim League (1906), which was a hundred percent communal and anti-national organization. Gandhi was disillusioned, however late, and felt so disturbed that at one stage he said : "he (Shaukat Ali) follows the law of non-violence with hatred in his heart."[12]

Before closing the episode it will not be impertinent to quote from Bipin Chandra Pal's letter of November 10, 1920, to Motilal Nehru : "but the last week has convinced me that Khilafat was only a cover for the Pan-Islamic propaganda. Hindu-Muslim unity is alright, but are we going to be fooled by those Pan-Islamists as the Government was one time? The *Khilafat agitation* spells a very serious danger to our cause. And excuse me for saying it, S.A. (Shaukat Ali) has been using Mr. Gandhi for his own ends." Then attacking directly the autocracy of Gandhi and the hero-worship of the people he added : "I did not like the latter's (Gandhi's) statement in the Subject Committee that he did not care *Swaraj*, he cared for Hindu-Muslim unity and the Khilafat. The Khilafat has precedence in his thought and endeavour over the Punjab tragedy. It is just here that I sense a great danger to let ourselves be led by him."[13] His prediction as early as 1920 : "a great danger to let ourselves be led by him." It was long before Subhas Chandra Bose revamped the issue. It may be mentioned, in 1923-24 Gandhi's Khilafat and Hindu-Muslim unity was marred by widespread Hindu-Muslim riots.[13a]

Bardoli Agitation

In 1921 to stir up the people with hopes and to win their unconditional allegiance Gandhi assured them *swaraj* within a year. It was amazing how a man like Gandhi who was initiated into the Congress only in 1920 and knew well that he had no non-violent army of his making in his hand could dare declare *swaraj* within a year? Gandhi had reason, apart from political. And that was to establish he alone "had discovered the path to liberation." To him the "country was almost reached the end, nothing to reproach him nor he had any reason to run away to the Himalayas."[14] All this was the voice of his 'inner vioce'. But when reality proved him failure, he rose up to avoid all responsibility and took resort to his characteristic nature : "My promise was conditional. . . I told the people : 'Fulfil these conditions and win *swaraj*.'"[15] He accused the people for violation of the conditions set by him. Thus, "I can only point out the means; it is then for the people to work and secure *swaraj*. I am a *vaidya*; I prescribe the medicine, explain the manner of taking it, mention the other things to be taken with it and specify the quantity to be taken every time. It is ultimately for the patient to act and do the best he can."[16] It shows Gandhi was not in command of the non-violent revolution but a mere *vaidya* and the people went to his chamber for a prescription. This was most unconventional and unconvincing to the intellectuals. Sir Sankara Nair, who was Congress President in 1897, said that the promise to attain *swaraj* within a year was "to mislead the ignorant masses which all intelligent supporters must have known to be impossible of attainment."[17]

Then in February 1922 Gandhi launched an agitation at Bardoli (Gujarat). Prior to that he had sent seven-day ultimatum to the Viceroy Lord Reading to change the heart of the Government. Perhaps the Viceroy had a smile in his face. The agitation was for general non-payment of taxes. The people as usual flared up. But suddenly Gandhi pulled himself back and directed the Congress, without consulting anybody, that it must take up constructional work like hand-spinning and hand-weaving instead. Why? Because some stray violence broke out at Chauri Chaura (United Province). There was resentment but it was the Dictator's Decree, so the Congress had nothing to do. To Gandhi such suspension of a movement might be politically unsound and unwise but religiously sound and wise. It was not possible for him to tolerate violence or to win freedom at any cost. His dictum : "I have discovered the *path* (*ahimsa*) and I will never abandon it."[18] From the point of political soundness such action is nothing else than mere amateurish venture playing with the future of the country. As to wisdom, it was not unknown to Gandhi – the long history of antagonistic relationships between the Muslims and the Hindus, the role of the British Government to fan the relationships, presence of violent temper of the people in general, absurdity of total non-violence and all others, yet why did he give a call for agitation? Was it because he came to sense that the agitation must face failure? Or was it to act as the 'buffer' to pacify the people's passion for upsurge because of his failure to deliver *swaraj* within a year? Or was it a half-way voice of 'inner voice'? Be that as it may, Gandhi was mentally humiliated. However, he consoled himself : "struggle for *swaraj* is the spiritual effort for me, a means for attaining *moksha*."[19] That is, he emphasised, *swaraj* was secondary to him, self-salvation was the object of his life.

Gandhi, however, confirmed *swaraj* overnight, if and only if, the people could wipe out violence from their hearts. He said: "had the Chauri Chaura murders not taken place the movement attempted at Bardoli would have resulted in the establishment of *swaraj*."[20] To follow him one may conclude: So long as violence remains in the soil and soul of India, India would remain dependent. As if, all over the world all the dependent countries became independent through conversion of their hearts from violence into non-violence. It was a grand escape clause for Gandhi to shed off all responsibilities of his venturesome experimentation with man and *ahimsa* – dependence and independence; servitude and salvation. His main target was, however, the militant revolutionists : "the revolutionaries have retarded the progress of the country. Their reckless disregard of the lives of their opponents has brought on repression that has made those that do not take part in their warfare more cowardly than they were before...The masses are not prepared for the repression that follows in the trail of revolutionary activities and unwittingly strengthen the hands of the very Government which the revolutionaries are seeking to destroy."[21] He branded the revolutionaries as "ignorant and misguided." Even he said : "those who... secretly or openly, give praise to the revolutionaries for their sacrifices, do harm to them and the cause they have at heart."[22] Certainly Gandhi had the cause and right to be vocal against the revolutionaries but he hardly subjected himself to self-criticism. When cornered under circumstances of his own creation he openly said that he was not omnipotent or omniscient; he was like many others and could do 'Himalayan blunder'. There was nothing odd in it. After all, 'man proposes, God disposes'; but not those not 'misguided' or 'thoughtless'. In this context Gandhi raised the question whether armed revolution was possible in a country like India : "They (revolutionaries) can and do applaud wholeheartedly the action of Mustafa Kamal Pasha and possibly De Valera and Lenin. But...revolutionary activity is suicidal at this stage of the country's life at any rate, if not for all time to come in a country so vast, so hopelessly divided and with the masses so deeply sunk in pauperism and so fearfully terrorstruck."[23] To counter-throw : The cause in revolution is 'plenty' or 'poverty'; 'fearfulness' or 'fearlessness'? Russia was a vast country yet the historic revolution took place there in 1917 when Gandhi was fully active with his *satyagraha* experiment. Every individual is revolutionary by nature but they are so systematized that their real spirit is forced to lie dormant that awaits the call of awakening. This is the history of spiritualism, history of materialism.

March to Dandi

The 1930 saw hectic activities of militant revolutionists and trade unionists. The Meerut Conspiracy Case (1929); Chittagong Armoury Raid (April 1930); Invasion of Writers Buildings (August 6, 1930); assassination of Lowman, Head of Intelligence Branch of Police, Bengal; and also of Simpson, Inspector General of Police, Bengal; murder of Peddie, Magistrate of Midnapore, Bengal; and his two successors are among many other remarkable events. This worried not only British Government but also Gandhi. The victory of armed revolution would mean the defeat of his *ahimsa* experiment, which was intolerable to him. He rose up to launch a fresh agitation to divert the people's minds from violence to non-violence as the only means to attain freedom. He announced that January 26 should be observed all over the country as the Independence Day.[23a] This was submissively approved by the Congress. Gandhi prepared a Manifesto which was a declaration of independence and a pledge of loyalty to the Congress, that is, to its supreme leader, to fight for *swaraj* only by non-violent means. Thus : "We recognize, however, that the most effective way of gaining our freedom is not through violence. We will, therefore, prepare ourselves by withdrawing, so far as we can, all voluntary associations from the British Government, and will prepare for all civil disobedience, including non-payment of taxes."[24] Apart from all other aspects, the implications of this Declaration were that a non-believer in non-violence and a challenger of the leadership of Gandhi must not have a place in the Congress. In this way Gandhi did tighten his belts against the militants from the constitutional point of view.

The Independence Day, also termed as the Day of Pledge to Gandhian policy and principle, was widely accepted and as such Gandhi was highly inspired again. Then for establishing *Purna Swaraj* (complete independence) Gandhi worked out an eleven point demand chart as the 'substance of independence', calling the Government to accept or reject it. He 'threatened' the Government that in case of rejection the whole country would go to the way of 'civil disobedience'. The irony is that Gandhi's 'Khilafat' Ali Brothers openly appealed to the Indian Muslims not to respond to the call of the Congress.

Gandhi after long deliberations announced the programme of his civilian movement on February 27, 1930. He had in mind the feelings of the people about his 'false' promise of *swaraj* in a year in 1921 and the disappointment of the people for his sudden suspension of Bardoli agitation in 1922. This time, as such, he was bent upon not to retreat. His pledge was 'Do or Die' (which incarnated in 1942 by a higher dimension in Quit India movement) until the goal was achieved. It was really thrilling. In *Young India* on February 27, 1930 Gandhi wrote : "This time on my arrest, there is to be no mute passive non-violence, but non-violence of the most active kind should be set in motion so that not a single believer in non-violence as an article of faith for the purpose of achieving India's goal, should find himself free or alive at the end of the effort." He said categorically that "civil disobedience once begun this time cannot be stopped so long as there is single civil resister left free or alive."

This time also Gandhi had lengthy communication with the Government but having no response as usual he ultimately decided to take up this programme in hand : 'March to Dandi' with his 70 loyal followers. The March was to him "a last religious pilgrimage." The object was to disobey the Salt Law. The programme was for three weeks on and from 12th March 1930. On 6th April Gandhi after having a purificatory bath in the sea began his civil disobedience by appropriating some grains of salt lying on the beach. This civil disobedience spur spread in some form or other all over the country.

The Government came down to encounter it with violence. Press Ordinance was imposed followed by other ordinances on 27th April and the Congress was declared unlawful. All this further flared up the public agony and the movement. The movement, however, maintained its non-violent character. But the Chittagong Armoury Raid (April 1930) shocked the British Government and as a result it became more brute. Gandhi was arrested on 5th May. Things were taking a violent turn. Some pacifists ran to the Government camp for some peaceful settlement. Then peace was restored through the Delhi Pact (also known as Gandhi-Irwin Pact). Both Government and Congress yielded to some conditions. The Congress agreed : Suspension of civil disobedience movement; participation of the Congress in the Second Round Table Conference to be held in London; withdrawal of demand for an investigation into the allegation of police atrocities. The Government yielded to: Release of all political prisoners involved in the non-violent movement, but not the revolutionists, possibly because they were common enemies of both the Government and the Gandhiites[24a]; withdrawal of ordinances; permission of peaceful picketing in the interest of domestic industries; permission to the people living within specified distance of the sea-shore to collect or manufacture salt free of duty.

Thus, Gandhi's first phase of 'Do or Die' died down peacefully, Gandhi felt relieved and the British Government might have blessed Gandhi for his honesty and loyalty in restoring peace.

Second Round Table Conference

The Congress did not join the First Round Table Conference. That Conference was the result of the Simon Commission report which was boycotted by the Congress. The non-participation of the Congress did not yield any effect of the Conferencc. The Government realized that without the cooperation of the Congress no problem could be solved. However, the Congress joined the Second Round Table Conference held in London. Gandhi alone represented the Congress in the Conference. His ego was that he alone could win over the heart of the Conference. What more is that he was novice about the details of the Conference. And all this in spite of his knowing that it was a conference "with all kinds oɪ non-descripts, flunkeys and self-appointed leaders arrayed against him like a solid phalanx."[25] The Congress was invited as one of the many other parties. The consequence was that Gandhi came out of the Conference with empty hands, even though he had warned the British Government : "Will you not see the writings that these terrorists are writing with their blood?"[26] The blood writings of the terrorists might have haunted Gandhi, least the British Raj, at least so long as Gandhi could function as the 'buffer'. Anyway, there the drama of 'March to Dandi' ended. It may be recalled that on December 6, 1921 Lord Reading in his speech at the British India Association and National Chamber of Commerce said : "I ask myself what purpose is served by flagrant breacher of the law for the purpose of challenging the Government and in order to compel arrest."

One Step Forward Two Steps Back

Gandhi was a half-way man : One step forward two steps back. In the words of Nehru : "Gandhi, for all his rock-like adherence to certain principles, has shown a great capacity to adapt himself to others and to changing circumstances... But from time to time he pulls himself up, as if he were afraid that he had gone too far in his compromising, and returns to his moorings. In the midst of action, he seems to be in tune with mass mind, responsive to its capacity and therefore adapting himself to it to some extent; at other times he becomes more theoretical and apparently less adaptable. There is also the same difference observable in action and his writings."[27] Long ago Chittaranjan Das, as placed by Subhas Chandra Bose, opined : "The Mahatma opens a campaign in a brilliant fashion; he works it up with unerring skill; he moved from success to success till he reaches the zenith of his campaign – but after that he loses his nerve, and begins to falter."[28] Nehru's observations carry meanings. Gandhi was a shrewd politician. He knew when to advance and to what length and when to retreat to advance again. He was not a man to lose nerves. He was too strong because of his 'rock-like' adherence to non-violence as creed for self-salvation. What he used to lose was the balance in his thought dashed by actions. When his creed to conquer hatred by love and untruth by truth came to the stage of collision with the 'rock-like' hearts of the *satans* he began to falter asking himself : Then what? *Swaraj* by violence, blood for blood? Absurd. For *swaraj* by violence was no *swaraj* to him. He preferred to remain under the domination of *satan* than to win independence on the dead body of the *satan*. It must be through conversion, compromise and be peaceful and legitimate.

Gandhi was unique in the sense that unlike the other prophets he did not preach 'follow me or go to hell'. For to him the people irrespective of faiths were ever ready to go to hell for material pleasure than to heaven for realization of Spirit. He observed the evils of disunity in 'follow me' and sought unity in 'follow non-violence' as the common means to enjoy collective real pleasure. It was not his mere wish and whim, it was truth to him. He fielded himself in politics only to establish it scientifically. The science of imperialism challenged his science of *ahimsa*. For the imperialist power had faith in force that could change the conditions of the world and consequently the character of man and society. The preachers may preach as they are doing for thousands of years but all is ever falling on deaf ears, while their deafness will vanish when they would be bombed by warring violent forces. This is the hard reality which made Gandhi falter from time to time. Nehru is apt to say on Gandhi : "The very nearness of that war became a challenge to him and a test of faith. If he failed at this critical moment, either non-violence was not the all embracing and basic principle and course of action he had believed it to be, or else he was wrong in discarding it or compromising with it. He could not give up the faith of a lifetime on which he had based all his activities, and he felt that he must accept the necessary consequences and implications of that non-violence."[29]

The 'necessary consequences' were accepted by Gandhi but the people for generations together had to bear the dire necessary consequences, in spite of their innocence. Here lies the greatest tragedy of heroism of *ahimsa*.

The cause of Gandhi's 'one step forward two steps back' was not only the effects of contradictions in 'means' and 'end'; there is also something else. Gandhi was by nature a hard-core loyalist to the British Empire. This was evinced long before he became a '*satyagrahi*'. At times he became so servile that he did not care to ask himself whether he was giving his services to the Empire for just or unjust cause. Thus, in a statement before the Court (1922), Gandhi said that his public life began in 1893 in South Africa. There he felt the racial discrimination as he had no rights as a man because he was an Indian. To him it was simply " an excrescence upon a system that was intrinsically and mainly good." As such he gave the Government his "voluntary and hearty cooperation, criticising it freely where I felt it was faulty, but never wishing its destruction." He did not render mere lip services to the Government. He was not a South African citizen, still when "the existence of the Empire was threatened in 1899 by the Boer challenge, I offered by services to it." He had never questioned himself whether Boer's challenge was socially and morally just or not. Then again in Zulu revolt he stood by the side of the Empire as an active organizer. The British Government awarded him : "I received medals and was even mentioned in despatches. For my work in South Africa I was given by Lord Hardings a Kaiser-i-Hind Gold Medal." Gandhi was the only national leader of India who was awarded with 'Gold Medal' by the British Empire.

Then came the crucial First World War (1914-1918). It was an opportunity to rise up against the British then involved in war. The Indian revolutionaries were organizing a national revolt in cooperation with Germany. Gandhi was then in London. What was he doing there? He stated: "When the war broke out in 1914 between England and Germany, I raised a volunteer ambulance corps in London consisting of the then resident Indians in London, chiefly students. Its work was acknowledged by the authorities to be valuable." His loyalty was in his flesh and blood and ever expansive : "Lastly, in India when a special appeal was made at the War Conference in 1918 by Lord Chelmsford for recruits, I struggled at the cost of my health to raise a corps in Kheda." Gandhi's servitude went so far that he did not hesitate to say that India could achieve her complete emancipation only within and through the British Empire. And unto the last in some form or other he did not betray his loyalty to the British Empire. For, after all, "British rule was on the whole beneficial to the ruled."[30] To elaborate, when Viceroy Lord Chelmsford invited Gandhi to participate in the War Conference in Delhi he became a bit hesitant in that how could he attend a War Conference having faith in *ahimsa*. The Viceroy knowing well the nature of Gandhi hit at his sentiment of loyalty : "If you agree that the Empire has been, on the whole, a power for good, if you believe that India has, on the whole benefitted by the British connection, would you not admit that it is the duty of every citizen to help the Empire in the hour of the need.[31] A letter from the Viceroy begging him to do participate in the Conference was enough for Gandhi's loyalty to flare up and bypassing his creed of '*ahimsa*' he made up his mind to participate. But what was the ultimate result of loyalty? The Viceroy was very clear-cut : "You may raise whatever moral issues you like and challenge us as much you please after the conclusion of the war, not today."[32]

To conclude, Gandhi's blind loyalty to the British Empire additionally made him a man : "One step forward two steps back."

NOTES AND REFERENCES

1. *Autobiography, op. cit.*, 530.
2. *Ibid.*, p. 531.
3. *Ibid.*, p. 534.
4. *Ibid.*
5. *Ibid.*, p. 537.
6. *Ibid.*, p. 554.
7. Collected Works of Mahatama Gandhi, *op. cit.*, Vol. 18, p. 203.
8. Makers of Modern India, ICHR, New Delhi, p. 3.

9. *Autobiography,* p. 583.
10. *Ibid.*, p. 516.
11. Collected Works, Vol. 18, pp. 203-204.
12. *Ibid.*, p. 158.
13. Sibdas Chakravarty, *Bipin Chandra Pal*, Chalantika Prakashak, Calcutta, pp. 437-440.

    In P.S. it was added : I understand that Dr. Kitchlew declared 'you Hindu, will have to fall in line with us, if you don't; you will see what the consequences will be."

13a The communal reactions underlying the *Khilafat agitation* are countable. The Hindus reactions in general : "You asked the Hindus to make common cause with the Mussalmans in *Khilafat agitation*. Your being identified with it gave it an importance it would never have otherwise received. It unified and awakened the Mussalmans. It gave a prestige to the Maulvis which they never had before. And now that the Khilafat question is over, the awakened Mussalmans have proclaimed a kind of jehad against us Hindus." Collected Works, Vol. 24, p. 136.

    A Mussalman friend wrote to Gandhi : "Your Hindu leaders in the guise of *shuddhi* and *sangathan* are trying to weaken the Muslim community... Under the circumstances, do you not honestly think that you are doing a great harm to this community by keeping the Mohammadans, a few of them of course, still in your camp." *Ibid.* p. 137.

14. Collected Works of Mahatama Gandhi, Vol. 21, p. 558.
15. *Ibid.*, p. 557.
16. *Ibid.*, p. 558.
17. *Ibid.*, Vol. 22, p. 512.
18. *Ibid.*, Vol. 21, p. 559.
19. *Ibid.*,
20. *Ibid.*, Vol. 26, p. 487.
21. *Ibid.*
22. *Ibid.*
23. *Young India,* April 9, 1925.

23a. Gandhi needed the services of Jawaharlal Nehru and his disassociation with Subhas Chandra Bose. Both Bose and Nehru stood for 'complete independence'. Gandhi assured Nehru of that and also the Presidency of Congress. Then Nehru switched over to Gandhi's camp. Then follows : "with a great fanfare, therefore, Jawaharlal, riding an elephant, led a procession to the banks of the Ravi, and on the 26th January hoisted the flag of independence. And since then the 26th January is celebrated as Republic Day." Wilhelm von Pochhammer, *India's Road to Nationhood*, Allied Publishers Pvt. Ltd., 1981, p. 519.

24. Subhas Chandra Bose, *The Indian Struggle*, 1935, Wishart Co. Ltd., London, 1935, p. 204.

24a. On April 8, 1929 Sardar Bhagat Singh and Batukeshwar Datta of Hindustan Socialist Republic Association threw bombs on the floor of the Indian Legislative Assembly in Delhi. It was when the Public Safety Bill was for the Assembly for adoption. None was injured. They surrendered, distributing copies of Red Pamphlet which declared their faith that a revolution would bring freedom to all.

Sardar Bhagat Singh and his two associates, Rajguru and Sukhdev, were executed on 23rd March 1931. In spite of assurance given by Lord Irwin, the Viceroy, that their execution would be postponed for the time being and would be taken up with all seriousness. This far and no farther. Even after signing the Gandhi-Irwin Pact Gandhi did show initiative to take up the matter. It was then current that Gandhi had prior knowledge that Bhagat Singh was already executed. On the contrary, in spite of severe opposition at Lahore Congress Gandhi moved a resolution congratulating Viceroy Lord Irwin on his providential escape when his train was bombed by a revolutionary.

25. Bose, *op.cit.*, p. 242.

26. At the Plenary Session of the Second Round Table Conference, Nov. 30, 1931.

27. Nehru, *Discovery of India*, p. 445.

28. Bose, *op. cit.*, p. 253.

29. Nehru, *op. cit.*, p. 443.

30. *Autobiography*, *op. cit.*, p. 196.

31. *Ibid.*, p. 516

32. *Ibid.*

5

A GREAT CHALLENGE

Subhas Chandra Bose

Subhas Chandra Bose was born on 23 January, 1897 at Cuttack (Orissa). His father, Janakinath Bose, was an eminent lawyer there. He had his school education in Cuttack. Therefrom he had his education at Presidency College, Calcutta. While in the college he was rusticated for two years in the year 1916 for his 'disobedience' in leading students against the high-handedness of Professor Oaten. Professor Oaten had manhandled some students who were also the class-mates of Subhas Chandra Bose. His reaction about the punishment was fine : "I had stood up with courage and composure in a crisis and fulfilled my duty. I had developed self-confidence as well as initiative, which was to stand me in good stead in future. I had a foretaste of leadership – though in a very restricted sphere—and of the martyrdom that it involves. In short, I had acquired character and could face the future with equanimity."[1] However, he completed his graduation from Scottish Church College, Calcutta, in 1917-19. Then he qualified himself in Indian Civil Service Examination in 1920. His inner urge was not to serve the British but to serve the people and free the motherland from British domination. He resigned from the service and left for India. He was then only twenty-three years of age. After arrival in India he hurriedly called on Gandhi. He placed before him three questions: (i) How were the different activities conducted by the Congress going to culminate in the last stage of the campaign, namely, the non-payment of taxes; (ii) How could mere non-payment of taxes or civil disobedience force the British Government to retire from the field and leave India with freedom; and (iii) How could the Mahatma promise *Swaraj* by his non-violent means within a year – as he had been doing ever since the Nagpur Congress. Gandhi might have passed some uneasy moments. In order to pacify the young revolutionary soul of Bengal he gave some abstract answers which could not satisfy Bose. Then at the end he advised him to go back to Calcutta and meet Chittaranjan Das. Bose obliged and since then he became a close associate of Chittaranjan Das. However, it gave rise to an awareness in him : "No great achievement, whether internal or external, is possible without a revolution in one's life."[2]

Philosophical Ideas

Since boyhood Bose was in search of an ideal person having irresistible moral appeal. While in the Ravenshaw Collegiate School, Cuttack, Beni Madhav Das, Headmaster of the school, had left a permanent impression on his youthful mind by his 'irresistible moral appeal'. Then when he was barely fifteen Ramakrishna Paramahansa and Swami Vivekananda entered into his life : "Ramakrishna's example of renunciation and purity entailed a battle royal with all the forces of the lower self. And Vivekananda's ideal brought me into conflict with the existing family and social order."[3] He organized a group of students for social service with spiritual bent of life. That is, he was becoming a self-revolutionary to bring in a radical change in the existing social system. Initially he wanted to realize the spiritual consciousness for which he visited, even without informing the family, a number of holy places in India to find a *Guru* (Preceptor). But could not find anyone. It gradually dawned on him that for spiritual development social service was necessary as a follower of Ramakrishna and Vivekananda. To him to serve the poor is to serve God. It gave him much pleasure to become one with the poor and serve them with heart and soul.

Subhas Chandra Bose was a student of philosophy. He read Hindu philosophy and was also well conversant with Western philosophy. He was a 'relativist' following Hegel. For to him 'truth' as known to us is not absolute, but relative and changes in the same individual during the process of time. Gandhi was also a relativist. But he was more subjectivist while Bose more objectivist. Bose said : "I am not prepared to take anything on trust. I must have first-hand experience." Then what about Absolute? He proceeded : "I am unable to get." His understanding was until he could go to 'super-mental constitution', that is, as long as he remained in 'common mental constitution' truth would remain relative. This also had relieved him from lots of philosophical controversy. Thus he found composure in the saying of Vivekananda : "Man proceeds not from error to truth but from truth to higher truth."[4] Here comes in the scope for widemost tolerance. It was also the perception of Gandhi.

As an ardent objectivist Bose discarded the doctrine of 'maya' (illusion). To him the objects are not illusions. What more: "If the world be real (not, of course, in an absolute but in a relative sense) then life becomes interesting and acquires meaning and purpose."[5] Further, to him 'reality' is not static but dynamic, ever changing, moving towards higher phase of existence. He had also realized that 'reality' is 'spirit' : "working with a conscious purpose through time and space."[6] What interests more: Why did Bose believe in Spirit? His answer : "Because it is a pragmatic necessity. My nature demands it. I see purpose and design in nature; I discern an 'increasing purpose' in my own life."[7] Further, it was to him "an intellectual and moral necessity." From reality point of view it is highly significant. Man degrades, degenerates and gets dehumanized only because of his lack of faith in Spirit. The Spirit is the unifying force, pleasure in living, learning and knowing the Absolute transcending the strains of lustful glamour of matter and materials. Thus, Bose's idea of Law of Progress manifests in : "Reality. . . is Spirit, the essence of which is Love, gradually unfolding itself in an eternal play of conflicting forces and their solutions."[8]

Social Ideas

Subhas Chandra Bose was a man of motion from nationalism towards internationalism. He was not a communist nor a Gandhiist but a socialist of Indian soil. His internationalism is rooted in nationalism. Thus, his idea of nationalism : Every single nation or individual has got a special trait or ideal of his own. He shapes his life in accordance with that ideal. Of internationalism : That internationalism is true which does not ignore nationalism, but is rooted in it. His clarion call : "Asia for Asians". For "the creation of an international society of nations can be possible only if we begin by setting up what I may call regional federations."[9] This would block domination of the international trade and finance and the nuclear force to unilaterally advance from the West to the East.

In social sphere Bose's idea of socialism is founded on five fundamental principles[10]. Justice : "we shall have to treat all men as equal. In order to make men equal we have to make than free"; Equality : "we must get rid of bondage of every kind—social, economic and political—and we must become fully and wholly free"; Freedom : "it only means the substitution of our own law and our own discipline in place of an externally imposed law and discipline"; Discipline : "whether for individual or for society, is necessary as a basis of life." The underlying force of all this is Love : "Unless we are inspired by a feeling of love for humanity we can neither be just towards all, nor treat men as equal, nor feel called upon to suffer and sacrifice in the cause of freedom nor enforce discipline of the right sort."[11] To Bose these five principles constitute the essence of his ideal of socialism. His concept of economic emancipation : "the right to work and the right to a living wage. . . a fair, just and equitable distribution of wealth. For this purpose, it may be necessary for the state to take over the control of the means of production and distribution of wealth."[12] His resolution of caste and communal problems : Cultural synthesis to resolve caste and communal problems. Of ethnic problems : Federation of republic states unifying through a strong central government. His approach to religious fundamentalism : Promotion of social consciousness oriented mass education. And to political fundamentalism : Pluralism leading to synthesis of doctrines. For the deprived and backward classes his call : Equal opportunity to all. Lastly, to him political freedom was freedom from slavery of the foreign power. The Gandhiites were little mindful about social and economic problems of the country and to draw a scientific outline of India's future social order. Instead, the powerful section of Gandhi wing was concerned with how to win freedom and wield power by exercising the Gandhian means of non-violence and its marginal section was busy with the Gandhian experimental philosophy of 'means and end' for self-realization of 'truth'.

Bose Contra Gandhi : Thoughts and Actions

Line of Thoughts

Gandhi did never take up politics as his profession or ambition. He had a spiritual mission in life. And that was self-realization through realization of the people which he discovered in politics: "I could not be leading a religious life unless I identified myself with whole of mankind and that I could not do unless I took part in politics."[13] It may sound odd but the underlying idea behind this oddness he was an experimental scientist. He came down to politics to experiment his model of conversion of devils rising above the spirit of mere preachings as the classical saints had done leaving the mankind within bare scriptures retaining all their devilish characters. It was a super-experimental venture unknown yet in world history. In other words, his venture was to experiment with an ancient thing in a new way in a new field. He realized the truth in it in his *satyagraha* spirit in *ahimsa*. In *ahimsa* he had realized 'truth' and for that he merged himself with the outer objects instrumentalizing politics as the bridge to enter into the hearts of the people. It was only for this cause politics was inseparable to him from religion. Contra, Bose had little or no faith in the idea of conversion of devils for realization of truth and salvation. To him nobody can convert anybody;

conversion is self-realization through self-revolution. One can preach, act–this far and no farther. Had it been then all would have been a Gandhi, a Mahatma. Subhas Bose's hard determination was to liberate India bearing in his heart that India was the key-stone to the world edifice and a free India would spell the destruction of imperialism throughout the world. Imperialism was the greatest hurdle in the way to culture self-realization. He was not in favour of muddling the minds of the people by inducting religion into politics. His reality was 'many in one'. It was most significant in a multi-religious country like India.

Both Gandhi and Bose were 'practical idealists'. But to Gandhi 'truth is spirit'; to Bose 'reality is spirit'. To Gandhi 'means' is one; to Bose 'many'. To Gandhi 'violence' ends in violence; to Bose violence is a storm that results in peace and brings in radical change in the system. Again, to Gandhi 'God is Love', that is, '*Ahimsa* is Love', for '*Ahimsa* is God'. That is, Love is a phenomenon of *Ahimsa.* Violence is not Love and as such it is irreligious. Thus, Gandhi spiritualized non-violence; contra, Bose spiritualized reality. Then, further, both Gandhi and Bose were relativists. But Bose was nearer to dialectical materialism as pronounced by Marx, Gandhi to objective idealism of Hegel.

To close up, the contrast between Bose and Gandhi in philosophical understanding lies fundamentally in 'means and end' philosophy of Gandhi. To Gandhi *himsa* (violence) is irreligious and 'untruth' and as such it was absolutely intolerable to him. To Bose 'means' is not the determining factor of 'end'. It is an open factor in 'many'. The 'cause' and not the 'means' was in the spiritual consciousness of Bose as the 'end and means' in Gandhi. In Gandhian philosophy there is no room for tolerance, only edict. To Gandhi whoever dared to violate his edict was a 'misguided' being and that being was intolerable to him. Sometimes that intolerance went so far that he could not resist to crush the 'misguided' by all possible *ahimsa* means as an astute politician. This resulted in rift within the Congress and disunity amongst religions and faiths.

The fun is that Gandhi had adopted the means of non-violent revolution to convince the people that his strategy was a necessity for the people had no arms in their hands. As if, had they arms in their hands he would owned violent means. In politics his philosophy had also left him in contradiction off and on. For 'policy' was subject to change while 'principle' was unchangeable to him. To Bose 'means' was an independent variable. This made Bose emerge as the emblem of unity, plurality and democracy, leaving Gandhi in an abstract world of truth.

Line of Actions

Subhas Chandra Bose and Gandhi both were possessed with their own lines of action for attainment of freedom. In the Presidential address at the Third Indian Political Conference in London, 1933, Bose had mentioned two paths of freedom : "One is the path of uncompromising militancy. The other is the path of compromise." Gandhi adopted the path of conversion by compromise, Bose the path of uncompromising militancy. To him freedom is an uncompromising right. He says : "There is no royal road to success in winning political freedom." He was confident enough : "We do not believe that India can achieve freedom without the use of arms". And "The movement of the future must be therefore made to rest on an objective and scientific foundation in keeping with the facts of history and of human nature." Bose's militancy does not mean that by nature he was a man of arms. His call was realistic : "Disarm, or we shall arm." India seeks "peace of a healthy life" not "peace of the graveyard". Gandhi is, however, otherwise. To him there should be periodical compromises with the devils for consolidating strength to advance step by step towards conversion. His contention is that a *satan* (devil) cannot be converted into a grand overnight. The *satan* requires psycho-spiritual treatment having compromising process which was only known to Gandhi. To Bose no compromise would be possible between the rulers and the ruled and the periodical compromises would not be enough without uncompromising miliant plan of action. Otherwise that would expose the weakness of the movements and benefit the rulers to consolidate more strength to rule on further. Thus, "A political compromise is possible only when there is some community of interests." Bose stood for 'armed force' totally, Gandhi discarded it totally. For "violence ever fails; passive resistance ever successful." He was firm in his stand for 'soul-force' or 'love force', which grows from within and is obtained by self-suffering and self-purification. All this was also within his knowing that "purest passive resistance can exist only in theory." Possibly Gandhi had realized the existence of sleeping Gandhi in the hearts of all the devils. He was not a sin-absorber but a sinner-converter. Be that as it may, there was tact in 'periodical compromises' and that was to wait for the conditions to revolt. To Bose conditions should be created by utilizing the emotions of the people at right time in right path. Thus, "the supply of our necessary resources depends on our ability to keep up the enthusiasm of the people and maintain the spirit of opposition towards the Government." To him the arms are the source of enthusiasm of the people and the spirit of opposition towards the Government. This was a 'psychological factor' to him. The world history of revolution stands in support of this.

Every movement must target a deadline. But in Gandhi's one after another movement Bose could not find any deadline. The Government might be paralysed by non-cooperation in its collection of taxes and revenues, non-cooperation of peasants and workers in production of goods for the needs of the war, boycott the British goods etc., etc.—then what? Would the foreign Raj then automatically collapse and withdraw from the soil of its colony? To Bose, backed by history : 'No'. The real foundation of the British Raj in India was the Indian army and police force. So long as they would remain loyal, the civil administration could function and the lives and the properties of the government officials and their supporters would feel quite safe and secure, the Raj would remain unhurt. To Bose what was needed was to awaken the spirit of nationalism among the Indian army and the police force, that is, to enthuse them to rise up against the slavery for the freedom of their motherland.

Gandhi ignored all this, possibly because 'revolt of army' meant 'civil war', and civil war meant violation of his creed of non-violence, self-suffering and self-purification. On the contrary, his reactions : "I shall spare no pains to frustrate their effort. Armed conspiracies against something satanic is like matching *satans* against *satan.*"

In order to strengthen the line of action Bose targeted 'complete independence'. Gandhi was hovering from time to time on that score. Complete independence seemed to him complete disloyalty to the British. He was inclined to live under the umbrage of the British Empire. He patched up *Swaraj* conveniently with 'Home Rule', 'Dominion Status', and even 'self-rule' or 'self-control', and 'abandonment of fear of death', etc. However, finally under pressure of circumstances he had to subscribe to *Purna Swaraj* or 'complete independence'. Bose was against untouchability towards other parties with different ideologies and means of actions provided they were prepared to fight unitedly for the freedom of the country. That is, if the 'cause" is common, means should not be any constraint in the path of unity. To Gandhi it was unacceptable. For to him 'means' was the sole determining factor of unity. As a result not only the Congress itself was split up into wings but even it was isolated from the diverse feelings of national unity. It was a great blunder in a multinational and multi-religious country like India. The British Raj took full advantage of this by adopting the colonial policy of 'divide and rule'.

Then, what for freedom, for whom freedom? This was not clear in the vision of Gandhi. For he lacked in objective foundations of freedom. Bose was strongly in favour of action with scientific plan and programme and having in hand the manifesto of social order for free India. To Bose the line of action should be modelled on propaganda, both negative and positive, and national and international. The negative aspect was to negate the lies that were propagated against India and the positive one was to draw the attention of the world towards the rich culture of India in all respects and also India's manifold grievances against the colonial rule. Gandhi was against international propaganda. For that would mean external interference and begging. On the other hand, to Bose international cooperation would rouse the sense of international cooperation for fulfilling both national and international interests. Gandhi was a self-sustained man. Bose was a man whose idea of sustenance and development was global cooperation. This is amply exposed in his thoughts of evolution of movement: "While every Movement draws its sustenance from the soil from which it springs, it also assimilates nourishment coming from outside — from the atmosphere, environment, etc. Internal sustenance and external nourishment are both necessary for a living Movement."[14]

Gandhi's means of 'non-cooperation' was not much appealing to the intellectuals. It was to them a short-lived adventure. Like many others, Rabindranath Tagore also could not support Gandhi's non-cooperation idea because it suffered from 'negation, exclusiveness and despair'. Gandhi, however, in his own style boldly upheld the faith in non-cooperation. Bose had no quarrel with Gandhi on his idea of non-cooperation as a policy. He praised him instead : "Though personally I believe that this method will not succeed in bringing us complete independence, there is no doubt that it has greatly helped to rouse and unify the Indian people and also to keep up a movement of resistance against the foreign government." Implicitly Bose had asked Gandhi not to hover but to accept either of the two historical paths. But Gandhi was all the way suffering from 'neither-nor' — 'neither sufficiently militant, nor sufficiently diplomatic'. Finally, the two minds started working in the opposite paths. Bose, a violent revolutionary, came out with the words : "We want to build up a new modern nation on the basis of our old culture and civilization." Gandhi, a non-violent revolutionary, worded : "India can be free this very moment if we turn our back on this modern civilization and go back to our ancient way of life, which embodied the right ethical principles." This was utopia to Bose as much as Bose was 'misguided' to Gandhi. Yet there was no fundamental difference between the two noble souls of the soil of India : "India of the past is not dead. India of the past lives in the present, and will live in the future."

A Critic of Gandhi

Subhas Chandra Bose was a well-educated nationalist revolutionary. He had studied indepth the roots and winds of colonialism and had first hand knowledge about the stand of colonialism in Europe. He had also clear idea how to uproot colonialism from India's soil and thereafter imperialism from the future political history of the world. He knew that power falls for its own poverty and at times waits for the crucial moment for a sharp knock from outside. He further knew how to mobilize resources and also when, where and how to move with time and conditions and what would be the new social order in a multinational country on the basis of 'unchangeable" values of the soil. Since his first visit to Gandhi in early twenties he was convinced that he was an out and out ethical man having no firm determination to free the country, but only to experiment in politics his dogmatic *ahimsa* for his own salvation. He was always in search of truth and freedom was a secondary to him. As a result he had no scientific means in hand to march on with the banner of freedom. He was an *Avatar* to unlettered religiously sentimental Hindu masses invoking much displeasures among the non-Hindu communities. So fanatic were the people that at Nagpur Congress in December 1920 when M.A. Jinnah, till then a Congress leader, addressed Gandhi as 'Mr. Gandhi' he was shouted down by the people in presence of Gandhi and insisted that Gandhi should be addressed as 'Mahatma Gandhi'. (How far that event made Jinnah to become a different Jinnah as the sole leader, Qaid-e-Azam, of the Muslim communities was known only to Jinnah.) The fact is, such was the image of Gandhi that even the top left winger Jawaharlal Nehru ever remained lying at his feet for blessing. Bose was built up with different ingredients. His conscience could never bend for position or power but only for cause and truth.

Bose was determined to draw an end of the 'absurd length' of Gandhian experimental movements with lives and time. He asked openly why *swaraj* still a distant dream although Gandhi himself was armed with 'purity of true character' and unprecedented following? His own answer lies in : (i) impure character, (ii) poor understanding of the character of the opponents, (iii) poor art of diplomacy, (iv) false unity of interests, (v) double role—the leader of an enslaved people and a world teacher who had a new doctrine to preach.

In his *The Indian Struggle* (1934) Subhas Chandra Bose paid high tributes to Gandhi. He saw in him 'India's man of destiny' and it was Gandhi who 'knew himself' – he knew his country's needs and he knew also that during the next phase of India's struggle the crown of leadership would be on his head. No false sense of modesty troubled him – he spoke with a firm voice and the people obeyed. Further : "The Indian National Congress of today is largely his creation. The Congress Constitution is his handiwork. From talking body he has converted the Congress into a living and fighting organization."[15]

At the same time he writes: "There is something in Mahatma Gandhi which appeals to the mass of the Indian people."[16] But what that 'something' possibly was not fully known to anybody. However, Bose writes : "Born in another country like Russia, Germany or Itlay he could have faced 'cross or the mental hospital'. But India was altogether a different country, suited best to Gandhi."[17] Gandhi perhaps also knew that otherwise he could not write in his *Hind Swaraj* (1909) : "Brute force is not natural to Indian soil. You will have, therefore, to rely wholly on soul-force." Bose proceeds to write : "The tradition and temperament of the Indian people is but one factor accounting for the former's (Gandhi's) success. If he had been in another epoch in Indian history, he might not have been able to distinguish himself so well."[18] He, however, could not resits to remark : "His loin-cloth was reminiscent of Christ, while his sitting posture at the time of lecturing was reminiscent of Buddha. How all this had earned a tremendous respect for the Mahatma in compelling the attention and obedience of his countrymen."[19] Thus, Gandhi posed himself as both Christ and Buddha in one and such was the madness of the people that some of them had installed the idols of Gandhi in temples. Gandhi did not like to be crowned as Mahatma or *Avatar* or Idol but he had never expressed repulsion to such idolism of the people. Bose was also vocal about Gandhi's style of functioning. To him he was virtually a 'dictator'. His word was the 'Dictator's decree'. He writes : "The leader of the Congress is Mahatma Gandhi—who is the virtual dictator. The Working Committee since 1929 has been elected according to his dictation and no one can find a place on that Committee who is not thoroughly submissive to him and his policy."[20] This character of Gandhi could not escape the eyes of Jawaharlal Nehru also. However soft, he writes: "Congress was dominated by Gandhi and yet it was a peculiar domination. . . .often Gandhi toned down his position to meet the wishes of others, sometimes he accepted even an adverse decision, in some vital matters for him, and the Congress. . . . But always he was symbol of India's independence. . . and it was such a symbol that people gathered to him and accepted his lead, even though they disagreed with him on other matters."[21] Thus, Gandhi was intolerable to 'inner democracy'. Even the Congress Constitution was made and revised from time to time by Gandhi according to his will and all important resolutions were his makings or subject to his ratifications even when he was not a primary member of the Congress. There he acted as the 'adviser' of the Congress. Thus, as 'dictator' he sometimes posed as 'democrat'. Bose illustrates this : "whenever any opposition was raised outside his Cabinet, he could always coerce the public by threatening to retire from the Congress or to fast unto death."[22] Besides, had he been a democrat and the 'symbol' of independence how could he declare one of his followers as his 'heir', the 'uncrowned king of India' inducting thereby the idea of 'dynastic democracy' to pollute democracy and human values in free India?

Subhas Chandra Bose dared criticize the Mahatma for it might have played to his mind that his confrontation with Mahatma was inevitable and desirable.

NOTES AND REFERENCES

1. Netaji Collected Works, Vol. 1, NRB, Calcutta, p. 80.

2. *Ibid.*, p. 54.
3. *Ibid.*, pp. 39-40.
4. *Ibid.*, p. 121.
5. *Ibid.*
6. *Ibid.*
7. *Ibid.*
8. *Ibid.*, p. 124.
9. Ref., *Netaji and India's Freedom,* Edited by Sisir Bose, Calcutta, 1975.
10. Speech at All India *Naujawan Sabha in Karachi,* April 5, 1931.
11. *Ibid.*
12. *Ibid.*
13. *Harijan,* Dec. 24, 1938.
14. Speech at the Third Indian Political Conference in London, 1933.
15. Subhas Chandra Bose, *The Indian Struggle,* 1920-1934, p. 328, Wishart & Co. Ltd., London, 1935.
16. *Ibid.*, p. 327.
17. *Ibid.*
18. *Ibid.*
19. *Ibid.*, p. 134.

    Notes

    Dress was not a fashion to Gandhi. There was politics in it. Gandhi writes : "During the *Satyagraha* in South Africa I had altered my style of dress so as to make it more in keeping with that of the indentured labourers, and in England also I had adhered to the same style for indoor use...One dressed in that fashion was sure to pass muster as a poor man." *Autobiography,* p. 440.
20. *Ibid.*, p. 27.
21. Nehru, *The Discovery of India,* p. 364.
22. *The Indian Struggle,* pp. 200-201.

6

DEFEAT OF GANDHI

Expulsion of Bose

Defeat

Subhas Chandra Bose was least hopeful about the prospects of the struggle for freedom under the leadership of Gandhi. He found "there is a great deal of vagueness and mental reservation in the minds of the leaders. Their programme is based not on radicalism but on adjustments—adjustments between landlord and the tenants, between the capitalist and the wage-earner, between the so-called upper classes and the so-called depressed classes, between men and women."[1] He reviewed (September 1929) the history of the Congress and categorized its phases into : (i) the age of *Swadeshi*, (ii) the age of anarchism, (iii) the age of non-cooperation. He then summarized the effects : The *Swadeshi* movement based on boycott of British cloth and salt tax forced the British Government to revoke the partition of Bengal and introduce Morley-Minto Reforms. The age of anarchism (1918-1919) moved the people's spirit to patriotism, fearlessness, self-respect and self-sacrifice, which compelled the British power to introduce the Reforms Act, 1919. Then came the age of non-cooperation, that is, the Gandhian age, and mass organization with the feelings not to cooperate with the British Government and thereby to destroy the foundation of the British Raj in India. But non-cooperation movement did not carry weightage to Bose. His conviction was that freedom could be achieved only by revolutionary movement organized by peasants and workers, men and women rising above all narrowness like castes, sex, religions. At heart he was a history-oriented militant revolutionary. To him India needed thousands of Jatin Das and raised slogan : "Bhagat Singh is dead, long live Bhagat Singh". They may be 'misguided patriots' to Gandhi, to him they were the real spirit of the people. His vision was that the last stage would come when active resistance would develop into an armed revolution and then would come the end of British rule in India.

Thus, from the very inception Bose was opposed to Gandhi's policy and principle. At a certain stage circumstances forced him to stand face to face with Mahatma to settle all about non-violent revolution and violent revolution. And also of the back-track of Mahatma to give new life to India as against the urge of the people to march with time. However, the proximate issue was about the authority of Gandhi to nominate the President of the Congress and direct the President to form the Working Committee with only those persons whom he would recommend, that is, with his 'yes men'. This power wielding tact of Gandhi cornered Bombay and Bengal, which were once at the helm of the Congress organization. Like Bose, Nehru was also not happy with the dictatorial role of Gandhi. He was a socialist ideologically yet a 'disciplined member' of the Congress under the rule of Gandhi. Bose was a revolutionary socialist and was a man of such spirit that he could never compromise with his conscience of conviction under any circumstances. Gandhi knew that and so he needed the services of Nehru to isolate Bose within the Congress. He nominated Nehru as the Congress President for two consecutive terms, 1936 and 1937. However, in the meantime the cloud of Second World War was moving in the -Western world. The leftists in India were getting restless to seize the war opportunity to struggle out freedom. Nehru, who was then the leader of the Congress left-wing, was sold out to Gandhi. Bose was then on the frontline. Gandhi conceived the nature of danger ahead and at once picked up Bose as the Congress President for 1938 as that would serve his purpose to bring in Bose under his control. But after being the President Bose began to work independently as President, and when necessary began to counter Gandhi knowing that he was the Mahatma of India. His public speeches, activities and campaigns exposed that not Gandhi but the Congress President had the right to lead the country unfettered by any remote control. In his Presidential speech at the 51st Session of the Congress at Haripur on February 19, 1938. Bose had provoked immense criticisms from the Gandhian-wing. In his speech he said that the British were at the cross-reads of history and cautioned the people against the British ingenuity that would seek by this or that constitutional means to divide India and thereby scuttle the transfer of power to the people of India.

Bose hit back the Gandhiites from different corners. He said that Gandhi was indifferent about rapidly changing phases of the world. The world before his eyes was one of 'spinning wheel' and not large-scale industrialization. To Bose in order to solve economic problems agricultural improvement would not be enough : "However, much we may dislike modern industrialism and condemn the evils which follow in its train, we cannot go back to the pre-industrial era, even if we desire to do so." He promoted Planning Commission which "will have to consider carefully and decide which of the home industries could be revived despite the competition of modern factories, and in which sphere large-scale production should be encouraged."

Nehru was appointed the head of the Planning Commission.[1a] The very idea of Planning Commission might have flashed before the eyes of the Gandhiites the 'terrified' picture of the Soviet Union, which within a very short period became a superpower by means of planned socialist economy. Bose was professed by the idea of no compromise with complete freedom as a matter of right. He said : "As Congress President, the writer did his best to stiffen the opposition of the Congress Party to any compromise with Britain and this caused annoyance in Gandhian circles who were then looking forward to an understanding with the British Government."[2] Following the Munich Pact in September 1938 Bose began to organize the people of India for a national struggle which would synchronized with the coming war in Europe. This move, though popular among the people in general, was resented by the Gandhiites who did not want to disturb the ministerial and parliamentary works of the Congress which was at that time opposed to any national struggle for freedom.

Then came the most crucial stage of confrontation that exposed the psyche of Gandhi about Bose. Gandhi allowed Nehru to hold the Congress Presidentship for two consecutive terms but in the case of Bose he took firmly the opposite stand. The reason is quite obvious. Gandhi knew that Nehru would never go outside his fold so long as all power was in his hands. But Bose was to him not a negotiable commodity. He believed not in 'mirage' of civil disobedience movement but freedom at any cost. He was prepared to compromise with the devil but not with freedom.

Bose was not a power-monger. He agreed not to contest the election for the Presidentship on condition that somebody else from the left wing must be given nomination. But such 'dictation' was unpalatable to Gandhi, for he was the 'law'. Bose was then determined to contest the election against Gandhi's nominee inviting profuse wrath of Mahatma. Gandhi took up the challenge. He gave his nomination to Pattabhi Sitaramayya. Bose won the election securing 1580 votes as against 1375. Gandhi was heavily shocked. It was for the first time since 1923-24 that Gandhi was so heavily shocked. Without any provocation from anywhere he came out to say: "The defeat is more of mine than his (Sitaramayya)." He had also made an unpleasant remark : "After all Subhas Babu is not an enemy of his country." It is 'unpleasant' in the sense that how could it come to the mind of Mahatma that after all Bose was not an enemy of the country. Is it that whoever would oppose Gandhi should be presumed as the enemy of the country? Bose's reactions were soft and mild. In a statement on February 5, 1939 he said : "It grieves me to find that Mahatma Gandhi has taken it as a personal defeat." Bose was really grieved as he had failed to win the confidence of Mahatma. Thus, "I do not know what sort of opinion Mahatmaji has of myself. But whatever his view may be, it will always be my aim and object to try and win his confidence for the simple reason that it will be a tragic thing for me if I succeed in winning the confidence of other people but fail to win the confidence of India's greatest man." But to Gandhi one must be with him or must leave him. There cannot be any compromise between *ahimsa* and *himsa*; truth and untruth—Gandhi and Bose.

Govind Ballabh Pant organized the 'Pant Resolution', passed by the Congress, the essence of which is that the Congress President must work as a 'puppet' under the supreme command of Mahatma Gandhi. Bose refused to act as the puppet President of the Congress. This had more relevance for this time he was democratically elected and not 'nominated'. Besides, he had never aspired to be the 'heir' of Gandhi. Yet he understood that his stand might cause split in the Congress. He was against that. The war wave was then moving towards the East as well. So unity was a vital necessity to struggle unitedly for freedom. In his Presidential address at Tripuri Session of the Congress on March 10, 1939 he predicted that world war was not at a distance and the "time has come for us to raise the issue of *Swaraj* and submit our national demand to the British Government in the form of an ultimatum." He specified six months time. This troubled Gandhi. *Ahimsa* is against involvement in war and *ahimsa* does not permit to take advantage when the enemy is in trouble. But to Bose the 'trouble' of the enemy was the 'golden opportunity' to free the motherland from the clutches of the enemy. This was Bose's call for "Quit India". But it was not appealing to Gandhi then. Gandhi summarily dismissed it as 'premature'. Possibly, his 'inner voice' did not respond then.

By that time all the members of the Working Committee resigned, save and except Nehru, who kept himself in between. Bose approached Gandhi for mediation, if not possible, at least his blessings in his efforts. But Gandhi refused to extend any help. The fun is in 1924 Gandhi took the initiative himself to settle his conflict with the Swaraj Party by withdrawing the names of the 'no-changers', that is, his followers—Rajagopalachari,

Vallabhbhai Patel and Banker—from the Working Committee, and, even he withdrew his 'spinning franchise'. However, he agreed to tribute 'congratulations', not 'blessings' as sought for, to Bose. His only say was that Subhas Babu should form the Committee by his own men and his men should cooperate with him on 'issue base'. It was an absurd proposition to Bose. It was a strategy of Gandhi as a challenge to his 'defeat'. It was the *ahimsa* means of non-cooperation to force Bose to resign. And also to discredit Bose about his inability to form a Working Committee of his own before the people who had hoped much from his leadership. Subhas Bose as a last attempt asked Gandhi: "I would beg to you to come back to active politics, become a four-anna Congress member and assume direct charge of the Working Committee."[3] Gandhi was not a fool to assume direct charge; his strategy was to act as the 'remote controller'—that is, full credit of success, no liability for failure. Bose's further approach : "Will it be open to me to get up at the meeting of the AICC and tell the members that you have advised the formation of a homogeneous Cabinet and the new Cabinet commands your confidence?"[4] But Gandhi was so uncompromising and vindictive that he was firm in his stand not to patronize Bose in any way. His simple reply : 'No'. Eventually Bose had to resign and thereby inflicting another and much greater defeat on Gandhi as that helped Bose to go down the history as 'Netaji' contra 'Mahatmaji'. And what was more amusing that Gandhi had to step forward to declare Bose as the "patriot of patriots".

What was the voice of Bose before tendering his resignation contra Nehru, who as President of Congress had to fall almost in the same trap? Bose's unshivering voice : "I had no desire to remain a dummy President, or to hang on to my office at any cost."[5] He addressed the people : "Self-respect, honour and duty towards my country demanded that I should resign, after having made all possible attempts to reach an honourable compromise and to avert a crisis within the Congress."[6] In short, Subhas Chandra Bose declined to surrender to a man, however Mahatma or Dictator he might be. He was a man possessed by the people and by individuality. His statement echoed the sentiment of Lokamanya Tilak who wrote to Gandhi in July 1915 about his 'complete surrender': "If the whole country wants it, I shall do so. But the small band of men is not the country."

Expulsion

The Gandhiites did not stop there. Their aim was to drive Bose out from Congress. So also Gandhi. By that time the Bengal Congress was divided into Gandhi-wing and non-Gandhi-wing. On one occasion Bose asserted his right to criticise the Congress High Command, that is, Gandhi, and he even demonstrated against the High Command. The High Command came down heavily and suspended Bose from the Congress Executive Committee for three years. He was thus isolated from the national forum. In this drama Gandhi played an important role. The 'show cause' resolution of the Congress Working Committee, August 9, 1939, on Bose was drafted by Gandhi himself, albeit he was not even a primary member of the Congress. Why not any other but Gandhi had to take up the job? For Gandhi had noticed that the members of the Working Committee felt shaky to draft a resolution for expulsion of Bose. For they knew that the people would not take it lying low. And hence Gandhi took up all responsibility to draft and expel Bose from Congress. In fact, since long Gandhi had been exercising moral pressure on Bose to leave the Congress peacefully : "I cannot recall a single instance in my life of having done what Subhas Babu has done, that is, defied an organization to which I owed allegiance. I could understand rebellion after secession from such an organization. That was the meaning and secret of non-violent non-cooperation of 1920."[7] Then again : "Of course the honourable course for you would be to leave the Congress."[8] It may be asked : Was the Congress a democratic organization or the organization of its 'maker'? And is it to threaten to retire or fast unto death of the supremo is the 'meaning and secret' of inner democracy of Congress on and from 1920? Had the Congress been a democratic organization no such domination and unpleasant things could occur. Bose's only fault was that he could not compromise with '*satans*' while the others could.

Forward Bloc

Since long Subhas Chandra Bose was thinking about formation of a party within the Congress with all disciplined leftists. This was because he was convinced that it would not be possible to hit out the Gandhiites from an undemocratic organization. After resigning from the Congress Presidentship on 29th April, 1939 he proceeded to form Forward Bloc. It was formed on 3rd May, 1939. Its primary objects were to fight more effectively against the Gandhian line of action and to win over the Congressmen then in the camp of Gandhi. He had marked that a very large number of Congressmen were being infected with parliamentary and constitutional mentality leaving the path of revolution. The immediate object of the Bloc was action-oriented : "an uncompromising struggle with British imperialism for winning India's independence. To this end, all possible means should be employed and the Indian people should not be hampered by any philosophical notions like Gandhian non-violence, or any sentimentalism like Nehru's anti-Axis foreign policy. The Bloc stood for a realistic foreign policy and a post-war order in India on a socialist basis."[9] Thus Bose virtually intended to declare war against Gandhi's 'non-violent means' and Nehru's pro-British political stand as the pre-conditions for pronouncement of war against the British imperialism All this made the Forward Bloc and its leader Bose as undeclared enemy of Gandhiites.

Ad Interim

Bose started assessing the national and international situations of that time to work out the strategy to stand against the British power. Britain declared war against Germany on September 3, 1939 and on the same day the Viceroy declared India a belligerent, and issued an ordinance to suppress the internal disorder. That is, no agitation would be allowed to force the

British to quit. On September 6, Gandhi issued a press statement after his meeting with the Viceroy Lord Linlithgow that India should cooperate with Britain in her hour of danger. His renewal of loyalty to the British Empire led a section of his followers to start propaganda that though they had demanded freedom for India at the same time they wanted Britain to win the war. To Bose it was a great betrayal to the cause of the Indians. He was strongly in favour of freedom by seizing full advantage of the golden opportunity offered by the war. Then what about the attitude of Nehru – a leftist and strongly anti-imperialist? What Bose studied : From 1927 to 1938, he had figured prominently in all the anti-war resolutions of the Congress, and then war broke out and Gandhi stood by British Raj, Nehru became a disciplined and trusted disciple of Mahatma and used all his influence to prevent the Congress from embarrassing the British Government while the war was on. However, the Working Committee adopted a resolution on September 14, 1939 and offered cooperation to Britain's war effort under certain conditions. The Viceroy reaffirmed on 17th October the pledge of Dominion Status and that would be only after the war and not now. This was not new for the first time. Ten years ago Viceroy Lord Halifax (Irwin) also assured Dominion Status on time. Bose pointed not only to diplomacy in 'reaffirmation' but also brought to limelight the mockery of the Allied powers who were vocal that they were fighting for 'freedom and democracy' usurping all democratic rights of the Indian people imposing ordinances.

Then on 29th October the Congress Working Committee adopted a resolution containing threat of civil disobedience movement. This much and no farther. The British Empire again opened negotiations sending persons and missions to prolong the demand : freedom here and now.

In June 1940 Bose had a prolonged discussion with Gandhi and his associates. By then the German troops were entering France and also into the other European states. In that meeting Bose asked Gandhi to launch a massive passive resistance campaign for it was the right time to win over freedom. But Gandhi simply smiled away the proposal. For to him the country was not prepared to undertake that task. However, he told Bose in his characteristic style to undertake that task and if his efforts became a success then his telegram of congratulations would be the first that would arrive Bose. It was a mild reminder to Bose that violent revolution was doomed to failure.

In April 1940, Forward Bloc started countrywide campaign of civil disobedience. On May 20, 1940, that is, immediately after Nehru made a statement : "Launching a civil disobedience campaign at a time when Britain is engaged in a life and death struggle would be an act derogatory to India's honour". Nehru's aim was to 'derogate' Bose in the eyes of the people. Gandhi also did not remain silent. His language was more crushing : "We do not seek our independence out of Britain's ruin. This is not the way of non-violence."[10] Gandhi was however in dilemma how could he support war effort having faith in non-violence.

Bose's anti-British and anti-war stand caused the British Government to arrest him and hundreds of his followers in early July 1940. In the meantime the Congress drama on cooperation to non-cooperation rolled on by rounds. On September 15, 1940 the Congress withdrew its offer of cooperation and approached Gandhi, who had retired from leadership, to take up all powers in his hands to lead the country. Gandhi agreed but was not inclined to launch any mass agitation. To Bose such a low profile of Gandhi showed that he still wanted to keep the door open for compromise and at the time when the golden opportunity was running out. After deep circumspection Bose arrived at the conclusion that India could win independence if she could play her part in the war against Britain in collaboration with those powers fighting against Britain. Further, the Indian freedom fighters should have firsthand knowledge as to what was happening abroad and then should be at one with other powers against the common enemy—the British Empire. He had also realized that the Gandhi-Nehru Company would never allow any mass agitation against the British Government so long as war continued. Bose's conscience did not allow him to remain blocked in British prison or detention and fenced by the Gandhiites. The war was a real 'golden opportunity' in his life to free his dear motherland, not for self-moksha or for power but for salvation of the people. He found the way and that was to fight from afar. He escaped from India and opened a new chapter in Indian political history.

NOTES AND REFERENCES

1. Netaji Collected Works, *op. cit.,* Vol. 6, p. 140.

1a. It is the common belief that Jawaharlal Nehru was the maker of Planning Commission. Nehru himself tried to cover up the truth as he wrote in his *Discovery of India* (1995 Edition, page 395) that "Towards the end of 1938 National Planning Committee was constituted at the instance of the Congress." But at that time Subhas Chandra Bose was the Congress President. Incidentally Nehru had the habit of distorting facts. Thus, in 1938 when the Congress sent a medical unit to China it had no approval of Bose, the President of Congress, because he was pro-Japanese. The fact is otherwise, *In an appeal to the people,* June 30, 1938, Bose stated : "The ambulance, together with the medical staff, will be a living emblem of India's sympathy and goodwill for the great Chinese people in the darkest hour in their history."

2. Netaji Collected Works, *ibid.,* Vol. 2, pp. 370-371.

3. Letter of Bose to Gandhi, March 31, 1939.

4. Letter of Bose to Gandhi, May 14, 1939.

5. Speech at Hazra Park, Calcutta, May 16, 1939.

6. *Ibid.*

7. Tendulkar, *op. cit.,* Vol. 5, p. 157.

8. *Ibid.,* p. 328.

9. Netaji Collected Works, *ibid.,* Vol. 2, p. 377.

10. *Ibid.,* p. 385.

7

SELF-EXILE

Indian National Army

The Second World War was a 'golden opportunity' to Subhas Chandra Bose to rise up with arms, as the last phase of non-violent non-cooperation, in collaboration with the enemies of the common enemy, that is, in collaboration with the Axis powers headed by Germany against the Allied powers headed by Britain. To Bose neither of the powers was warring for globalization of democracy and freedom. It was an imperialist war to re-divide and colonize the world by themselves. To the colonial countries it was an opportunity to liberate themselves standing against the common enemies. To Bose the British imperialist power was the 'common enemy' of India. It should be forced to quit India taking all advantages of the war situation. His urge grew up as he continued to study the advance of the German troops step by step towards Britain. He had made up his mind to escape from India to have unconditional cooperation of the Axis powers as well as of the Soviet Union, which was at that time maintaining distance from the war.

Subhas Chandra Bose was at that time in prison without trial. There he went on 'hunger strike' that forced the Government to intern him at his house. There his 'instinct and deliberations' led him to leave the country. Later by broadcast from Azad Hind Radio on July 6, 1944 he expressed the role of his 'instinct' to Gandhi : "I can assure you, Mahatmaji, that before I finally decided to set out on this hazardous mission, I spent days, weeks and months in carefully considering the pros and cons of the case. . . By going abroad on a perilous quest, I was risking not only my life and my whole future career, but what was more, the future of my party. If I had the slightest hope that without action from abroad we could win freedom, I would never have left India during a crisis. If I had any hope that within our lifetime we could get another chance—another golden opportunity—for winning freedom, as during the present war, I doubt if I would have set out from home."

In order to remove 'suspicion' about the object of his escape Subhas Chandra Bose addressed Gandhi as the 'Father of our Nation' seeking his blessings and good wishes in this holy war of India's liberation and added to idealize the passion of Gandhiji: "There remains but one question for me to answer with regard to the Axis powers. Can it be possible that I have been deceived by them? I believe it will be universally admitted the cleverest and the most cunning politicians are to be found amongst Britishers. . . If British politicians have failed to coax or coerce me, no other politicians can succeed in doing so. And if the British Government, at whose hands I have suffered long imprisonment, persecution and physical assault, has been unable to demoralize me, no other power can hope to do so. I have never done anything which could compromise in the least either the honour or the self-respect or the interest of my country."

Targeting those who were vocal that Subhas Chandra Bose was a 'traitor', he broadcast to Gandhi : "After having served my people so long to the best of my ability, I could have no desire to be a traitor, or to give anyone a justification for calling me a traitor."

Self-Exile

Leaving all this aside, let us proceed. On June 16, 1941 Subhas Chandra Bose left India in disguise.[1] He reached Peshawar. The Kirti Krishak Party, a separate unit of the Communist Party of India organized in Punjab, helped him in this adventure. His intention was to have a place in the Soviet Union, the 'fatherland of socialism', himself being a socialist in ideas. But the Soviet

Union showed a cold shoulder. The Russian Ambassador in Afghanistan suspected a British game behind Bose's escape. In the meantime, Germany and Soviet Union entered into a non-aggression pact and thus Russia became an ally of Germany. Naturally, the Soviet Union was reluctant to become an enemy of Britain. It preferred maintaining distance. However, the German Ambassador and the Italian Ambassador in Afghanistan managed to have a visa for journey of Bose to Germany via Russia.

Bose arrived in Berlin on March 28, 1941. Hitler came to power in Germany in 1933. He was a soldier who fought during the First World War with always a struggling sword in hand. The defeat of Germany in that war was intolerable to him. He was an ultra nationalist and a racist indepth. His remote mission was to globalize racism by his doctrine of nazism. He had a very low idea about the Asians. He used to call the fighters for India's freedom *Asiatic jugglers* and the Japanese a *yellow man*. The 'white' should only be the universal colour. He liked to see India remain under the British rule than any others. He went so far as to state : "loss of India by the British Empire would be a misfortune for the rest of the world, including Germany itself." Later, however, he repented for not taking advantage of anti-colonial feelings of the non-European races. And all this was in 1940 when : "All Islam vibrated at the news of our victories. The Egyptians, the Iraqis and the whole of the Near East were all ready to rise in revolt. Just think what we could have done to help them, even to incite them, as would have been both our duty and in our interest."[2]

Had Hitler stood by the side of the oppressed nations then history would have adorned him as the liberator of colonial countries. Whereas the credit had been usurped by the British as the warrior of world democracy and freedom. Hitler had to repent for that : "Further, this futile policy has allowed these hypocrites, the British, to pose, if you please, as liberators in Syria."[3]

Bose conferred with Hitler on May 29, 1942. In that Conference he asked the Great Dictator face to face seeking clarification of Germany's attitude towards India. This had reference to Hitler's 'Mein Kampf'. Hitler said : "He had previously taken a stand solely against certain tendencies according to which the subject nations were supposed to build up a untied front against the oppressors. In view of the weakness of these nations he considered this to be completely wrong."[4] Bose made it clear that "India was not the old philosophical one, but a new modern and active India."[5] The point is : could Bose dare dialogue all this with the Great Dictator face to face on the soil of Germany had he been a 'fascist' or 'nazist', which the Congress and the communists were saying about?

There in Germany Bose had organized a regiment with the Indian soldiers in captivity equipped with German weapons. At that time he was convinced of post-war disintegration of the British power and the rise of American imperialism as the world power. In July 1941 Japan concluded a joint defence pact with Indo-China. At that time Britain, USA and Holland froze Japanese interests and in October the oil supplies to Japan were stopped. Then Japan declared war against the USA, Britain and Australia on December 8, 1941. Bose was keenly studying the developments in East Asian front. His object was to open a second front against the British in the East along the Indian frontier. Towards the end of October 1941 he had a meeting with the Japanese Ambassador in Berlin. Finally, he left for Japan, which was also advised by Hitler : "to quickly exploit the chance of an internal revolution in India with the enemy pressure from outside".[6]

Indian National Army

The East Asian war broke out in 1940. Germany, Italy and Japan signed a treaty of military alliance on September 27, 1940, Japan involved in war with the Allied powers. In December 1940 three Indian soldiers who were captives in the British prison in Hong Kong escaped and sought refuge in Japanese Army. The General Staff of Japanese Army intended to help India's independence movement for driving out the Western powers from the East for mutual interests.

The three captives were sent back to Bangkok where they formed the Indian Independence League (IIL). Amar Singh was its head assisted by Pritim Singh. The aim of the League was to lead India's liberation movement from overseas. Its slogan was historic : *Viswas Eikta Balidan* (Faith Unity Sacrifice). Mohan Singh, who was a Captain in British Indian Army, played the key role in organizing the Indian National Army (INA; also known as Azad Hind Fouj). The INA was a wing of IIL. Each and every one in the INA was imbued with patriotic feelings and pledged to 'faith, unity, sacrifice' heart and soul. The INA worked together with the Japanese Army on condition that Japan would not ask for any concession from the League.

In March 1942 the Indians from the different parts of South East Asia assembled in Tokyo under the leadership of Rash Behari Bose.[7] Subhas Chandra Bose conveyed his congratulations from Berlin stating that although Germany, Italy and Japan were sworn enemies of the British imperialism yet we would have to have our independence by ourselves.

By then Japan had gained more strength to force the British to surrender or retreat from East Asia. Thus, Japan captured one after another : Hong Kong, Philippines, Malaya, Burma, Singapore, Java, Sumatra, Borneos. The circumstances were such that the IIL and INA needed a new and dynamic leader who had revolutionary image in India and abroad. The IIL requested Subhas Chandra Bose to come to the East to open a second front in the East against the British to march forward with the Indian National Army to Delhi in cooperation with the Japanese troops to force the Anglo-American forces to quit the Indian soil. After a great turmoil Bose arrived in Tokyo on May 16, 1943. Rash Behari Bose greeted him and handed over leadership to Bose on July 4, 1943.

Subhas Chandra Bose on assumption of Presidentship of the Indian Independence League addressed the Conference held in Singapore on July 4, 1943 : "Friends, the time to start an armed struggle for freedom has come. Military service and loyalty to the mother country are the most essential things necessary to achieve our goal of freedom during the war."[8] He cautioned the countrymen : "The British may offer promises which I must tell you are made to ensure you. Any compromise with the British will be sheer loss for us, and will prove detrimental to our interests. We must be ready for sacrifice and action."[9] On June 18, 1943 he addressed Mahatma through a press statement : "The enemy that has drawn the sword must be fought with the sword. Civil disobedience must develop into armed struggle. And only when the Indian people receive the baptism of fire on a large scale will they qualify for their freedom."[10] Again, on June 21, 1943 : "But what I want to point out is that by compromise the British politicians will never recognize India's independence, but will only try to bluff the Indian people."[11] In short, Bose's message both to Mahatma and to British : 'No compromise'.

Provisional Government of Free India

On October 21, 1943 the Indian Independence League at its meeting in Singapore formed the Provisional Government of Free India. Bose took the oath : "In the name of God, I take the sacred oath that to liberate India and the thirty-eight crores of my countrymen I, Subhas Chandra Bose, will continue this sacred war of freedom till the last breath of my life."[12] Further : "Even after winning freedom, I will always be prepared to shed even the last drop of my blood for the preservation of India's freedom". The main object of the Provisional Government was to conduct the last war against the British and their allies in India. In his speech Bose repeatedly said that a new government would be established in India based on the free will of the people. He addressed : "It remains now to start the final struggle for freedom. This will begin when the Indian National Army crosses the frontier of India and commences its historic march to Delhi. The march will end only when the Anglo-Americans are expelled from India and the Indian National Flag is hoisted over the Viceroy's House in New Delhi".[13]

The Provisional Government of Free India was recognized by eight countries by November 1943. The countries were :

Japan, Burma, Croatia, Germany, National Government of China, Italy and Thai. On October 24, 1943 at 12.55 a.m. the Provisional Government declared war against Britain and the USA. And within two hours San Francisco broadcast this information over radio. In order to counter apprehension of a section of Congressmen and the propaganda of the British that Bose was going to replace the British rule by the rule of Japan, Subhas Bose broadcast : "If the British Government could not befool me with its blandishments, no other nation on earth can do."[14] It may be mentioned here that the Japanese Prime Minister Tojo declared Japan's intention to transfer the Andaman and Nicobar Islands to the Provisional Government of Free India, which he did. On January 8, 1945 the Provisional Government of Free India appointed a Chief Commissioner for the Islands. The Andaman and Nicobar Islands were renamed *Saheed* and *Swaraj* respectively.

To Delhi, To Delhi

The slogan of the Provisional Government of Free India : "On to Delhi". The Indian National Army marched forward to the Indian boarders on and from February 4, 1944 and attacked the Arakan Mountains near Indo-Burma border and step by step reached Kennedy Peak on March 18 and saw the soil of India. The Japanese Prime Minister Tojo declared on March 22, 1944 that all the areas of India occupied by the Japanese troops would be placed under the jurisdiction of the Provisional Government of Free India. His historic declaration : "The purpose of Imperial Japan is to destroy the power of the enemy and to transfer the whole of India to Indian hands. All areas occupied in the course of Japanese advance will be immediately placed under the administration of the Provisional Government of Free India. I shall expect that the patriotic Indian people will welcome the advancing armies of INA, that the liberated areas will rapidly grow larger and larger and complete independence will come." He proceeded : "The independence of India is the common desire of all Asia and it is in keeping with world conscience. . . I sincerely hope and pray that the Indian soldiers will be able to overcome all difficulties and fighting unitedly continue their advance on the road to victory. I once again declare to the world that Imperial Japan is firmly resolved to make all efforts to help in this task."[15]

This declaration might have convinced the world as a whole and softened the anti-Japanese stand of Gandhi but became a burning spectre of Bose to Nehru & Co.

The INA continued to advance and reached Kohima on April 6, 1944 and on May 7 the INA crossed the Indo-Burma border and entered into India from the South. Then for the first time in the British Raj history the Indians as independent Indians hoisted an April 14, 1944 the flag of independence on Indian soil of Mairang in Manipur. Unfortunately, the INA could not advance further because of intermittent rains that had destroyed the supply routes.

All this when the war situation took a turn in favour of the Allied powers. And this was mainly for the entry of the USA into Allied powers with mighty navy and air forces. The Allied forces defeated the Axis forces in South Africa in May 1943 and invaded Italy on September 3, 1943. On October 19, 1944 the US troops landed in Philippines. In the meantime the Tojo Cabinet resigned and a new Cabinet was formed led by Koise on April 22, 1944. Undaunted Bose addressed his countrymen on April 4, 1944 : "The Provisional Government of Azad Hind will continue the armed struggle until the Anglo-American forces are annihilated or expelled from India."[16] But the war situation was further rapidly deteriorating. Germany surrendered unconditionally on May 7, 1945. To proceed to close up, the brutality of American imperialism went so far that the United States atombombed Hiroshima and Nagasaki (Japan) on 6th and 9th August 1945 respectively. All this when Japan was in the process of surrender. Japan surrendered unconditionally on 14th August 1945, formally signed on September 2, 1945.

Anyway, Bose was reluctant to leave Japan. But under pressure of circumstances he intended to fly over to the Soviet Union with some of the trusted members of his Cabinet. Finally, he, accompanied by his close associate Habibur Rahman, boarded a bomber plane of the Imperial Japanese Army for landing in the capital of Manchuria where he would be bailed out to the Russian armies, which were then heading towards South, to work out his own ways and means there. On August 18, 1945 the plane crashed after it took off from Taipaei Airport. Bose "died" in that accident and Rahman was severely injured.

Whatever may be the irony of fate Subhas Chandra Bose's patriotism and conviction remained continuous. In his Special Order of the Day of August 17, 1945 he said : "And Delhi is our goal. The sacrifices of your immortal comrades and yourselves will certainly bring victory. There is no power on earth which can keep India in bondage. India will certainly be free and that too, soon, Jai Hind!"

NOTES AND REFERENCES

1. Some political analysts hold that strategically Bose had committed Himalayan Blunder and admitted defeatism by his adoption of the line of escapism. He escaped from virtually the imprisonment of the British and the Gandhians. The Forward Bloc was too feeble a challenge to Congress. He might have followed the line of Lenin to lead the party and people from afar. But Lenin had strong ground of his own in Russia while he had negligible. Mahatma was there to guide or misguide the people. He was still then the 'law' to the people. Had he been in India his revolutionary image and activities could have reduced the weight of the durbar of the Congress-League-Communists with the British Raj for the people were at heart against division of India.

   There is reason in all this. But can any revolutionary give away the 'golden opportunity' in apprehension of partition of the country or in expectation of gaining freedom as a gift? Bose had followed the historical line. If the war did not take the turn in favour of the Allied powers, the entry of Bose into his motherland would be inevitable. Then by his war and unity image he could wipe out all disunities by all means of democracy. Bose took a chance, for the accident he could not be held responsible.

2. Netaji and India's Freedom, *op. cit.*, p. 272.
3. *Ibid.*
4. *Ibid.*, p. 315.

5. *Ibid.*, p. 311.

6. *Ibid.*, p. 313.

7. Rash Behari Bose (May 25, 1886–January 21, 1945) was a militant revolutionist. He hurled bomb on Viceroy Hardinge on December 23, 1912 at Chandni Chowk in Delhi. Hardinge fainted and fell back in shock. He in association with the Gadhar Party of Punjab planned an all-India armed upsurge on February 19, 1915. This was foiled because of spying of Kripal Singh, also a revolutionist. He then escaped to Japan in 1915. There he remained underground for long eight years. Then in 1923 he started openly movement for India's freedom there.

8. Selected Speeches of Subhas Chandra Bose, *op. cit.*, p. 178.

9. *Ibid.*, p. 179.

10. Netaji and India's Freedom, *op. cit.*, p. 338.

11. *Ibid.*, p. 340.

12. *Ibid.*, p. 351.

13. *Ibid.*, p. 352.

14. Rash Behari Bose : His Struggle for India's Independence, Edited by Radhanath Rath *et al*, Biplabi Mahanayak Rash Behari Bose Smarak Samiti, Calcutta, 1963, p. 486.

15. Netaji and India's Freedom, *op. cit.*, p. 388.

16. *Ibid.*, p. 389.

8

SPECTRE OF BOSE
Gandhi at Cross-Roads

At Cross-Roads

In March 1939, keeping in view the world war on the Western horizon, Subhas Chandra Bose as the Congress President proposed that the Congress should serve immediately an ultimatum to the British Government demanding independence within six months and simultaneously prepare for a national struggle. The proposal was opposed by the Gandhi-wing and it took such a turn that eventually he had to resign and face expulsion from the Congress at the instance of Gandhi and thereafter to form Forward Bloc. On September 3, 1939 Britain declared war against Germany. The Viceroy immediately after declared India a belligerent and issued an ordinance for suppression of internal disorder. On September 11, 1939 the Viceroy also announced postponement of inauguration of the Federal Constitution during the war period. All this annoyed Gandhi in that the British Government did not even mind to take the consent of the Indians prior to declaring India as a belligerent. War means violence, violence means war against the creed of Gandhi's non-violence. Gandhi as such was in dilemma where and how to stand with his creed in the breast and the torch of *ahimsa* in the hands as the means to win the world, India being a belligerent country.

The Congress took up the matter and on September 14, 1939 the Congress Working Committee in its meeting condemned Fascism and Nazism of the Axis forces of Italy and Germany and showed softness for the anti-fascist and anti-nazist stand of the Allied forces of Britain and France. However, it showed displeasure for declaring unilaterally India a belligerent. At the same time it maintained the Congress loyalty to the British Empire assuring cooperation with the Empire in its war effort. To Congress, mostly organized by Nehru, it was not an imperialist war but 'international war' – the war of liberation of the world from the domination of racism for the global cause of 'freedom and democracy'. The Congress sought for cooperation of equals. For it was only a free India that could fight together with the Allied forces against the Axis forces. Thus, the Congress demanded, rather expected, positive and unequivocal declaration of India's independence beforehand. In short, let India be free and then let India to be an ally of the Allied forces. The Congress had reason behind this. It had bitter experience during the First World War (1914-1918) when the British Empire made many lofty promises during and after the war but ultimately betrayed the nation. For instance, the British Prime Minister Llyod George appealed to India to cooperate with the British Empire by participating in the war conference and hinted that the hour of independence of India was near at hand. Gandhi, a born loyalist of the Empire, at once extended his unconditional cooperation to the Empire as its citizen. His hope was if not today day after today the heart of the Empire would get converted into *ahimsa*. He was however gifted with Rowlatt Act, which he designated as Black Act. Thus being taught a lesson the Congress this time sought positive response from the Empire : "The real test of any declaration is its application in the present, for it is the present that will govern action today and give shape to the future. . . It will be infinite tragedy if even this terrible war is carried on in the spirit of imperialism and for the purpose of retaining this structure which is itself the cause of war and human degradation."[1]

But the British Empire was firm as ever in its stand of no-compromise with the Congress demand for freedom here and now. So also the Congress not to come out from its creed of *ahimsa* and conversion or to disturb the Empire during the war period. Thus, the Congress had been suffering from conflict and contradiction. The conflict was between the rulers' attitude of no-compromise with the demand for independence and the Congress demand of no-compromise with independence and the contradiction in its means of movement for freedom without any disturbance to the rulers' war effort, leaving aside the basic contradiction between war and non-violence. In order to pacify the urge of the people to win freedom at any cost Gandhi took up the tact of taken protest directing the Congress governments in the eight provinces to resign followed by his innovative 'individual satyagraha' as against mass movement of non-cooperation. And side by side the Congress raised the 'moral issue' in public not to profit by taking any means of bargaining in war effort. The Congress Working Committee declared that it would "continue to explore the means of arriving at an honourable settlement, even though the British Government had banged the door in the face of the Congress."[2] So noble was the mind of the Congress that it did not falter to pronounce that this war was a 'holy war'— war for world freedom and democracy.

Thus, the music is that it was Gandhi who once said : "If the British wish to document their right to win the war and make the world better they must purify themselves surrendering power to India." Then his comments on the American President Roosevealt's formulation of Four Pillars : "Do they include the freedom to be free? We are asked to fight for democracy in Germany, Italy and Japan. How can we when we have not get it ourselves."[3] The Congress politics in 'holy war' was to divert the attention of the people from freedom movement to holy cause of the war waged by the British Empire against the Axis powers. This was also to help uplift the Gandhian creed of *ahimsa* and win freedom through peaceful and legitimate means.

But the people cannot be befooled for long. They were growing insurgent. At the annual session of the Congress at Ramgarh in March 1940 the Congress decided to launch civil disobedience movement and asked the people just to get prepared. In the meantime, another attempt was made to arrive at some settlement with the British Government. C.R. Rajagopalachari was the negotiator between the Government and the Congress which worked out that the Viceroy in cooperation with all the parties would form the national government. However, reluctant, Gandhi and Nehru accepted the settlement on moral grounds to oppose the Fascism and Nazism. At that time Subhas Chandra Bose was in the blacklist of the Congress, that is, Gandhi. However, he was not sitting idle. The annual session of the Congress at Ramgarh had to face massive demonstration of the strength of Forward Bloc. The Bloc had been making periodical demonstrations through anti-compromise conferences. Shortly, Subhas Chandra Bose was put to prison (June 1940). Prior to his arrest, to repeat, he had a talk with Gandhi and with his close associates on war policy but found Gandhi non-committal on mass agitation against the British Government. His reasoning was that the country was not prepared for undertaking such movement.

By then the German troops were fast advancing towards their neighbouring states. France collapsed. Britain was seized with alarm. Nehru on May 20, 1940 came out speaking loudly: "Launching a civil disobedience campaign at a time when Britain is engaged in life and death struggle would be an act derogatory to India's honour."[4] Gandhi was pleased. And he too said : "We do not seek our independence out of Britain's ruin. That is not the way of non-violence."[5] Thus, what was the 'golden opportunity' to Bose and the people was 'immoral' and 'derogatory'. Gandhi's morality suddenly rose so high that let India be ruined but not Britain, even in spite of its devilish character of no-compromise with the legitimate demand of India for independence.

In the meantime, Gandhi had retired from the leadership of the Congress. It was because he discovered in the AICC resolution of September 16, 1940 that there was no line of creed of *ahimsa* in the resolution of non-participation of the Congress in Britain's war effort. It was simply a strategy. It may be recalled that Gandhi gave up the primary membership of the Congress in 1934 to think, work and move independently with his means and end philosophy.

On July 27, 1940 at the Congress meeting at Poona the Congress offered cooperation with Britain on condition of declaration of independence. The Viceroy's reply came on August 8 which was virtually negative. The Forward Bloc was going through its campaign of anti-compromise that continued to stir up the people's urge and disturb the mental balance of Gandhi on compromise with the Government at any cost. The Congress was at the cross-roads as also Gandhi. Feeling much helplessness the Congress finally approached Gandhi to take up the leadership again. Gandhi agreed and resumed his leadership. On September 15 the Congress withdrew its offer of cooperation and bestowed all power upon Gandhi to lead the country in his own way. Gandhi then started campaigning half-heartedly keeping ever the door of compromise open. Subhas Chandra Bose escaped from the grip of the imprisonment.

Spectre of Bose

Subhas Chandra Bose addressed the people of India from Berlin on March 13, 1942 :

> "Some Indian nationalists even went on to the extent of announcing that, should the British satisfy their national aspirations, they would be prepared to help them in this war. To this appeal British statement paid no heed. They never gave an unambiguous reply which would have earned the goodwill of Indians. With characteristic hypocrisy and fraud, they have again made an obscure declaration.
>
> "Friends, it is crystal clear that in British decline alone lies the hope of India's independence. Every Indian who works to strengthen the British hands betrays the cause of his motherland. Such a man is a traitor to India. Whoever opposes Indian patriots and sides with the British is no better than Mir Jafar or an Umi Chand of the present generation."[6]

How displeasing the address was to Gandhi and Nehru who

were indirectly designated 'traitors of India', and how much it was pleasing to the British rulers who found in it more emotion of rousing anti-Axis feelings in Gandhi and Nehru, this can easily be guessed.

Gandhi became worried about the spectre of Bose whom he kept out twice from being the Congress President by denying to give him his nomination. In 1939 election Bose 'defeated' Gandhi and became the Congress President for two consecutive terms and now that very Bose addressing the people from the Axis Camp advising them that "their first duty would be to carry out a thorough destruction of British military objectives in India, and prevent India's raw material, wealth and youth from being harnessed by the British to their war effort".[7] On the opposite side Gandhi cautioned the people : "Subhas Babu will bring German troops to oust the possessor; Germany is under no obligation to deliver India from bondage. Therefore, Subhas Babu's performance can only fling India from frying pan to fire".[8] It is beyond the comprehension of history how the enemy of 'common enemy' has no obligation to deliver India from bondage. This also exposed Gandhi's duality about Bose. At heart he did not like the existence of Bose but in lip service Bose was a 'patriot of patriots' to him. How a true patriot of patriots could be so 'misguided' that he was throwing his motherland from frying pan to fire? What was the measure of his judgement that Bose was 'misguided' and not he himself?

Gandhi's apathy towards Bose was further exposed in his interview with a journalist in May 1942 when he said that the people were very happy when Subhas Babu said over the radio that there were no differences between him and Gandhi and also that Gandhiji was now out to fight for liberty at any cost. Gandhiji's reactions : "I cannot possibly appreciate the compliments he is paying me. . . 'At any cost' does not exist in my dictionary. It does not, for instance, include bringing in foreigners to help us in our liberty. I have no doubt, it means exchanging one form of slavery for another, possibly much worse".[9] When in November 1941 the war clouds appeared in the Far Eastern horizon Gandhi became further alert. He made it clear to Bose : "I do not feel flattered when Subhas Babu says, I am right. I am not right in the sense he means. For there he is attributing pro-Japanese feeling to me. If I were to discover that by some strange miscalculation I had not realized the fact that I was helping the entry of the Japanese in the country, I should not hesitate to retrace my steps".[10]

The Japanese troops were advancing rapidly and within a week Singapore surrendered to Japan on February 15, 1942. The troops then after fighting the Malayan campaign advanced towards Burma. The British army was forced to retreat from Burma. The mental strength of the British administration was then tottering and to Gandhi the victory of the Axis powers was a certainty. To him then the only course open was to compromise with the British Empire and then with the aid of the British defence forces to fight unitedly against the Japanese invaders to defend the country.

Japan's war success switched Gandhi's attention from West to East. His assessment was that Japan was advancing to invade India to colonize her, although she was propagating herself as the liberator of India : "The Japanese are broadcasting every day that they do not intend to keep India — their only purpose is to help us win our freedom. I do not welcome their sympathy or help. I know they are not philanthropists."[11] Gandhi had no issue of philanthropy in international politics. But the international politics rests on common national interests and when fulfilled disunity follows for a higher form of unity again. Japan must have interest in India. It was not for colonization of India. For that era was fast dying out with the culmination of the Second World War. Its interest was in India's vast resourceful market. The rise of imperialism was largely because of the poverty of some struggling small countries with poor natural resources as that of Britain and Japan. Britain showed no interest to Quit India not for its lust for India's territory but for its interest in India's resources over which it had monopoly.

However, the fear psychosis made Gandhi desperate to come to terms with the British Government. He had also felt the pulse of the masses who were growing more and more pro-

Japanese. He said : "possibility of a large number of Indians going over to the Japanese side — if they effected a landing on the Indian shores — as we knew happened in Burma, Malay, and as far as I know, Singapore too."[12] The Congress was also getting prepared. At the AICC meeting on May 1, 1942 the following resolution was adopted : "The Committee repudiates the idea that freedom can come to India through interference or invasion by any foreign nation, whatever the professions of the nation may be. In case an invasion takes place it must be resisted. Such resistance can only take the form of non-violent non-cooperation."[13] Obviously the target of the resolution was Subhas Chandra Bose. But Bose at no time or nowhere had said freedom through third party's interference or invasion. He sought international cooperation for assertion of freedom as the birth right. It was Nehru who had begged the US President Roosevelt for 'interference' and Gandhi ever made Britain to be the 'third party' to win freedom through peaceful transference of power. Anyway, the resolution once again confirmed the Congress loyalty to the Empire : "Not to put any obstacle in the way of British forces will often be the only way of demonstrating our non-cooperation with the invader."[14] Whereas the call of Bose : "a thorough destruction of British military objectives in India".

Gandhi was absolutely at the cross-roads being haunted constantly by the spectre of Bose. He always felt as if the Japanese troops were "knocking our gates" and seemed convinced that "Japan will not rest till India is wholly in her hands." At a certain stage his axiomatic belief was that the defeat of the British was inevitable and the only and last resort was to fight together with the British against the Japanese invaders. He asked the British to remain in India until the invader was crushed : "Don't leave India to Japan, but leave to Indians in an orderly manner."[15] This happened when he recollected the situations in Burma and Malay where-from the British army retreated leaving them "neither to God nor to anarchy, but to the Japanese." Such slavish mentality played in his mind because he knew the non-violent non-cooperation would be a fun to keep the Japanese at bay. The most tragic event was that he had lost influence in his leadership : "I have no confidence to direct the people's energy in a channel in which they have no interest."[16] He was hovering. Sometimes, he was suspicious about the declaration of Japan of India's independence and felt secure in the lap of the British : "I am more interested than the British in keeping the Japanese out. For Britain's defeat in Indian waters may mean only the loss of India but if Japan wins, India loses everything."[17] In substance : "If Bose wins, Gandhi loses everything", which was inconceivable to Gandhi, a man, above all, possessed by his idea. At times he became so crude as to say that the "non-violent resisters would refuse them (Japanese invaders) to help, even water." Then some other times disgusted with the British no-compromise attitude he said : "The presence of the British in India is an invitation to Japan to invade India. Free India will be better able to cope with the invasion. Unadulterated non-cooperation will then have full sway."[18]

Gradually Gandhi became soft towards Japan : "Japan's quarrel is not with India. She is warring against the British Empire. If India were freed, her first step would probably be to negotiate with Japan."[19] Nehru vehmently opposed this : "The whole background of the draft is one which will inevitably make the whole world think we are passively linking up with the Axis power."[20] Nehru's stand was to resist invasion at any cost. That is, resistance of entry of Subhas Chandra Bose at any cost, otherwise his future would be totally ruined. Sometimes he became so emotional that he advised the people to resort to 'guerilla warfare', which was dismissed by Gandhi as a 'nine days wonder'. Then over-stepping the Congress creed of *ahimsa* he said : "We should fight in every way possible with non-violent means and with arms, by making it a people's war, by raising people's army, by increasing production and industrialization."[21] He all along tried to console himself that Subhasist sentiment or actual pro-Japanese sentiment was practically nil for no one wanted to change masters. Although he himself was aware that Bose in his great escape had risked his life as the 'patriot of patriots' not to change masters but to liberate the motherland by any means. He was however candid to confess that those who were pro-Japanese "were influenced by the broadcasts being made by Subhas Chandra Bose who had secretly escaped from India the year before."[22]

Cripps Mission

The spectres of Bose and Japan and the rapid collapse of the British colonies in the East worried also the British diplomats. They were feeling the need and urgency of cooperation of Indians in their war effort. The British War Cabinet headed by Winston Churchill sent Sir Stafford Cripps to India with some set proposals (See Appendix I) to offer. Sir Cripps arrived in India in April 1942 and placed forward the proposals, which were all for future and not for the present, seeking cooperation in their war effort for the present. The proposals provided self-determination and the right of the provinces to form separate independent states. The right to non-accession was also allowed to the princely states some six hundred in number. Gandhi at once rejected the proposals as 'post-dated cheque on a failing bank', and advised Sir Cripps 'to take the first plane home'. In this context Gandhi looked back : "Far back, Lord Minto, the Viceroy, declared that the British had to keep Muslims and Hindus apart in order to facilitate the domination of India." And "Cripps proposals divided Hindus and Muslims more than ever."[23]

The AICC resolved on May 1, 1942 that the proposals of Sir Stafford Cripps : "have led to greater bitterness and distrust of that Government and the spirit of non-cooperation with British has grown. . . the British Government functions as an imperialist government and refuses to recognize the independence of India or to part with any real power."[24]

The Congress once more realized the real character of British imperialism. Subhas Bose also addressed the nation over the Azad Hind Radio from Germany on March 25, 1942: "Britain wants to achieve a two-fold purpose. She desires, on the one hand, to utilize to the fullest extent India's resources for the whole Empire, and, on the other, to force thereby the enemies of Britain to attack Britain's military base in India, so that the Indian people may be provoked into voluntarily entering the war as Britain's ally."[25]

Gandhi, a man professed by 'inner voice', waited for the 'voice'. On time the 'voice' voiced : "Quit India". Enough for Gandhi.

NOTES AND REFERENCES

1. Jawaharlal Nehru, *Discovery of India,* pp. 418-19, J.L. Nehru Memorial Fund, Teen Murti House, New Delhi, 1995.
2. *Ibid.,* p. 434.
3. Interview with Louis Fischer, June 7, 1942, Collected Works, Vol. 76, p. 439, *op. cit.*
4. *Netaji Collected Works,* Vol. 2, pp. 384-385, Netaji Research Bureau, Calcutta, 1981.
5. *Ibid.,* p. 385.
6. Selected Speeches of Subhas Chandra Bose, S.A. Ayer, pp. 128-129. Publications Division, Ministry of Information and Broadcasting, GOI, 1962.
7. *Ibid.,* 128.
8. *Harijan,* 19.7.42, Collected Works, Vol. 76, p. 282.
9. Collected Works, Vol. 77, p. 181.
10. *Ibid.,* p. 182.
11. Interview with Louis Fischer, June 7, 1942, Collected Works, Vol. 76, p. 442.
12. To a foreign Journalist, July 15, 1942.
13. Collected Works, Vol. 76, *op. cit.,* p. 425.
14. *Ibid.*
15. *Ibid.,* Vol. 77, p. 168.
16. Tendulkar, Vol. 6, *op. cit.,* p. 128.
17. Collected Works, Vol. 77, p. 164.
18. Tendulkar, Vol. 6, p. 81.
19. *Netaji Collected Works,* Vol. 2, *op. cit.,* pp. 389-399.
20. *Ibid.,* p. 389.

21. Collected Works, Vol. 77, *op. cit.*, p. 192.
22. Nehru, *Discovery of India, op. cit.*, p. 469.
23. Collected Works, Vol. 76, *op. cit.*, p. 437.
24. *Ibid.*, p. 424.
25. S.A. Ayer, *op. cit.*, p. 133.

9

QUIT INDIA
Farce and Betrayal

The Scenario

The dismissal of Cripps proposals gave way to political turmoil which is well graphed by Nehru in his *The Discovery of India.*[1] To him the abrupt termination of Cripps negotiations was not only a surprise but also unpleasing. For the hasty decision of Gandhi had left the country at the point of no hope of a settlement with Britain nor even to defend the country with the power of violent arms of the British against the aggressor Japan. He felt that the chance of invasion was growing and the civil administration of India was suffering from a nervous breakdown. To him there were rays of hope with the advent of American air and army on Indian soil. The British authorities were even then could not rest trust on the Indians and were afraid of the Congress proposal of organizing popular fronts. In April the Congress expressed its deep resentment at this policy and treatment. This shows that the British attitude was let the Congress depend on the British but the British would not depend on the Congress. They bore independent character and policy.

The Gandhi-wing, then largely under the leadership of Nehru, advised the people not to interfere in any way in Anglo-American imperialist forces operations as that would be giving of indirect aid to the invader. Instead, if the invading forces sought to take possession of any Indian territories they must resist unto death. The logic behind this was that the death of even a limited number, innocent as they were, would raise national spirit of resistance. Thus, to the Gandhi-wing, not the British but the Japanese were the number one enemy of India.

Running for 'inner voice'

Gandhi was growing impatient : "If I am impatient of the British yoke, I am so because India's sulliness and suppressed delight of the man in the street over British overseas reverses are dangerous symptoms which may lead to the success of Japanese designs upon India, if they are not dealt with in the proper manner."[2] Gandhi felt that the voice of the people and the voice of the Gandhi-wing were just opposite. It was a danger signal and so an immediate agitation must have to be launched that could deal with both the people and the British in the proper manner. It was for him : "that the time has come during the war, not after it, for the British and the Indians to be reconciled to complete separation from each other. That way alone lies the safety of both."[3] Why so much urge for separation disowning loyalty? At the end of 1942 Gandhi said : "I have waited and waited, until the country should develop the non-violent strength necessary to throw off foreign yoke. But my attitude has now undergone a change. I feel that I cannot afford to wait. If I continue to wait, I might have to wait till doomsday." His mind might have been swelled up with the Black Rowlatt Act as he said : "The whole idea keeps blossoming out within me. The original idea of asking the British to go burst upon me suddenly. It was the Cripps fiasco that inspired the idea. Hardly had he gone, when it seized hold of me."[4] And the idea was 'Quit India'—the solid voice of the 'inner voice'. The 'voice called for no prior plan and programme, only the message : 'Do or Die' ('*Karenge Ya Marenge*'). It did not mean 'kill or be killed'. Its "true meaning is that we must do our duty and die in the course of performing it, if necessary. To die without killing is the badge of a *satyagrahi*. If we had lived upto that ideal we would have won *swaraj* by now."[5] Thus, Gandhi tactfully pacified the pro-Cripps Congressmen like Nehru and at the same time took up the *ahimsa* means to reverse the attention of the people from Japan to Britain, with hopes of peaceful settlement with the British Government.

On August 7, 1942 the AICC adopted 'Quit India' resolution (See Appendix II). Its basic features : Non-violence; Every man and woman must be prepared to be his/her own leader; All must carry out 'all I (Gandhi) say' : "God has vouchsafed to me a priceless gift in the weapon of *ahimsa*"; Shed tears for China and Russia, the victims of Axis powers.

The headlines of the directives : (i) On the day of *hartal* no processions, no meetings to be held in cities; (ii) Every *satyagrahi* should vow that he will free or die; (iii) All students of government institutions should come out and those who are sixteen years of age should join the *satyagraha*; (iv) If excesses are there by the Government the people should offer resistance and endure penalty; and (v) Tax, salt and land, not to be paid.

All this was '*satyagraha* and passive resistance', how-ever old and obscure that might be. Gandhi was not hopeful about the success of his 'Quit India' venture. For it was within his knowledge that his 'non-violence' was represented by a hopeless minority. However, he inspired the people with the feelings : "It is only when individuals go out to seek and face death that the nation will survive."[6] He had also warned the people : "I can say that so far as they are contrary to non-violence, they can never have my approval."[7]

The 'Quit India' resolution of the Congress was the result of impatience of Gandhi who had been haunted con-stantly by the spectre of Bose and also of the re-discovery of Nehru that Bose in afar was not insignificant in public feelings: "While we were doubting and debating, the mood of the country changed, and from a sullen passivity it rose to a pitch of excitement and expectation. Events were not waiting for a Congress decision or resolution. . . It was clear that, whether Gandhiji was right or wrong, he had crystallized the prevailing mood of the people. There was a desperateness in it. . . It was better to jump into the unchartered seas of action and do something, rather than be the time objects of a malign fate."[8]

Thus, the function of the 'inner voice' apart, the 'Quit India' was for the Congress a compulsion to "jump into the unchartered seas of action", however childish it might be, to do 'something', rather than to be reduced to 'nothing'. In other words, the 'Quit India' was a thoughtless action and not a logical operation. Mentally Gandhi was also growing a bit violent : "If a man holds me by the neck and wants to drown me, may I not struggle to free myself directly?"[9] He found no harm to compromise with war and violence if that would be an absolute necessity. Even he expressed his urge to take up arms in hand : "I would rather see India freed by violence than enchained like a slave to her foreign oppressors."[10]

All this does not mean that Gandhi became a new soul. His faith in non-violence and loyalty to the British Empire remained as before. He said : "I feel myself to be a greater friend of the British now than ever before. One reason is that they are today in distress."[11] It may be mentioned that the 'Quit India' resolution was drafted by Gandhi, moved by Nehru and seconded by Patel.

Nehru addressed the Congress that the Anglo-American armies would be allowed to defend India against the invasion of Japan as non-violence was too poor a weapon to hit back the invaders. The Congress President Abul Kalam Azad and Gandhi made it clear that before finalization of the Quit India movement they would appeal to the British Government and the United Nations : "For an honourable settlement, which while recognizing the freedom of India, would also advance the cause of the United Nations in the struggle against the aggressive Axis powers."[12] But so poor was the reading of the Congress of the political mind of the United Nations and the depth of its loyalty to the British Empire that it had to bear the humiliation when the British Prime Minister Winston

Churchill cleared off that "democracy and freedom" was not for the colonial countries. The American President smilingly accepted the doctrine.

Challenge against Challenge

The Governor-General-in-Council published a resolution on 8th August 1942 that the Government was determined to meet the 'challenge' contained in the resolution of the Congress. Gandhi and all other leaders of the Congress were arrested on 9th August. Before going to prison Gandhi left the instruction, possibly to know the number of his true followers : "Let every non-violent soldier of freedom write out the slogan 'Do or Die' on a piece of paper or cloth, and stick it on his clothes, so that in case he died in the course of offering *satyagraha*, he might be distinguished by that sign from elements who do not subscribe to non-violence."[13] It was very much stimulating to record oneself as the true follower of Mahatma and at the same time to be an asset of his that would help him to pronounce that his experiment failed because of the betrayal of the people; if succeeded it was because of non-violence.

Bose from Germany

Subhas Chandra Bose broadcast from Germany on August 31, 1942 : "The campaign that is now going on in India may be described as non-violent guerilla warfare. . . we should spread out our activities all over the country so that the British police and military may not be able to concentrate their attack on one point." Then he added : "I am in a position to offer you some suggestions as to how this present campaign should be brought to a victorious end. The object of this non-violent guerilla warfare should be a two-fold one. Firstly, to destroy war production in India, and secondly, to paralyse the British administration in the country."

The Gandhians had no intention to 'destroy' or 'paralyse' the British administration. Their urge was to protect the British war production so that the Congress could fight unitedly with the Anglo-American forces from the soil of India against Japan *vis-a-vis* Bose to win freedom as a gift for siding with the war-effort of the British Empire.

The British Government did its best to massacre all the broadcasts of Bose so that they could not reach the doorsteps of the people of India. Besides, such idea of non-violent guerilla warfare sounded evil to the Gandhi-wing.

The Government's excesses exceeded all limits of endurance of the people yet violence did not take any serious turn. The non-violence opportunity apart, the Government had the cooperation of the Muslim League and the Communist Party of India as both were 'hand-in-gloves' with the Government. The disturbance continued for a month or two. The British Prime Minister Winston Churchill addressed the House of Commons : "The disturbances were crushed with all the weight of the Government."[14] This was the price which had to be paid by Gandhi for his non-violence and loyalty not to disturb the war-effort.

The movement was crushed by the end of September 1942. Consequently, all eyes fell on Gandhi. Gandhi disowned all responsibility as in 1921 when he declared *swaraj* within a year. His ground was that the people violated the creed of non-violence. This time he shirked all responsibilities on the ground that he was outside the movement as he was under detention and according "to the canons of *satyagraha* when a civil resister was imprisoned, authority vested in him automatically came to an end."[15] But how could it be convincing when everybody knew that Gandhi and all his lieutenants would be thrown into prison and he himself in apprehension of this worked out what was to be done by each and every *satyagrahi* resister in his and their absence. Does it not mean that guidelines were 'thoughtless' that had 'misguided' the *satyagrahis*? Gandhi, however, was evasive in this matter. Instead he accused the Government for excesses, which was not anything unusual.

Back to Pavilion

Although Gandhi was in detention he did not fail to observe the development of the Quit India movement upto the end. On December 31, 1942 he sent a 'personal letter' to his 'personal friend', the Viceroy Lord Linlithgow. Lord Linlithgow wrote back on January 13, 1943 : "You wish now to retrace your steps and disassociate yourself from the policy of last summer." Then again on January 25 he wrote : "If, therefore, you are anxious to inform me that you repudiate or you disassociate yourself from the resolution of the 9th August and the policy which that resolution represents, and if you can give me the appropriate assurances as regards the future, I shall, I need not say, be very ready to consider the matter further."

The history wonders how did Lord Linlithgow dare write such letters to Gandhi knowing that it was Gandhi who was in command of the Congress and the sole promoter of the Quit India resolution? The man who was professed by the idea and who only that day raised his 'inner voice' "Do or Die" could comfortably absorb the advices of his 'friend' Viceroy Lord Linlithgow? Whereas Gandhiji's trusted 'heir' Pandit Jawaharlal Nehru adversely reacted. In his prison diary he recorded : "With all his very great qualities he had proved a poor and weak leader, uncertain and changing his mind frequently." Then further on August 5, 1944 : "I feel that I must break with this woolly thinking and undignified action—which really means breaking with Gandhi. I have at present no desire even to go to him on release and discuss matters with him what do such discussions lead to?"[16] But it was Nehru who suggested to "jump into the unchartered seas of action" to do 'somcthing' to thwart the entry of Bose into India.

The reactions of Subhas Chandra Bose from afar : "Non-violence is the life-long creed of Mahatma Gandhi. But so far as the people are concerned, it is only a tactic, a temporary tactic, a tactic which is temporarily useful. But they will take up arms as the times change." Further : "India will get freedom through an armed struggle coupled with a civil disobedience movement." Then again : "Freedom cannot be given by others. Indians should win it through their own struggle and sacrifice."[17]

Mr. Amery, Secretary of State, snubbed Gandhi further : "There can be no question of the Government of India entering into negotiations. . . so long as there is the danger of recrudescence of troubles. . . or until they made it clear to the authorities that they have abandoned their whole policy to control India by illegal methods and are prepared to come to an agreed settlement with ourselves and their fellow country-men."

The defeat of the historic Quit India Movement was a great victory for the British Government. After the victory Amery called for unconditional surrender with repentance and penance. For it was within the experience of Amery that so long as the Indian soldiers and police and administration would remain loyal to the British Government the non-violent agitations would cause no danger to the existence of the British Raj. And about the 'agreed settlement' it was known to them that the 'fellow countrymen' would never come to agreement with Hindus so long as the British remained in India. And about the loyalty of Indian soldiers upon whom the whole safety of India and the fate of Allied cause so largely depended there had been nothing to worry as they were fighting like one with the Allied forces overseas. Actually, to the British Empire Gandhi's non-violent non-cooperation was 'sesame' and his 'unto death fast' was nothing but 'political blackmailing'. In this context it may be said that Gandhi did never try to rouse anti-British feelings in the rank and file of the Indian soldiers lest his *ahimsa* creed was marred by violence and the British Government felt disturbed during war time thereby facilitating the entry of the Japanese troops.

Change of Scenario

Being frustrated Gandhi informed his decision of resorting to 'fast for twentyone days'. He expected some 'reciprocal action' as he had gained during Lord Irwin that led to 'Gandhi-Irwin' Pact. But Lord Linlithgow summarily dismissed his threat as 'political blackmail', later by Lord Wavell as magic 'sesame' that had opened the Ali Baba's Cave. Gandhi was then 74 years old and was released from detention mainly on health grounds on 6th May 1944. By that time the war trend was favourable to the Allied powers. But yet then the British Government and Gandhiites were being haunted by the spectre of Bose who was then moving towards Indian soil with his Azad Hind Fouj.

In the meantime, Lord Linlithgow was replaced by Lord Wavell. He reminded Gandhi that the offer of unqualified freedom after the end of hostilities was conditional and prior to that there would be no change and the duty of the Majesty would be to safeguard the interests of the racial and religious minorities and the depressed classes and their treaty obligations to the Indian states. All this meant no freedom until the communal problems and depressed class affairs were settled under the arbitration of the 'third force' which itself was the creator, fueller, fanner of all internal frays and feuds by its tool of 'divide and rule'. Thus, the picture that flashed before the eyes of the Gandhiites was that partition was inevitable so that the last course remained open to them, to Gandhi, once again : Unity first then freedom.

Role of Communal Muslims

M.A. Jinnah, leader of the Muslim League, found in the Quit India Resolution, 1942, the following : (i) Immediate grant of complete independence, that is Hindu Raj; (ii) A Constituent Assembly that would be dominated by the Hindu majority. That is, it would be a Hindu Constituent Assembly to constitute Hindu Raj. In order to enforce Hindu Raj the Quit India resolution decided to resort to mass civil disobedience at the supreme command of Gandhi. Thus, the command of the

Dictator of the Congress "would be a death blow to Muslim India."

Jinnah was very consistent and explicit in his stand : Pakistan by division of India on two-nation basis. He proclaimed this while the Cripps Mission was functioning. In contrast the Hindu Mahasabha pronounced : "India is one and indivisible", and the Sikh : "We shall resist by all possible means separation of the Punjab from the all-India Union." However, the Muslim League was determined to oppose the Quit India Movement by all means. To the Muslims India must not be allowed to win freedom until the Muslims won Pakistan. Jinnah's strategy was : "in the Muslim majority provinces they should be prepared to hoist Muslim League flag and capture power from the Hindus. Invasion by the Japanese would be a signal for the fight with the Hindus rather than with the Japanese who would naturally place the stronger party in power."[18]

The Communists

Marx theorized capitalism in such an assumptive way as if the fall of capitalism was inevitable as and when it would reach in natural course at the stage of full pregnancy. But it proved wrong. Lenin was an experimental revolutionary socialist, contra determinist Marx. He visualized imperialist war in the 'weak link' of the capitalist world paving the way for social revolution ushering in socialistic capitalism that would develop into socialism to communism. His prediction was not totally wrong. The Russian socialist revolution took place during the First World War and then within twenty-five years the Second World War broke out in the capitalist world. The Soviet Union took the stand 'wait and see' how and how far the warring capitalist powers were being destructed making placement for world socialism. The Communists of India at that time cried out it was an 'imperialist war' and dressing themselves as 'nationalists' took up all means to liberate India from the yoke of the British imperialist power involved in the war. Their manifesto : "Revolutionary utilization of the war crisis for the achievement of National Freedom". The Communist Party of India (CPI) condemned the Congress for its 'neither-nor-policy' against the British Government and designed Gandhi as the 'astute leader of the bourgeoisie' and itself launched mass struggle against Gandhian policy of compromise. In rural areas the party raised the slogan : "*na ek pai, na ek bhai*" ("not a pie, not a brother") to the British Government. In the industrial areas it organized widespread strikes to stall war productions and supplies as the modified form of violence. Its observation about the Gandhian war-time policy : "The future under Gandhism is to lose all that the Congress has built up so far."[19]

A turn came in 1941. On June 22, 1941 Germany suddenly invaded the Soviet Union cutting off Stalin's dream when Germany and Soviet Union were tied up with non-aggression agreement. The dream was "The friendship of the peoples of Germany and the Soviet Union, cemented by blood, has every reason to be lasting and firm."[20] Hapless Soviet Union then feeling helpless ran to the Allied powers to become one with them. The CPI then fell into dilemma. Only yesterday it raised its voice against the British Government as a 'nationalist' party for the liberation of the 'motherland' and now when it found its 'socialist fatherland' was in grave danger without the alliance with the Allied powers it would have to take an opposite stand. That is to reverse the slogan 'revolutionary opportunity' and condemnation of Gandhiites for adoption of the policy of compromise. It took the strategy of "two war" : War in the Western Front 'imperialist war' and in the Eastern Front 'people's war'. At once Stalin snubbed the party calling that "war is indivisible" and directed the party to raise the slogan "people's war" in place of "imperialist war". This strengthened Nehru's slogan of "international war" waged by the Allied powers for globalization of democracy and freedom. Immediately after the communists started saying: "We consider this war to be the People's War, a war of world liberation in which the Indian people in their own interest must participate to win their own liberation."[21]

Thus, the Congress and the communists came closer in helping the British in their war effort, contra Subhas Chandra Bose, then spectre of both. The CPI was highly rewarded by the Government. The party was declared illegal in 1934, which was revoked in 1942, when Gandhi called for 'Quit India' offering the '*mantra*': 'Do or Die'. During the movement the Congress leaders were in prison while all the Csommunist leaders were freed, of course, on condition that they would help the Government in war effort. They upheld the condition and wherever there was attempt by anybody to bring about a strike in any mill or factory they stood between the organizer and the labour to create a cleavage in the workers. Thus, both the Muslims and the communists betrayed the 'Quit India' movement : Muslims for Pakistan and the communists for the cause of their 'socialists fatherland'.

Thus, the British Raj was feeling highly secured. For the Congress was begging for 'compromise and exist', the Muslim League to 'exist and Pakistan', and the Communists to 'exist for existence of socialist fatherland'.

Communists on Bose

What was the communists' stand about Bose? Was he a 'spectre' to them? 'No'. To them the 'spectre' was the Axis powers which had been haunting the Soviet Union. And as such because Bose was in cooperation with the Axis powers for liberation of India, he was to them a 'Quisling', 'the advance guard of Tojo and Hitler', 'a deceased limb that must be amputated', 'a fifth columnist', 'the henchman of Japanese imperialist', etc. etc. So he 'must be wiped out as a political past'. They threatened him with dire consequences if he dared enter into the Indian soil. In a signed article B.T. Ranadive, a communist stalwart, in the CPI's journal *People's War* on January 10, 1943 wrote : "Bose's mercenary army of "liberation" of rapine and plunder will feel the wrath and indignation of our people if it dares set its foot on Indian soil to enact acts of pillage and robbery." The fun is that the communists did never claim that they were the sons of the soil of India for they were above all geographical boundaries : "They have a world to win."

Farce and Betrayal

Gandhi stirred up with the '*mantra*' "Do or Die" only when after long three years he could understand that the British demanded India's dependence and not independence. In the morning of 9th August 1942 when he left the message : 'We get our freedom or die', his mind was full with the feelings that if necessary he would fight alone against the whole world to finish the noble task of freedom. It was all emotion, not determination. Determination must have the foundation of well-thought-out plans and programmes having determined, trained and disciplined army under command. Instead, Gandhi had in his hands and lips : "Don't leave India to Japan, but leave India to Indians in an orderly manner."[22] Was this begging not to thwart the entry of Subhas Chandra Bose?

Bose was Gandhi's real spectre. At that time the British Empire was rocked by the Axis powers and the Soviet Union was at the edge of surrender to German troops. That was an opportune time for Gandhi to spread the *mantra* 'Do or Die' to coerce the British to come to terms. The British came to India for their own interests and not to modernize the Indian culture and economies. Such was their interests that the British Prime Minister Winston Churchill had to say : "The loss of India would be final and fatal to us. It could not fail to be part of a process that would reduce us to the scale of a minor power."[23] Gandhi's pleas and coercions must not be the prime cause of this reduction to 'minor power'. The British would leave for their own cause at their own time. Besides, the British knew how far a man like Gandhi could rise up to force the British to quit. He ever wished. Thus : "I want hundred thousand people to march on Viceroy's palace and dash their heads against its doorsteps to commit 'harakiri' in front of its gates, to allow themselves to be killed rather than tolerate the present stage of things."[24] It was a call of a non-violent revolutionary indeed! But why Gandhi himself did not commit 'harakiri' in front of the Viceroy's palace? Instead he advised the Indian army to consider themselves as Congressmen and act according to their conscience as Congressmen and only to disobey measures against the Congress and the people fighting in non-violence, and not to revolt against the British command for the cause of freedom of their motherland. Further, as a strategist, why did he leave the people to self-leadership during the Quit India Movement? Is it not anarchy?

The observations of the socialist Congressman Jayaprakash Narayan on failure of 'Quit India' Movement are relevant here: (i) Lack of efficient organization of the revolutionary forces; (ii) After the first phase of the rising was over there was no further programme placed before the people. There was nothing in the vision of Gandhi about the 'next phase'. Possibly the first phase was enough for Gandhi to attain *swaraj*. Gandhi might not be 'misguided' but his guideline was such that it was doomed to failure.

Gandhi's own confession : "In 1942, I said I was sailing out on unchartered waters. I will not do it now. I did not know the people then. I know now what I can do and what I cannot."[25] Without knowing his own army Gandhi started commanding — what does it indicate? What sort of excuse is this? Is it that all the venture was to measure the progress of his experimental *ahimsa*? Is it not a farce? Is it not a betrayal to the nation? And all this for self-salvation at the cost of thousands of lives and the futurity of the country?

However harsh and tough one may be in criticizing the egocentricity of Gandhi it should have to be taken that the Quit India Movement roused new consciousness among the people to fight for freedom with a vow to do or die until the goal was achieved, which had alarmed the British that they had lost the support base of the people. In case of invasion the people would stand by the invader as their friend and even if the British came out victorious they must have to leave India transferring power to the people however truncated by diplomatic means for their narrow interests.

NOTES AND REFERENCES

1. Nehru, *The Discovery of India, op. cit.,* pp. 464-465.
2. Tendulkar, *op. cit.,* Vol. 6, pp. 118-119.
3. *Harijan,* May 3, 1942.
4. Tendulkar, *op. cit.,* Vol. 6, p. 100.
5. Collected Works, *op. cit.,* Vol. 84, p. 420.
6. *Ibid.,* Vol. 77, p. 455.
7. *Ibid.*
8. *The Discovery of India,* p. 475.
9. Tendulkar, Vol. 6, p. 170.
10. Romain Rolland, Mahatma Gandhi, Publications Division, GOI, 1976, p. 32.
11. Tendulkar, Vol. 6, p. 153.
12. *The Discovery of India,* p. 478.
13. Tendulkar, Vol. 6, p. 174.
14. *The Discovery of India,* p. 485.
15. Tendulkar, Vol. 6, p. 255.
16. Stanley Wolpert, *Nehru : A Tryst with Destiny,* Oxford University Press, Reviewed by A.G. Noorany in The Statesman, Calcutta, April 11, 1997.
17. At Press Conference held at Tokyo, June 19, 1943.
18. Quit India Movement, British Secret Documents, Edited by P.N. Chopra, Internet, New Delhi, 1986, p. 96.
19. In CPI's official journal, '*Communist*', March 1941.
20. Valentin Berezhkov in Stalin's Error of Judgement in International Affairs, Moscow, September 1989, p. 19.
21. Arun Shourie, Did the Communists Strike a Secret Deal with the British in 1942, *The Illustrated Weekly of India,* March 18, 1984, p. 12.

22. Collected Works, Vol. 77, p. 168.
23. Freedom at Midnight, *op. cit.*, p. 55.
24. Quit India Movement, British Secret Documents, *op. cit.*, p. 385.
25. Interview with Lousis Fischer, July 17, 1946.

10

PARTITION
Some Developments

Onwards to Vivisection

Following the defeat of Quit India Movement Gandhi again entered into the phase of settlement. Viceroy Lord Wavell in his speech broadcast on June 14, 1945 said that pending the settlement of the communal issue a new Executive Council would be formed giving placement in it to equal proportion of caste Hindus and the Muslims. This was possibly the first time that the British Government had dared divide the Hindu community politically into castes and term Congress as an organization of 'caste' Hindus. And also the first time the Muslim League which was out and out a communal organization and whose contributions to the freedom struggle were not only non-cooperative, but destructive, was taken as a 'political party'. The Viceroy also announced that the main task of the Government would be to persecute the war against Japan with utmost energy till Japan was utterly defeated. Japan, that is, Indian National Army, that is, Subhas Chandra Bose, was the common enemy of all the threes : British Government, Muslim League, Congress. So there was no point of disagreement on that effort. Gandhi, however, raised objection to the term 'caste'. This had stalled the formation of the new Executive Council. However, Lord Wavell kept all at bay. Side by side he recommended reminding Gandhi that the Cripps 'post-dated cheque' 'stands in its entirety'.

Lord Wavell convened a conference at Simla in which Gandhi did not participate directly. The representatives of the Congress and also of all other parties attended the conference. But it could not advance to settlement because of the hard stand taken by Jinnah that all the Muslim members of the Executive Council should be the members of the Muslim League. For the League was the only organization representing all the Muslims of India. To him the Congress was a Hindu organization. This irked Abul Kalam Azad, President of Congress, who held that to yield to such communal claim would tarnish the national character of the Congress.

About Muslim League

Abul Kalam Azad in his *India Wins Freedom* has briefly sketched the historical evolution of the role of Muslim League. He has classified the League's history into three phases. The League was established in 1906 in Dacca. It owed its origin to the efforts of Nawab Mushtaq Husain. It was declared that the objects of the League would be to strengthen and develop a feeling of loyalty to the British Government among the Muslims of India. The other object was to advance the claims of the Muslims against Hindus and other communities in respect of service under the crown in order to safeguard the interests and rights of the Muslims. Thus the League was feudalistic by birth and loyalist in character. The League from the beginning opposed the political independence of India. For in that case it might lose the special privileges for the Muslims as now from the British Government. Incidentally, it may be mentioned that the Morley-Minto reforms scheme was announced in December 1906. Then a deputation of Muslims leaders led by Aga Khan placed the demand that the Muslims should have a certain number of seats reserved for them to be voted only by the Muslim voters. That is, the demand for 'separate electorate', which was granted in the Indian Councils Act of 1909. However, to the League, the Congress was a disloyal organization of rebels. The British Government was happy as it found in the League the very instrument that could be used to confuse and scuttle the freedom movements of the Congress, whenever needed.

The second phase, according to Abul Kalam Azad, of the League surfaced when the British Government had to introduce some reforms under the pressure of the Congress. In that phase the strategy of the League was to remain aloof from the political struggle but when the stage of distribution of reform package was tabled it used to come forward with claims for the Muslim community. The Government at once reacted favourably. This created confusion in national demand and the Congress felt cornered. This was a great victory of the League much to the pleasure of the British Government.

The third phase of the League became apparent during the Second World War. This phase has been clearly displayed by Azad : "Mr. Jinnah had now become the leader of the Muslim League and felt that he must take advantage of every difference between the Congress and the Government for transfer of power, Mr. Jinnah would in the beginning remain silent. If the negotiations failed he issued a milk and water statement condemning both parties."[1] Thus, the Muslim League was such a 'political party' which had no political activities in a colonial country, instead ever used to look for difference between the two warring forces, Congress and the British Government, to place the demands of the Muslims raising all possible communal issues. Finally, its demand was Pakistan for the Muslims of India and Hindustan for the Hindus of India on the basis of the League's two-nation concept. To the League it was the only way to resolve distrust and disunity between the Muslims and Hindus. It was not surprising to the British for they knew that only the creator of distrust and disunity could destruct the distrust and disunity, and none else.

This amazed Gandhi : "I find no parallel in history for a body of converts and their descendants claiming to be a nation apart from the parent stock. If India was one nation before the advent of Islam, it must remain one in spite of the change of faith of a very large body of her children."[2] But this simple fact was not propagated by Gandhi nor by the Congress among the poverty-stricken unlettered Muslim communities who were under the clutches of Muslim fundamentalists, Muslim feudal lords and the parental posture of the British Government. Gandhi tried to penetrate into the Hindu 'untouchables' but not into the area of Muslim 'untouchables' to the caste-oriented Hindu communities. Such was such that the Muslim League found enough comfort to grasp and exploit the gap in the link of interactions between Hindus and Muslims.

About Jinnah

M.A. Jinnah was a lawyer by profession, Englishman by character, unreligious in outlook and was closed to moderates like Dadabhai Naoroji, himself being a Congress leader, and was also a close friend of Gokhale, the political *Guru* of Gandhi. His Hindu-Muslim unity stand made him the 'Ambassador of Hindu-Muslim Unity'. His outlook was so broad that he said : "but for real new India to arise all petty and small things must be given up. She is now India irredenta and to be redeemed all Indians must offer to sacrifice not only their good things but all those evil things they cling to blindly—their hates and their divisions, their pride in what they should be thoroughly ashamed of, their quarrels and misunderstandings."[3] This proves Jinnah was a novel patriot, not a narrow politician and far away from all sorts of communalism.

Then why such a patriot Congress leader had to retire from Congress and left for London to live there as a person? And then what made him to join the Muslim League to become a 'communalist' to lead the League as its supremo? And how could he struggle for Pakistan and how could he utter that if he was granted a sovereign state he would invade India with foreign help? The clue of all the causes might be traced in the political life of Subhas Chandra Bose who had also retired from Congress, left for Germany and emerged as Netaji contra Mahatmaji. Jinnah emerged as the 'father of Pakistan' contra Gandhi 'father of the nation'.

The psyche of Jinnah may also be studied in his attributions that Gandhi was the 'sole dictator and interpreter of the Congress' and was trying 'to subjugate and vassalize the Muslims under a Hindu Raj and annihilate the Muslims'. He did recollect that once Gandhi worked under him at the time of Lucknow Pact and also that Nehru worked under him in the Home Rule Society. If Gandhi by winning the Hindus could be the 'father of the nation' then why by winning the Muslims he could not be the 'father of Pakistan'? In short, who is the creator of "father" Jinnah, the British or Gandhi?

Venture of Unity Again

The political scenario was so changing and the divisive mind of the British was becoming so powerful that they would not leave India until and unless the condition laid down by the Empire of Hindu-Muslim unity was fulfilled. Gandhi was then forced to step back to his primary stage of unity first then freedom. Although his past experience had taught him that it would not be a success so long as the British worked as the 'third force'. However, desperate Gandhi finally approached Jinnah to have a durbar with him.

Durbar with Jinnah

Gandhi realized that the stage of political agitation had come to an end, Jinnah had become the supreme of the Muslim League and the League had become the second largest political organization of India. He was also convinced that the British would always stand by their 'favourite wife'[3a], the Muslim League. Thus, under duress Gandhi had to step down at the lowest step of his political ladder.

The Muslim League over the nose of Gandhi passed a resolution at its Lahore session in March 1940 (Lahore Resolution) on its demand for Pakistan. Jinnah in his Presidential speech said : "The Muslims are a nation, according to my definition of a nation, and they must have their motherland, their territories and their state."[4] Jinnah further elaborated the definition of nation in his letter to Gandhi on August 12, 1944: "We are a nation of hundred millions, and what is more, we are a nation with our own distinctive culture and civilization, language and literature, art and culture, names and nomenclature, sense of value and proportion, legal laws and moral codes, customs and calendar, history and traditions, aptitude and ambitions; in short, we have our own distinctive outlook on life and of life. By all canons of international law we are a nation."[5] There was a straight answer to this straight presentation : Leave India for your own homeland to live comfortably within one nation giving up lust for others' territories. Gandhi was a different man. His reactions :

"Partition means a patent untruth. . . I must rebel against the idea that millions of Indians who were Hindus the other day changed their nationality on adopting Islam as their religion."[6] That is, could a Hindu today being a Muslim tomorrow change his genetic characters, social culture and civilization overnight. This aspect of Gandhi is irrefutable. His passion for 'rebel' had mass approval. But perhaps his 'inner voice' was silent over confrontation with 'sword-force', again by mere 'soul-force'. So he had adopted the policy of conversion by the force of reasons.

War of Attrition

The object of the war of attrition was to convert the communal Muslims into nationalist Muslims. Jinnah was a violent experimentalist with no clear idea of Pakistan, while Gandhi was a non-violent experimentalist with speculative idea 'truth'. Both Gandhi and Jinnah entered the field of conversion which was the first round to Jinnah to fight out (*Lar-ke-Lenge*) Pakistan and final round to Gandhi to convert or retreat for ever from politics. Jinnah was responsive. On 11th September 1944 he wrote to Gandhi : "I am anxious to convert you to my point of view, if possible. I urged you that the only solution of India's problem is to accept the division of India as Pakistan and Hindustan, as briefly laid down in the Lahore Resolution of March 1940."

In his letter on 15th September 1944 addressed to Jinnah Gandhi raised 15 basic points around the Lahore Resolution for elucidation, some of which are : Is the goal of Pakistan pan-Islamic? Is the demarcation to take place during the pendency of British rule? If affirmative, the proposal must be accepted first by Britain and then imposed upon India, not evolved from within by the free will of the people of India? What is your definition of 'minorities'? Will you please define the 'adequate, effective and mandatory safeguards' for minorities?

Gandhi seemed to have missed one and conclusive point, although that would be meaningless for the deaf ears : How the Muslim minorities to be left behind in Hindustan would live together under the Hindu Raj and if they could why not a larger number as that would be more comfortable to resist the tyranny of the Hindu Raj? Had there been democratic raj instead would it not be desire to gain more protection and privileges for the minorities? In short, why the adventure to snatch out a large number of Muslims throwing at random a reduced number of them at the 'prey' of Hindu Raj?

Be that as it may, Gandhi's understanding was that Jinnah wanted to convert all non-Muslims into Muslims as embodied in pan-Islamism : "Will the two nations become one if the whole of India accepted Islam?"[7] However, Jinnah did not track back. He tried to give point to point reply of the 15 point letter of Gandhi, however evasive, unhistoric and ungeographical. He attacked Gandhi : "You aspire to represent all the inhabitants of India, I regret I cannot accept that statement of yours. It is quite clear that you represent nobody else but the Hindus." Further, "You represent nobody but yourself." Such remark because Gandhi was not even the primary member of the Congress. Then Jinnah reminded Gandhi : "As long as you do not realize your true position and the realities, it is very difficult for me to argue with you, and it becomes still more difficult to persuade you, and hope to convert you to the realities and the actual conditions prevailing in India today."[8] Thus, Jinnah's "Law of Jungle" excelled Gandhi's "Law of Love" so much so that Jinnah, to repeat, could utter publicly to injure the sentiment of

Gandhi : "You represent nobody but yourself!"

To sum up, following lots of correspondences and face-to-face discussions both Gandhi and Jinnah came to the conclusion that the war of attrition was to be resolved in war of division.

The main causes of collapse of conversion :

1. Jinnah's act of conversion was based on 'realities and the actual conditions prevailing in India', while Gandhi's on 'truth', that is, 'reality' contra 'truth'. To Gandhi the 'actual conditions' were surperficial, which were the creation of the British.
2. To Jinnah true welfare of the Muslims and the rest of India lay in division of India, as resolved in Lahore Resolution, while to Gandhi it would but ruin the whole nation.
3. To Jinnah the Quit India Resolution of the Congress "is inimical to the ideals and demands of Muslims in India", while to Gandhi "Independence does mean as envisaged in the AICC Resolution of 1942".
4. To Jinnah settlement of division of India into Pakistan and Hindustan first and then joint action for ouster of the British, while to Gandhi first ouster then settlement. The settlement is an internal affair between two brothers, there is no scope for the 'third force" to interfere. To Jinnah that mean automatic imposition of Hindu Raj on the minority Muslims. Thus, Gandhi's stand : 'Quit then Settlement'; Jinnah's : 'Pakistan then Quit". This is because to Gandhi the British were the 'evil force', to Jinnah a blessing in disguise.
5. Gandhi offered 'a territorial unit' by way of 'self-determination' and that would be only after complete independence, while Jinnah's contends : "Ours is a case of division and carving out two independent sovereign States by ways of settlement between two major nations, Hindus and Muslims, and not of severance or secession from any existing union, which is non-existent in India.[9]

However late, Gandhi understood Jinnah was no longer the Jinnah of his time. He informed Jinnah that "an ocean separated you and me in outlook." Yet in his characteristic way he begged "Believe me, I approach you as a seeker"; "do not disappoint me"; "allow me to address the meeting of the Council of the Muslim League etc." Gandhi even addressed not 'Mr. Jinnah' but as 'Dear Qaid-e-Azam' (leader) and then 'Bhai' (brother) but Jinnah was growing more and more firm, enthused with more confidence. The weakness of Gandhi was an asset to Jinnah.

Finally, Gandhi felt tired and fed up with Jinnah's diplomacy. He then attacked Jinnah, however unbecoming to a man of his stature : "Jinnah is an evil genius. He believes he is a prophet"; "is suffering from hallucination"; "He really looks upon himself as a saviour of Islam"; "he is a maniac". Gandhi was so irked that he had also made some untasty remarks about the Muslims: "The Muslims are religious fanatic but fanatics cannot be answered with fanaticism", Islam is brotherhood. But "as a matter of fact it is the brotherhood of Muslims. Theosophy is the brotherhood of man."[10]

The irony is that Gandhi did get no justice either from the British nor from Jinnah. Then blaming God as the sole 'disposer' he gradually came down to the prevailing conditions which were created by the British in alliance with the Allied powers and in connivance with their 'favourite wife', which had no democratic vision nor any sense of tolerance, instead was ever fuelled with distrust and hatred. His too much passivity in conversion idea was also a contributing factor.

To look back on May 26, 1938 Gandhi along with Subhas Chandra Bose, then Congress President, conferred with Jinnah for harmony. Even at that time Jinnah dared to offer some pre-conditions for an agreement between Hindus and Muslims, which are extremely obnoxious and completely unsecular in character : (i) '*Vande mataram*" should be given up; (ii) Muslim majority provinces must be affected by territorial redistributions or adjustments; (iii) Practice of cow slaughter by the Muslims should not be interfered; (iv) Muslims right to call *azan* and perform their religious ceremonies should not be interfered in any way;

(v) Share of the Muslims in state services should be fixed in the Constitution; (vi) Muslims' personal law and culture should be guaranteed by statute; (vii) Congress should withdraw opposition to the Communal Award; (viii) Use of Urdu shall not be curtailed; (ix) Representation in local bodies should be governed by the principles underlying in Communal Award; (x) Tricolour flag should be changed, alternatively the Muslim League flag should be given equal importance; (xi) Recognition of the Muslim League as the one and only authoritative and representative organization of Indian Muslims.

The effects of tolerance instead of isolation measure went so far that the Congress Working Committee was pleased to recommend : "whenever and wherever *Vande mataram* is sung the first two stanzas should be sung, with perfect freedom to their organizers to sing any other song of unobjectionable character, in addition to or in place of *Vande mataram.*"[11] It was known to the Congressmen that *Vande mataram* was not a Hindu religious cry, a political slogan. Even Gandhi admitted that this slogan stirred up while the people of India were asleep. Thousands had sacrificed their lives shouting for the last time : *Vande mataram*. Even no other religious minded sects had any objection to sing or shout *Vande mataram* except the conservative Muslims. Incidentally, the clever Congress leaders, including Gandhi, replaced *Vande mataram* by the INA slogan: '*Jai Hind*'— the slogan of violent revolutionaries, who were above all sorts of communalism.

Reactions of Bose

1944 was a crucial year for India. In a historic prediction Subhas Chandra Bose addressed the people of India from somewhere in Burma on September 12, 1944 : "Friends and countrymen...you are all aware that Gandhiji and Mr. Jinnah are discussing the Hindu-Muslim question. . . We Indians in East Asia are today fighting for a free and a united India. . . we are resolved to create a united and free India. . . we have realized that to divide a country will ruin it economically, culturally and politically. . . We can easily solve the minorities problem once we are free from foreign domination...I vehemently opposed the Pakistan scheme for the vivisection of our motherland. . . the Congressmen who want to come to a compromise with Britain have decided to swallow the bitter pill of Pakistan."

Then addressing the young Indian Muslims : "Will you be a party to the vivisection of your motherland? What will your status be in a divided India? Therefore, my friends, if you want freedom you must fight for it and kick the British out."[12]

Thousands had sacrificed their lives in the struggle for free and united India and the Indian National Army were fighting in East Asia for the same cause while the Congress and League conspirators were busy with the scheme of vivisection of the country. Bose called for 'kick the British out'. But who would kick them out? Gandhi, Jinnah or Nehru? Gandhi was then sinking; Jinnah was rising up in arms; and then what about Nehru? He studied the communal problem of India in 1931 and said : "I repeat that the communal problem does not affect the masses."[13] To him it was a 'fear complex' and communalism was 'an amazing farrago'. Gradually he became a changed man. He preferred 'joint electorates' and subscribed to Gandhi's tact of civil disobedience movement to 'divert the attention of the people from the wretched communal wranglers of today."[14] When the war came to the East Asia both Gandhi and Nehru became horrified and advanced towards Jinnah-British nexus to fight together against the Japanese invaders, truly, the force of Indian National Army of Subhas Chandra Bose. The joint appeal of the Congress and the League to the British Empire was not to Quit India leaving her in the hands of the invader. As neither Islamic sword-force nor Gandhi's soul-force could resist the entry of the Indian National Army. If Bose could have an entry Jinnah's Pakistan idea would vanish, Gandhi's last hope of transfer of power through legitimate and peaceful means would remain unfinished and Nehru's lust for personal power unfulfilled. So unanimity was on visisection as quick as possible to avoid INA, direct action threat of Jinnah, uncertainty of the continuation of the British on Indian soil, and not less important, Nehru himself was tired of struggle and jail. He was then only 57. He was a revolutionary socialist! Bose's definition of 'revolutionary', as he was, : "A true revolutionary is one who never acknowledges defeat, who never feels depressed or disheartened."[15]

Cabinet Mission

1945 marked the end of Second World War. The United States atom-bombed Hiroshima and Nagasaki on 6th and 9th August 1945. Following bombing Japan capitulated on 15th August and formally surrendered on 2nd September 1945. On July 26, 1945 the Labour Party came to power in Britain. Attlee became the Prime Minister. The spectre of Bose and INA was invisible by then. But there appeared another and more dangerous spectre — the war effects on world economies — which was haunting most Britain, it being the number one in world economic power prior to the war. Incidentally, it was bombed heavily by Germany during the war. Its economy was on the verge of ruination. A settlement with India, which too was at grips of economic crisis, became imperative.

On March 15, 1946 the British Prime Minister Attlee in a statement said : "My colleagues are going to India with the intention of using their utmost endeavours to help her to attain her freedom as speedily and fully as possible. . . I hope that India and her people may elect to remain within the British Commonwealth." The colleague-members of the Cabinet Mission were : Lord Pethick-Lawrence, Secretary of State for India, Sir Stafford Cripps, President of the Board of Trade, and A.V. Alexander, First Lord of the Admiralty. Cripps was well known to India because of Cripps proposal of 'post-dated cheque' for India's independence.

The Cabinet Mission arrived in India on 23rd March 1946. The Mission organized a Conference in Simla on 5th May 1946 with the participation of representatives of four each from the Congress and the Muslim League for mutual settlement of communal issues. The Congress put forward constitution of a federal government having only three portfolios assigned to the Centre : Defence, Foreign Affairs, Communications. The Muslim League's stand was Pakistan. But Pakistan was not acceptable to the Mission for "almost universal desire, outside of the Muslim League, for the unity of India." That did not mean the Mission was totally against division of India. In a sense it was a diplomatic stand to throw the thankless task of partitioning the country to the leaders of all the political parties of India. The 'divide and rule' policy of the Empire was enough for disseminating the unity of the Hindus and Muslims. Thus, the Mission viewed that they were "greatly impressed by the very genuine and acute anxiety of the Muslims lest they should find themselves subjected to a perpetual Hindu-majority rule." The 'unity of India' was not the last word to the Mission : "This consideration did not, however, deter us from examining closely and impartially the possibility of partition of India." The Mission in its scheme kept open enough loopholes for the birth of Pakistan. However, the delegates in their statement on May 16, 1946 expressed : "We are therefore unable to advise the British Government that the power which at present resides in British hands should be handed over to two entirely separate sovereign States." Prior to that they had examined the composition of the sovereign state of Pakistan as claimed comprising two areas; one in the north-west consisting of the Provinces of the Punjab, Sind, North-West Frontier, and British Beluchistan; the other in the north-east consisting of the Provinces of Bengal and Assam. Instead they gave greater weightage on the Congress scheme of federal structure with greater autonomy to the Provinces. It was to placate the majority communities initially.

Reviewing the moods and demands of all the parties and also the urgency of the British to Quit India the Mission placed for consideration of the parties its 'basic form' of India's new Constitution. The features of which are :

1. There should be a Union of India, embracing both British India and the States, which should deal with the following subjects : Foreign Affairs, Defence, and Communications; and which should have the powers necessary to raise the finances required for the above subjects.
2. The Union should have an Executive and a Legislature

constituted from British Indian and States' representatives. Any question raising a major communal issue in the Legislature should require for its decision a majority of the representatives present and voting of each of the two major communities as well as a majority of all the members present and voting.

3. All subjects other than the Union subjects and all residuary powers should vest in the provinces.
4. The States will retain all subjects and powers other than those ceded to the Union.
5. Provinces should be free to form Groups with executives and legislators, and each Group could determine the Provincial subjects to be taken in common.
6. The Constitution of the Union and of the Groups should contain a provision whereby any Province could, by a majority vote of its Legislative Assembly, call for a reconsideration of the terms of the Constitution after an initial period of 10 years and at 10-yearly intervals thereafter.

The objects of the 'basic form' was not imposition but "to set in motion the machinery whereby a constitution can be settled by Indians for Indians." This arbitration was a compulsion as otherwise there was no hope "of getting the two major communities to join in the setting up of the constitution-making machinery."

The constitution-making would take time. In between an Interim Government was a necessity. So it was to be formed with the support of the major political parties, that is, Muslim League and the Congress. The Mission addressed the Indians that its labour "will enable you to attain your independence in the shortest time and with the least danger of internal disturbance and conflict". It cautioned India : "The alternative therefore be a grave danger of violence, chaos, and even civil war." It also reminded the leaders : "There is the grave danger of famine to be countered." The substance of the mission of the Mission : Accept the British framed model of new constitution or face violence, chaos, and even civil war. The British knew more than all others that everything would be solved but that would be only through violence and chaos and dependence on external powers. This was enough to horrify Gandhi and amuse Jinnah.

Reactions of Gandhi

In a written message on May 20, 1946 Gandhi said : "After four days of searching examination of the state paper issued by the British Cabinet Mission and the Viceroy on behalf of the British Government, my conviction abides that it is the best document the British Government could have produced in the circumstances. It reflects our weakness, if we would be good enough to see it. The Congress and the League did not, could not agree. We would grievously err, if at this time, we foolishly satisfy ourselves that the differences are a British creation. The mission have not come all the way from England to exploit them. They have come to devise the easiest and the quickest method of ending British rule. We must be brave enough to believe their declaration until the contrary is proved.

"The authors of the document have endeavoured to say fully what they mean. . . Their own purpose is to end British rule, as early as may be. They would do so, if they could, by their effort, leave a united India, not torn asunder by internecine quarrel bordering on civil war. They would leave, in any case... they descended to the plains of India, and devised a worthy document for the purpose of setting up the constituent assembly which should frame India's charter of independence, free of any British control or influence. It is an appeal and an advice. It has no compulsion in it.

"The mission are entitled to warm congratulations for the first step in the act of renunciation which the statement is. Since other steps are necessary for full renunciation, I have called this one a promissory note."[16]

Thus, Cripps 'post-dated cheque' within four years became a 'promissory note'. The 'promissory note' was passed in the session of AICC on July 7th by a majority of 204 to 51. Gandhi was displeased with the oppositions. He identified Jayaprakash Narayan in particular who had threatened to promote *hartal* on 9th August. Gandhi reminded him that he was offered a seat on the Working Committee by the Congress President Pandit Jawaharlal Nehru, and now stood up against the views of the President. He also reminded him that to Gandhi the constituent assembly was the substitute of *satyagraha*, and there was no occasion for a fast or civil disobedience. For his inner urge was that the British must quit and in an orderly manners.

Not only Jayaprakash and company, the Congress socialists, opposed Gandhi's renunciation in the proposals of the Cabinet Mission, even 'yes man' Babu Rajendra Prasad and 'Sardar' (Vallabhbhai Patel), who had earned this 'nickname' from Gandhiji and 'even flaunts it as compliment', were opposed to him. But there was nothing to worry so long as Panditji would with him. He had already nominated Nehru as the Congress President in 1946 and the 'Prime Minister' of the proposed Interim Government. Gandhi told Nehru that he must wear the crown of 'thorns' for the sake of the nation and he had agreed. That is, Nehru was going to be the first 'unelected' Prime Minister of independent India. A great promotion was going to take place before the eyes of 'yes man' and 'Sardar'.

Reactions of Jinnah

On June 6, 1946 the Muslim League in its meeting of the Council of the All-India Muslim League found after careful consideration of the statement of the Cabinet Mission and examination of relevant documents officially issued on May 16, 1946 that the Muslims' demand for Pakistan was considered as "unwarranted, unjustified, and unconvincing" in spite of the admission that the Mission "were greatly impressed by the very genuine and acute anxiety of the Muslims lest they should find themselves subjected to a perpetual Hindu majority rule".

The League had discovered the 'loopholes' and so resolved: "inasmuch as the basis and the foundation of Pakistan were inherent in the Mission's plan by virtue of the compulsory grouping of the six Muslim provinces it was willing to cooperate with the constitution-making machinery proposed in the scheme outlined by the Mission, in the hope that it would ultimately result in the establishment of complete sovereign Pakistan." Then it was for these reasons the League resolved to join the constitution-making body and it would keep in view the opportunity and right of secession of provinces or Groups from the Union which had been provided in the Mission's plan by implication.

The Council of the All-India Muslim League reiterated that the attainment of the goal of a complete sovereign Pakistan still remained unaltered and called the Muslims of India to get prepared for the achievement of which they would, if necessary, employ every means in their power and consider no sacrifice or suffering too great.

Thus, in the Cabinet Mission proposal of Grouping Jinnah found the loopholes to ensure the right to secession and formation of sovereign Pakistan, while to Gandhi they were an admission of the right to self-determination within the Union of India. Thus, again, while Gandhi was in the dreamland of 'complete *swaraj*' by means of 'soul-force', Jinnah to win 'complete Pakistan' by means of 'sword-force', leaving the matter to the future to judge the real relation between 'means' and 'end'.

Direct Action : The Great Calcutta Killings

The next phase of the Cabinet Mission was the formation of Interim Government. Viceroy Lord Wavell called for immediate formation of an Interim Government. Nehru as the President of Congress requested Jinnah to join the coalition Government. Jinnah refused raising the old voice that only the Muslim League would nominate the Muslim members in the Interim Government for it was only the League that represented all the Muslims of India. This was unacceptable to the Congress which claimed itself as national organization. Lord Wavell dropped the idea of formation of the Interim Government. Then at the direction of Prime Minister Attlee he called the Congress to form the Government with or without the representatives of the Muslim League.

On July 29, 1946 the Council of the All-India Muslim League passed a resolution on Direct Action. Thus, Jinnah retaliated declaring 16th August as the 'Direct Action Day'. Calcutta was his target, where the Muslims were in majority and the Government was headed by Suhrawardy, a follower of Jinnah. The Government declared 16th August as public holiday having understanding with the local leaders of the Muslim communities to make the action one-sided. The Muslim communal extremists and gangsters secretly propagated among the Muslims that the Hindus were going to kill all the Muslims in Bengal and called them to arm themselves and kill the Hindus before they kill them (the Muslims). The action continued from 16th to 19th August. According to official version 4,000 persons were killed and 10,000 injured. But the number of persons killed was not less than 6,000. The British military officer in the area wrote: "It was unbriddled savagery with homicidal maniacs let loose to kill and to maim and burn. The underworld of Calcutta was taking charge of the citizen."[17] Gandhi's shock : "This much is clear that if the people are, probably, not ready for the exercise of non-violence of the brave, they must be ready for the use of force in self-defence."[18] The Congress Working Committee in its meeting in Delhi on 27-30th August 1946 recorded the direct action atrocities in Calcutta : "It appears that the processionists carried big bamboo sticks, swords, spears, daggers, axes, which they brandished when ordering the people to shut their shops from the early morning of August 16, and mercilessly assaulted anybody, who declined or hesitated to close his shop. Stabbing and looting started early in the day, and guns are said to have been used by hooligans in many places. . . resulting in the death of several hundred persons and looting and burning of property worth crores of rupees.

"There was practically no police, nor even the traffic police, to be seen on August 16, and even the precaution of sending the foot and mounted police to accompany the processions, as is done with in the *Moharam* and other processions, was not taken. Even when the police were available, they rendered no help to peaceful citizens, and frantic appeals for help to the officers in-charge of the police stations were not heeded and the people were told to save themselves as best as they could."

What an emblem of Muslim Raj for Hindu minorities in Pakistan : Such was such that Sir Roy Bucherzon, the British Commander, wrote to Jawaharlal Nehru on 13th November 1954 (Nehru Papers) : "Neither then (16th August 1946) nor afterwards, did one member of that Government give me any real assistance in bringing order out of disorder."

The Great Calcutta Killings flared up communal riots in Amritsar, Multan, Rawalpindi, Ahmedabad. The Sikhs and the Punjabi Hindus jointly retaliated. Bihar and the United Province were also not sitting idle. This indication of communal civil war satisfied both the British Government and the Muslim League, however dismal to Gandhi and Nehru. Even in this countrywide turmoil the Interim Government was formed on February 2, 1946. The Muslim League did not participate in it. The Prime Minister Jawaharlal Nehru and the other members of his cabinet rushed to Gandhi for his blessings. They were received with garlands of handspun yarn. It being Monday, day of silence of Mahatma, his written message was read out to them : "You have been in my thoughts since the prayer. Abolish the salt tax. Remember the Dandi March. Unite Hindus and Muslims. Remove untouchability. Take to khadi."[19] To Gandhi it was an auspicious day, a red-letter day in India's history, a step towards complete independence. He congratulated and thanked the British Government for having resolved an age-old issue between Britain and India by peaceful settlement. It was useless to revive bitter memories. Such was the pleasure of Mahatmaji when the Bengal Famine and the Great Calcutta Killings were dazzling before the eyes of the people!

Soon after the Muslim League felt that all power was going to be absorbed by the Congress and it was being isolated by the British. However, consultation was going on among Wavell, Nehru and Jinnah about the participation of the Muslim League in the Government. Then on 13 October 1946 Jinnah informed Wavell that the League had decided to nominate five members to the

Interim Government as scheduled. One of the nominees of the League was Dr. B.R. Ambedkar[19a] a member of the Schedules Castes Federation, who was opposed to the Congress right to speak for the 'untouchables'. The League joined the Government on 26 October 1946. Its aim was to sabotage the Government from within and without to create such an impasse that both the British and the Congress would be compelled to yield to the League's demand for Pakistan. This was echoed long age in the speech of Ghazanfar Ali Khan at a public meeting in Delhi : "The aim of our direct action is to paralyse Nehru's Government which will vanish like the historic half-day rule of Nizam the Water carrier." He also warned Britain that "the Muslims will resist such a government with their blood." Liaquat Ali Khan, a stalwart of the Muslim League, was allotted the ministry of finance. He was clever enough in tactics to stall the functioning of the government, especially Home, which was in the hands of Patel, by controlling the flow of finance.

Flow of Mountbatten

The British Prime Minister Attlee was fast growing impatient. The Great Calcutta Killings and almost India over communal riots were not a happy event to him. He seemed determined to transfer power to India by June 1948. Lord Wavell was replaced by Lord Mountbatten. On February 20, 1947 Attlee stated in the House of Commons that the British Government was determined to hand over responsibilities to the authorities established by a constitution approved by all parties in India in accordance with the plan of the Cabinet Mission by June 1948. In a White Paper there were indications that if there was no unity between Hindus and Muslims and also between the other communities India would face division. But the mark of unity was nowhere on the horizon. The Congress being hopeful of transfer of power, as committed by the British Empire, became very active for the formation of the Constituent Assembly. As scheduled the Constituent Assembly met at Delhi on 9th

December 1946 without the representatives of all parties. Then it met for the second time on 20th January 1947. Earlier the Working Committee of the Muslim League at its Karachi meeting resolved that the Constituent Assembly was illegal and should be dissolved. Thereafter the Congress demanded that the Muslim League representatives should resign form the Interim Government, if it refused to join the Constituent Assembly. But the League claimed that it had right to remain in the Interim Government without joining the Constituent Assembly. The Congress threatened to resign from the Government if the British Government failed to act favourably. A deadlock was there. This made Attlee's announcement of transfer of power by this or that means by June 1948, difficult.

The Muslim League leaders realized that the Congress leaders were impatient for transfer of power and the 'direct action' would compel them to yield to their demand for Pakistan. What was needed was only a bit patience. And exactly Nehru and Patel were hand-in-glove to settle the matter by partitioning the country, vivisecting Punjab and Bengal. Incidentally, these two provinces were not in good books of the Congress because they were militant by nature. If the affairs of these two provinces could be managed then by handing over the Muslim-dominated North-West and North-East territories to the League the transfer of power to Hindus and Muslims would be possible peacefully and legitimately, if the consent of the people could be procured. Patel was convinced that Pakistan would not long. Nehru's ambition was to wield State power as soon as possible as the successor of Gandhi. Then at the initiative of Patel on March 8, 1947 the Congress Working Committee passed a resolution : "During the past seven months India has witnessed many horrors and tragedies which have been enacted in the attempt to gain political ends by brutal violence, murder and coercion...Therefore it is necessary to find a way...This would necessitate division of the Punjab into two provinces so that the predominantly Muslim part may be separated from the predominantly non-Musllim part."[20] Gandhi called for an explanation from Patel. He replied:

"It was adopted after the deepest deliberation. . .But you are of course entitled to say what you feel right."[21] Then Gandhi asked for his 'heir', Nehru, whose version : "in fact it was based on reality." Gandhi might have felt where he was then in Congress.

The Sole Arbitrator

Lord Louis Mountbatten was a cousin of the British Emperor. He was also the Allied Commander of South-East Asia (1943-1946). He was a diplomat and statesman as well. Mountbatten landed on Indian soil on March 22, 1947. He was relatively young, only 47 years old. He was ever proud of his achievement as the liberator of East Asia from the clutches of Japan. Now he was bent on liberating Britain from the clutches of India which had raised war of independence since the *Sepoy Mutiny* (First War of Independence), 1857 and by now became desperate to force the British Raj to quit. It is really a wonder that within only five months this young Commander could transfer power to the hands of Indians 'peacefully and legitimately'. More so, he had to tackle such veteran stalwarts : Gandhi, Nehru, Patel, Jinnah, and also Liaquat Ali Khan. They were all aged persons. He was fortunate to have in his possession two "contact men" : V.P. Menon and V. Krishna Menon. The former was close to Vallabhbhai Patel and the latter to Jawaharlal Nehru. Mountbatten had unofficial friendship with Nehru and Krishan Menon while they were in England. Nehru was conversant with British culture and character, so also Krishna Menon, and as such there was no much problem.

Prior to leaving for India Mountbatten met Sir Stafford Cripps and Lord Wavell to assess who was who in Indian politics and had gathered a good profile. Cripps was less elaborative. His important observation was on Gandhi : "He could destroy, but couldn't create." Wavell was elaborative. His comments about Gandhi : "absolute in the clouds — purely idealistic. He would appear to have no practical solution whatever." About Nehru : "He's very clever; he's full of Idealistic ideas. . . has no political experience whatsoever." About Jinnah : "absolutely hopeless. . .

a pure Englishman by education, by outlook and by affection."[22]

Durbar

Mountbatten preferred to meet the top leaders : Gandhi, Nehru, Patel and Jinnah, one after another to avoid acrimony and extract evenly the hidden reserves in the mind of each. He found in them some common qualities : Every one of them had passed middle age and spent their lives arguing with each other; Well versed in agitation, dedication to independence and had absolutely no idea of administration; All were lawyers and nearly well versed in British constitutional law; independence was merely the culmination of their lifetime's effort, but what to do with independence was little known to them; Their human lives were completely submerged in their political action. Patel was a bit exception as he was tough and rough to tackle with.

Mountbatten's own assessment : Nehru "was an extraordinarily intelligent man. . . I was completely in step with him. . . Nehru was a first class chap." That is, Nehru was not a problem but a friend of Mountbatten.

Then about Gandhi : "Gandhi had no key at all." Then who had key in hands? Mountbatten : "The key to the whole thing obviously was Jinnah." To him neither Gandhi nor Nehru "it was Jinnah and Patel. They were the two people." That is, whoever could win Nehru would win Gandhi. Patel was 'rough and tough'. And Jinnah : "If Mr. Jinnah had died of this illness (suffering from tuberculosis) about two years earlier, I think we would have kept the country unified." "He was the evil genius."[23]

Formularized Arbitration

Mountbatten felt from the very beginning that he was saddled with the 'idiotic' Interim Government consisting of 15 members, 6 Muslims, 6 Congress, 3 others. That is, any vote was always (9-6) in favour of what the Congress wanted and unacceptable to the Muslim League. Then Moutbatten had a brain-wave : "I had the idea of breaking the government up and making two governments, the government of the future India and the government of the future Pakistan. And this was a sort of formula that I devised that they would have the opposite side sitting with them. This kept them busy, they were busy, working on partition and the transfer of assets."[24]

Thus, formularizing partition Lord Moutbatten advanced step by step towards the goal. Then he started drafting his plans and programmes. According to him, his first step was for a unified India; if failed, a centre with the functions of external affairs, defence and communications. The 'unified India' sooner became a myth. The alternative course was set out in the formation of 'plan' which was sent to London on May 2, 1947. But the details of the plan were not made public. Mountbatten summoned Nehru on 8th May. There on 10th May be showed the draft plan to Nehru before it was made public for discussion. Nehru's comment : "This is absolutely unacceptable, this is the Balkanization of India, this is exactly what we don't want to present."[25] Apprehending crisis in the all-party conference scheduled to be held in Simla on 17th May it was deferred until 2nd June.

On June 2, 1947 a meeting was held. Those present were Nehru, Patel, Kripalani (Congress President), Jinnah, Liaquat Ali, Sardar Nishtar, and Baldev Singh. Mountbatten announced as the alternative of the Cabinet Mission plan the British Government's new proposals. The proposals were accepted without dissension. On 3rd June the plan was officially published. The gist of the plan was to give option to the provinces to join or not to join Pakistan, that is, to force North-West Frontier to join Pakistan and partition of Punjab and Bengal into East and West.

The June 3 plan was accepted by Congress and Sikhs, reservation was from the stand of Muslim League. Mountbatten took a firm stand even knowing that the key of the situation was in its hand and the old Gandhi held nothing at all in his hands. He told Jinnah that if he wanted partition he must have partition of Punjab and Bengal. Jinnah said : "So you insist on giving me a moth-eaten Pakistan" Moutbatten, as the arbitrator, had enough confidence in himself. He said : "You call it a moth-eaten Pakistan I don't even want you to take it at all if it's as moth-eaten as that. I'd really like you to leave India unified."[26] Jinnah's reactions — Pakistan was no cause to him, cause was Hindu Raj : "No, I don't want to be a part of India. I'd sooner lose everything than be under a *Hindu Raj.*"[27] Besides, how a man like Jinnah could swallow defeat to Hindus?

Then as advised by Moutbatten Nehru (Congress), Jinnah (Muslim League) and Baldev Singh (Sikhs) turned up at 7o'clock at the All-India Radio Studio in Delhi to broadcast to their followers to accept the plan peacefully. After the broadcast of Lord Mountbatten, one after another stood before the microphone. The people had neither the intellect nor any urge to know what had been going on over their heads. They were busy to resist bloodshed and protect their huts and farms from communal fray. It was a great opportunity for the leaders of all communities to betray the people and the nation.

In real perspective the broadcast was the public announcement of the great historical victory of the 'trios' in transferring power to the people and winning power for the people according to the will of the people peacefully and legitimately. The history must have smiled then. The Jallianwala Bagh banner-holder Punjab and the Bengal that in 1905 stirred up the national spirit of sleeping India revolting against the partition of the province, the homeland of *Bande mataram*, Netaji Subhas and Swami Vivekananda, must on time reveal who were the real patriots and who were the real traitors, who actually ran after truth, who after untruth. The new generations must take up, research and rewrite the history placing right persons to the right places.

The next step of Lord Mountbatten was to transfer power with 'reckless speed'. Why so? Mountbatten had his say : "The reason was that neither side would cooperate with each other. I could feel the damn thing simmering. It's like standing in the edge of a volcano and feeling the moment of explosion."[28] May be the INA trial and revolt of Indian Navy were before his eyes.

Mountbatten fixed 15th August as the date of transfer of power. Why 15th August? It was an auspicious day to Mountbatten. He liberated East Asia from the hands of Japan which surrendered on 15th August 1945. 15th August 1947 was the second anniversary day of liberation. Then arrived the day of liberation of Britain and India from the clutches of each other winning for both the benefit of interdependence through the forum of Commonwealth under the British Crown. So let the day of India's independence be 15th August. He discussed only with Nehru prior to fixation. But thereafter it was found that to the Indian astrologers 15th was inauspicious. Nehru put forward a dramatic idea to transfer the power at midnight of 14th August, 1947. The day was not propitious to the astrologers and all could be performed smoothly while the rest of the world would remain asleep.

Lord Mountbatten was pleased to appoint Jawaharlal Nehru as the Prime Minister of free India. Nehru also asked the Lord to stay as Governor-General of India. Gandhi was not displeased. On the morning of 15th August Mountbatten announced in the Constituent Assembly : "I have the honour to be the Governor-General of Independent India. I am your servant." Thus, in fee India Pandit Jawaharlal Nehru became the first Prime Minister appointed by Viceroy Lord Mountbatten, and Mountbatten the first Governor-General of free India.

On August 14, 1947 the Dominion of Pakistan was heralded at Karachi. There Jinnah announced : "The two Indias are parting as friends and will continue to be friends for ever." Nehru, his counterpart in Delhi on 14 August, 1947, voiced aloud: "At the stroke of the midnight hour, while the world sleeps, India will awake to life and freedom". He concluded his speech with the INA slogan : '*Jai Hind*' (and not '*Bande mataram*' lest the Muslims flare up again). The flag of free India was hoisted amidst cheers and shouts : '*Jai Hind*', '*Mahatma Gandhi Ki Jai*', '*Pandit Nehru Ki Jai*', '*Lord Moutbatten Ki Jai*', '*Lady Mountbatten Ki Jai*', even, '*Pandit Mountbatten Ki Jai*'.

Thus, the second anniversary of the defeat of Japan, INA and Bose was celebrated with pomps and splendours organized jointly by the British and the Congress.

Mountbatten stayed on as the Governor-General of India for ten months and then backed to Navy by June 1948. But during the nine months since August, according to some modest estimate, 14-16 million Hindus, Sikhs and Muslims were forced to leave their homes and over 6,00,000 were killed.[28a] And that was not the end, just the beginning of the game of flits and kill and get killed to protect communal interest, which is going on as on today. Such was the noble character of vivisection of the country, 'peacefully and legitimately'.

Gandhi : In Search of Truth

Lord Mountbatten in his address on 15 August 1947 said : "At this historic hour, let us not forget all that India owes to Mahatma Gandhi, the architect of her freedom through non-violence. We must miss his presence here today and would have him know how much he is in our thoughts."[29]

Exactly, at this historic hour where was Mahatma Gandhi? His successor, the 'uncrowned king of India' was going to be crowned by the British chief representative in India, and the people were shouting, '*Mahatma Gandhi Ki Jai*', where was he? On that 'auspicious' day Mahatma Gandhi was at Beliaghata in Calcutta. In Calcutta the Independence Day was being celebrated with deafening shouts : 'Hindu-Muslim Unite': '*Jai Hind*'. However, he did not participate in any functions. He observed the Independence Day undergoing twenty-four hour fasting and spinning and there was no special ceremony in his camp.

Gandhi was in Calcutta to stand by the side of the Muslims. The Hindu refugees were pouring in thousands from East Bengal (East Pakistan) into West Bengal. This influx, the Bengal Famine 1943-1944, the Great Calcutta Killings 1946 over-heated the Calcutta communal atmosphere. In this atmosphere suddenly the

Muslims, now deserted by Jinnah & Co., found in Gandhi their 'Godfather'. Shaheed Suhrawardy, the brain behind the Bengal famine and Great Calcutta Killings, came forward to stand by the side of Gandhi for restoration of Hindu-Muslim unity. At the request of Gandhi Suhrawardy addressed a prayer meeting of Gandhi. In that meeting the Muslims flew Tricolour Flag. Hindus were also admitted to mosques and the Muslims to temples. Gandhi was so enthused that he said "the delirious happenings remind me of the early days of the Khilafat movement."[30]

Suhrawardy and Gandhi lived together in a Muslim *manzil* in Beliaghata where the Muslims were reported to be in suffering. The house was occupied on 13 August and on the following day the Hindus and the Muslims in thousands began to embrace one another and shouted : '*Jai Hind*'; '*Hindu-Muslim be One*'. There was also stray cry from a section of the people : '*Long Live Hindustan and Pakistan*'. Gandhi found no wrong in it. For "all the three parties accepted Pakistan." That is, it was the people's mandate. But not long ago he said : "I have called Pakistan a sin. Can I cooperate to make a sin a success? God cannot belie Himself."[31] What a changed man! However, the slogans emotioned Gandhi and it seemed to him as if there never had been bad blood between the Hindus and the Muslims and his joy of fraternization was leaping up from hour to hour.

Calcutta Miracle Vanished

In Calcutta anti-Gandhi feelings developed so much so that in the evening of 31 August there was a demonstration against his peace mission. So worried that Gandhi had to write to Sardar Patel : "What was regarded as the 'Calcutta Miracle' has proved to be a nine days wonder". On September 1 Gandhi in a press statement said : "This was about 10 p.m., Calcutta time. The young men began to shout at the top of their voices. My sleep was disturbed. . . I heard the window-panes being smashed. . . The old Muslim lady in the house. . . and a young Muslim stood near my matting, I suppose, to protect me from harm.

"The noise continued to swell. Some had entered the central hall and began to knock open the many doors...My vow of silence admitted of my breaking it on such occasions, and I broke it and began to appeal to the angry young men to be quiet...Their ears were closed against reason.

"I clasped my hands in the Hindu fashion. Nothing doing. More window-panes began to crack...A lathi blow missed me and everybody round me. A brick aimed at me hurt a Muslim friend standing by. . . Meanwhile, the police superintendent and officers came in. They did not use force. They appealed to me to retire. Then there was a chance of their stilling the young men. After a time the crowd melted."[32]

Thus, Gandhi was rescued by the police force, which was hardly available during street fighting communal forces. Curiously, Gandhi did not apply his *ahimsa* means in this case. The means: "Go in the midst of rioters and prevent them from indulging in madness or get killed in the attempt. But don't come back alive to report failure. The situation calls for a sacrifice on the part of top rankers."[33]

Gandhi seemed to be a different man in the actual field of action.

Then Gandhi took up his coercive resort : fasting to touch the hearts of those who were behind the goondas. He intended let the leaders of different organizations come forward with written pledge that they would fight for the communal peace. But it was a problem for the leaders to sign a pledge to avoid the situation. However, from Gandhi's point of view, let it be so, but the tension would come down and let the commonmen knew what force had his fasting in purifying one's heart.

The Muslims were worried about the fasting of Gandhi. A leading leader of the Muslim League appealed to Gandhi not to go to fasting : "Your very presence in our midst is an asset to us. It was a guarantee of our safety. Do not deprive us of it." However, a pledge document was prepared and signed by the leaders of Hindu Mahasabha, the Muslim League and others and carloads of handgrenades and arms were surrendered to Gandhi. Gandhi seemed pleased and relieved and discontinued his fast after seventy-three hours. It may be mentioned that Shurawardy was reluctant to sign the pledge document as a cut piece on the plea that he might any time be called to Pakistan.

About the 'Calcutta Micracle' Gandhi was quite senseful that it was a magic not 'miracle' : "From the very first day of peace, that is, from August 14th last, I have been saying that the peace might only be a temporary lull."[34] He had the feelings: "His doctrine did not count for much among the people today and yet it was his duty to give his advice whether they acted upon it or not."[35]

In spite of all the adversity Gandhi had gathered greater strength and confidence and made up his mind to move to Delhi.

To Delhi

While Gandhi was in Calcutta what was the communal scenario in Punjab and Delhi? In short, twelve of the Punjab's districts were aflame, and there was effective administration in Delhi. To what extent Nehru's dependence on Mountbatten, the Governor-General of India, went down is well highlighted by Larry Collins and Dominique Lapierre in 'Freedom at Midnight.'[35a] On 4th September 1947 V.P. Menon rushed to Simla with the plea : 'Your Excellency, you must return to Delhi.' When Mountbatten showed reluctance Menon said : 'The situation has got very bad since Your Excellency left. Trouble has broken out here in Delhi. We just don't know how far it's going to go. The Prime Minister and Deputy Prime Minister are both worried. They think it's essential for Your Excellency to come back.'

Mountbatten : "They've just got their independence. The last thing they want is the constitutional chief of state coming back and putting his fingers in their pie, I am not coming. Tell them." Then, 'All right, V.P., you old swine, you win. I'll come down'.

Next round on 6 September 1947 was with Mountbatten and Nehru and Patel. The Prime Minister and Deputy Prime Minister looked to the Governor-General 'like chastened schoolboys'. The situation in Punjab and Delhi was out of control and Nehru admitted their inability to tackle with. He said : 'We have no experience...Our experience is in the art of agitation, not administration. We can barely manage to run a well-organized government in normal circumstances. We're just not up to facing an absolute collapse of law and order.'

Nehru stepped forward with greetings and request : "You are a professional high-level administrator...You English can't just turn this country over to us after being here all our lives and simply walk away. We're in an emergency and we need help. Will you run the country?" Further : "We'll pledge ourselves to do whatever you say."

Mountabatten : "If anyone ever finds out you've turned the country back to my hands, you will be finished politically."

Nehru clever enough : "Well, we'll have to find a way to disguise it, but if you don't do it, we can't manage."

Mountbatten : "But we must agree that nobody finds out about this. Nobody must know you've made this request. You two will ask me to set up an Emergency Committee of the Cabinet and I will agree. Will you do that?"

At once both Nehru and Patel agreed.

Then with all power in hands, Mountbatten took a tough stand : If the security guards on trains failed to open fire on their assailants, round up its security guards and sort out those who were wounded, then court-martial and shoot the rest on the spot to have salutary effect on the guards' discipline.

It seemed the Gandhi-wing .was convinced that not soul-force but sword-force that would only be effective to ensure discipline and restore peace. And what was most disgraceful was that the first government of free India did not hesitate to sell out the dignity of the nation to the domination of an Englishman.

In Delhi

Gandhi arrived at Delhi on September 9, 1947. He was placed in Birla House and not in the Bhangi Sweepers' Colony for security reason. Gandhi was shocked to learn the communal frenzy. He declared : " I must apply the old formula 'Do or Die' to the capital of India."[36] Nehru countered the fanaticism of Gandhi addressing the nation : "Indeed, the military are still masters of the situation and they will be still more masters very soon."[37]

Shortly after Gandhi's arrival Muslim delegates continued to flood the Birla House to apprise the plights and pangs of the Muslims at the hands of Sikhs and Hindus. Gandhi agreed not to leave for Punjab until peace was restored in Delhi. Such was the intensity that the Sikhs and Hindus were determined to force the Muslims out from Delhi. Their argument was that the Muslims who had divided the country had no right to live in India. Once they raised the slogan : '*Hanskeliya Pakistan, Larke lenge Hindustan*', now it was the right time to cry out '*Larke lenge Paksitan*' ('Got Pakistan by laughing, We'll get India by fighting' turned to 'We'll get Pakistan by fighting'). Gandhi felt helplessness : "I invoke the aid of the all-embracing power to take me away from this 'vale of tears' rather than make me a helpless witness of the butchery by man become savage."[38] What a peaceful transference of power and where was the Jinnah, the protector of Muslims? Lives of millions of innocent people were being drained out! So disgusted that Gandhi in *Harijan Sevak* wrote on 15 September : truth and non-violence should be removed from the Congress Constitution."

There was enough reason behind it. Himself he was growing indeterminist. After conditional accession of Kashmir to Indian Union troops were sent to Kashmir to protect the territory from Pakistan aggression. Gandhi expressed no displeasure. He dismissed this violence as the government's policy in which he could not interfere. Instead, he praised their activities for they were doing according to their conviction and liberty. As if, the government is something which is above the people whose creed is non-violence and art is non-cooperation.

Fast for the Last Time

Gandhi went to fast at noon of January 13, 1948. To him it was not a hasty decision. It was the result of four days heart-searching and prayer. He said that his fast was against no one party or group or individual exclusively, yet it excluded nobody. It was addressed to the conscience of all, expecting to attain Calcutta Miracle again.

On 13th January 1948, Gandhi attended his evening prayers as usual. However, there was in the air that Patel was anti-Gandhi in his operation of 'self-purification' and against Nehru's passivity towards the Muslim Leaguers. Patel to dispel all this informed Gandhi to do anything he might wish. In reply Gandhi asked him to give top priority to the disposal of Pakistan's share of the cash assets withheld by the Indian Government. Then within twenty-four hours of the commencement of the fast the Cabinet met round his fasting bed to reconsider the issue. The adverse reactions became spontaneous. At night some Sikhs and others demonstrated before the Birla House, shouting : 'Blood for Blood', 'We want revenge', 'Let Gandhi die'.

The Cabinet at the instance of Gandhi, then on fast, decided to release wealth worth Rs. 55 crore. The amount was held up because of the aggressive attitude of Pakistan towards Kashmir. The Government communique stated : "This decision is the Government's contribution, to the best of their ability, to the non-violent and noble effort made by Gandhiji in accordance with the glorious traditions of this great country, for peace and goodwill."

It was a great victory of Gandhi. But Sardar Patel could not take it kindly. Immediately after Patel left for Delhi for '*burden of work*', in spite of Gandhiji's request not to leave, leaving behind a message : "I cannot do otherwise than I am doing now. And if thereby I became burdensome to my lifelong colleagues and a source of distress to you and still I stick to office, it would mean that I let the lust of power blind my eyes and so unwilling to quit. You should quickly deliver me from this intolerable position."[39]

On 17th January Gandhi's health alerted the doctors. They asked for ending the fast without delay. Gandhi set out seven conditions to end his fast. The conditions are: All communities once again live in Delhi like brothers in perfect amity; The annual fair at Khwaja Qutabud-Din Mazar will be held this year as in previous years; The Muslims will be able to move about in all localities as they could in the past; The mosques which have been left by the Muslims will be returned and no area would be forcibly occupied that has been set apart for the Muslims; The Muslims who have left Delhi will be allowed to come back and even to carry on their business as before; All this will be done by personal efforts and not with the help of the police or the military; And pledge: 'We request Mahatmaji to believe us and to give up his fast, and continue to lead us, as he has done hitherto.'

The above conditions were incorporated in the declaration of the Central Peace Committee, consisting of 130 members representing all communities formed under Rajendra Prasad, including representatives of R.S.S. and Hindu Mahasabha. For none was inclined to take the responsibility of 'fast into death' of Mahatmaji.

On the basis of the Declaration Gandhi broke his fast on 18th January at 12-45 p.m. A drama took place. When all left the place Nehru stayed on. Then he told Gandhi that he had been fasting with him from the day before. Gandhi was deeply moved and sent a note to Nehru : "Now break your fast. May you live for many long years and continue to be *Jawahar* (the jewel) of India. Bapu's blessing."[40]

Once Gandhi wanted abolition of the Congress as it lost its basic character. Possibly after the 'Bapu's blessings' to the 'Jewel' he changed his opinion. On January 27 he wrote on 'Congress Position' : "The Indian National Congress, which is the oldest national political organization and which has after many battles fought her non-violent way to freedom, cannot be allowed to die. It can only die with the nation."[41] However, he proceeded to form a new Congress. For that purpose he sketched a draft constitution for the Congress : "Though split into two, India, having attained political independence through means devised by the Indian National Congress...has outlived its use. India has still to attain social, moral and economic independence in terms of its seven hundred thousand villages as distinguished from its cities and towns. . . For these and other similar reasons, the A.I.C.C. resolves to disband the existing Congress organization and flower into a Lok Sevak Sangh."[42] Thus, in the draft constitution Gandhi subtly claimed that India won freedom by his means of *ahimsa* and left a point for his Jawahar, the Jewel, to take up 'panchayat' form of social reconstruction, with confidence.

Then arrived Friday, the 30th January 1948. At 4 p.m. Sardar Patel went to see Gandhi at Birla House. Gandhi knew the friction between his 'heir' Jawahar and his 'Sardar' Patel. He spent with Patel for one hour. He thereafter left him at 5-10 p.m. to attend the prayers. As he was passing through the cordoned path crowded with people. Nathuram Godse[43] came forward and fired point-blank three shots in quick succession. He collapsed uttering : 'Hey Rama'.

NOTES AND REFERENCES

1. Abul Kalam Azad, *India Wins Freedom,* p. 118.
2. Collected Works of Mahatma Gandhi, Vol. 78, p.101, Publications Division, Ministry of Information & Broadcasting, GOI, 1965.
3. Bolitho Hector, *Jinnah,* p. 65.

3a. Bamfield Fuller, Lieutenant-Governor of East Bengal, said this openly. Quoted in Azad's *India Wins Freedom,* p. 5.

4. D.G. Tendulkar, *Mahatma,* GOI, Vol. 5, p. 268.
5. Collected Works, *op. cit.,* Vol. 76, p. 407.
6. Tendulkar, *op. cit.,* Vol. 7, p. 271.
7. Collected Works, *op. cit.,* Vol. 78, p. 101.
8. *Ibid.,* p. 408.
9. *Ibid.,* p. 411.
10. Louis Fischer's Report of *Interview with Gandhi* on July 17, 1944.
11. Collected Works, *op. cit.,* Vol. 66, p. 297.

12. Selected Speeches of Subhas Chandra Bose, S.A. Ayer, Publications Division, Ministry of Information & Broadcasting, GOI, 1962, pp. 223-225.
13. Nehru Selected Works, Vol. 5, Sangam Books, p. 284.
14. Letter to Mohammad Alam, October 29, 1933.
15. S.A. Ayer, *op. cit.,* p. 238.
16. Tendulkar, *op. cit.,* Vol. 7, pp. 119-120.
17. *Ibid.,* p. 198.
18. *Ibid.,* p. 198.
19. *Ibid.,* p. 198.

19a. Gandhi was not happy with B.R. Ambedkar : "One has to be very careful indeed when dealing with a man who would become a Christian, Muslim or Sikh, and then be reconverted, being guided by whim pure and simple." Tendulkar, *ibid.,* p. 154.

20. B.K. Ahluwalia and Shashi Ahluwalia, *Sardar Patel Rebel and Ruler,* p. 76, Akbe Group, New Delhi, 1981.
21. *Ibid.*
22. Larry Collins & Dominique Lapierre, Mountbatten and the Partition of India, Vol. 1, p. 21, Vikas Publishing House Pvt. Ltd., New Delhi, 1982.
23. *Ibid.,* p. 44.
24. *Ibid.,* p. 49.
25. *Ibid.,* p. 57.
26. *Ibid.,* p. 43.
27. *Ibid.,* p. 44.
28. *Ibid.,* p. 50.

28a. Leonard Mosley, *The Last Days of the British Raj,* p. 279, Jaico Publishing House, Bombay, 1961.

29. Tendulkar, *op. cit.,* Vol. 8, p. 80.
30. *Ibid.,* p. 82.
31. Collected Works, *op. cit.,* Vol. 84, p. 385.
32. Tendulkar, *op. cit.,* Vol. 8, p. 103.
33. *Ibid.,* p. 101.
34. *Ibid.,* p. 104.
35. Collected Works, *op. cit.,* Vol. 85, p. 464.

35a. See pp. 313-316.

36. Tendulkar, *op. cit.,* Vol. 8, p. 112.

37. *Ibid.*

38. *Ibid.,* p. 145.

39. *Ibid.,* p. 260.

    "his (Gandhi) influence is largely negative or even destructive and directed against the only man who has his feet firmly on the ground, Vallabhbhai Patel." Lord Mountbatten to the HMG, Personal Report No. 16, August 9, 1947.

40. Tendulkar, *op. cit.,* Vol. 8, p. 268.

41. *Ibid.,* p. 282.

42. *Ibid.,* p. 284.

43. Nathuram Benayak Godse, a Maharashtrian, was actively associated with RSS and Hindu Mahasabha. He watched closely the activities of Gandhi and marked his sense of placating the Muslims to have Hindu-Muslim unity. The Great Calcutta Killings (1946) organized by the Muslims shocked him so also the partition of his dear motherland India and the atrocities on Hindus and Sikhs in Pakistan. While in India Gandhi was going on fast after fast for the protection of the Muslims. Godse's passion crossed over when he found how Gandhi coerced the Cabinet to change its decision of withholding wealth worth Rs. 55 crore payable to Pakistan for Pakistan's aggression towards Kashmir. To Godse Gandhi was the 'Father of Pakistan'. He then made up his mind to remove Gandhi from the earth as the devout son of his motherland India.

    In his statement at the trial court on 8th November 1948 Godse said that in future the historians would correctly determine the real value of his deed. His conscience was clear. He said that in the court of super law he would be declared innocent.

    Godse and one of his associates Narayan Apte were hanged on 15th November 1949.

11

FATHER OF PARTITION
Facts and the Figure

Introduction

Who is the 'Father of Partition'? To Nehru : 'Reality'; To some others : 'Inevitable'; To Gandhi : 'Impatience'. People do not like to the illusioned by abstraction. They demand concrete answer to their concrete question : Who was that person? In the limelight comes in : Patel, Gandhi, Nehru. Let us make an attempt to search out that noble person : 'Father of Partition'.

Maulana Abul Kalam Azad identified Vallabhbhai Patel as the 'founder' of partition : "It would not perhaps be unfair to say that Vallabhbhai Patel was the founder of Indian partition."[1] His reasoning is that Patel was much annoyed and irritated at the actions of the Muslim League members in the Interim Government that at a certain stage he openly said that he was prepared to have a part of India if only he could get rid of Muslim League. Azad had also sensed that Patel was 'sentimentally attached' to the idea of partition. Maybe. But what was he? Was he a Gandhi or Nehru? Relatively he was too tall a man. Besides, Azad identified Patel as the 'founder'. But the people want to identify the 'father'. This may call for a distinct conception of 'father'. Founder is not father. Founder is one who founds. Father is something else. Gandhi was the 'father'. According to his version 'father' is 'maker'. He said : "If he is called in all sincerity the "Father of the Nation", it was true only in the sense that he had had a great hand in making the

Congress what it had become after his return from South Africa in 1915."[2]

Thus, the 'maker' is the 'father'. Gandhi was the maker of the Congress when the organization had lost all its dynamic characters.

To follow again Azad : How did he identify Nehru? His answer was inexplicit. He wrote : "I have often wondered how Jawaharlal was won over by Lord Mountbatten. He is a man of principle but he is also impulsive and very amenable to personal influences."[3] Nehru was the 'heir' of Gandhi. Gandhi was a man professed by unwavering faith in *ahimsa*. He never compromised his 'principle' with his 'policy' nor was he amenable to any personal influence, where circumstances were such he simply retired to his self. Nehru being his 'heir; what sort of 'man of principle' was he that he was 'very amenable to personal influences'? Azad, however, made an oblique remark focusing Lady Mountbatten : "Most attractive and friendly temperament influenced Nehru."[4]

Azad might not be unaware of the attractive character of Lady Mountbatten : "often, over tea, a stroll in the Moghul Gardens, or a swim in the viceregal pool, she had been able to charm Nehru out of his gloom, redress a situation and subtly encourage her husband's efforts."[5]

Azad did not identify Gandhi in any way, possibly because he was to him a passive spectator.

It appeared in the minds of some people that Jinnah was the 'Father of Partition'. Azad had separate version : "India was divided not by the Muslim League but by the Congress."[6] The Muslim masses were simply betrayed by the League : "Jinnah had deceived them and left them in the lurch."[7] He had assured them "they would be regarded as a separate nation and would enjoy the right of determining their own future."[8] Thus, Azad had identified the Congress as the 'father', that is, either Patel, Nehru or Gandhi, and not Jinnah.

Gandhi : Maker to Founder

Gandhi's great ambition was to experiment with his South Africa-oriented '*satyagraha*' model on Indian soil. He joined the Congress not to be made but to make it in his own way for his own purpose : "I could only join an organization to affect its policy and not to be affected by it."[9] Straightway, he entered the Congress to utilize that national organization for his adventerous experiment with people, politics and salvation. It was then high time for him for the Congress was at the cross-roads. He offered the organization his *mantra* : non-violent non-cooperation. The people were enthused.

Gandhi launched his campaigns, agitations, movements in his action line of 'one step forward two steps back' that brought him at the cross-roads. His 'policy and principle' of two-in-one became absolutely inoperative. The break-up of war and violence all over the world, direct action and blood flow all over India, uncompromising attitude of the British Empire, domination of Nehru's 'reality' in Congress, 'impatience' of the people in the streets made Gandhi a changed being. This transitional phase is well narrated by Azad. He rushed to Gandhi to apprise him that Nehru and Patel were durbaring with the Viceroy Lord Mountbatten to chalk out plans to vivisect India. Gandhi's immediate reactions: "If the Congress wishes to accept partition, it will be over my dead baby."[10] This voiced the same voices : "Vivisect me before vivisect India"[11]; "Let the whole nation be in flames; we will not concede one inch of Pakistan."[12]

But after the meetings with Mountbatten and Patel, Gandhi became a completely changed man : "What surprised and shocked me even more was that he began to repeat the arguments which Sardar Patel had already used."[13] His conscience however pinched him : "I have called Pak a sin. Can I cooperate to make a sin a success? God cannot belie himself."[14] Then he blamed himself : "Man proposes God disposes constantly proves true in my cases."[15] In June 1947 half an hour before the beginning of his morning prayer he in much low voice said : "Today I find myself alone. Even the Sardar (Patel) and

Jawaharlal think that my reading of the political situation is wrong and peace is sure to return if partition is agreed upon. They did not like my telling the Viceroy that even if there was to be partition, it should not be through British intervention or under the British rule. They wonder, if I have not deteriorated with age."[16] It can easily be conceived the mental agony of this great soul to witness, the vivi-section of India before his vivi-section.

To conclude, Gandhi was the 'maker' of the Congress and as the maker with absolute power in his hand led the nation step by step at the threshold of partition. Then he had to draw a full stop. There the Gandhi's chapter was closed.

Rise of Nehru : Mutual Interests

In Indian politics Nehru was next to Gandhi. How he became so and what was his relationship with Gandhi?

Nehru was the son of Motilal Nehru, an eminent lawyer and also a Congress leader. He was affluent enough and lived a luxurious life. Nehru was sent to England for education. He was then only fifteen. Living there for seven years he came back home in 1912 after graduating from Cambridge University and procuring barristership. Thus he was built up in Western culture that made him known, even to Gandhi, as half-Englishman. Nehru had interest in politics. He was a close observer, a political analyst, socialist in ideas and modern in outlook. He had the sensibility to adjust with time and trend, however unhealthy that would be to his ideas and conscience. This made him revolutionary in thoughts and temper but conservative and capitulatory in deed. His ambition was to wield power in his hands to transplant his ideas in his own ways. To him whoever had power in hands could win the people.

In all respects he was contra Gandhi. He had never accepted Gandhi as his '*Guru*'. Gandhi's 'Policy' of *ahimsa* was to him the means to redress the slavery of the nation and his 'end' was mere some ethical principle. Gandhi had black-listed Nehru as a left-winger but not inconvertible as that of Subhas Chandra Bose. Gandhi had also marked the image of

Nehru as a socialist propagandist among the workers. Thus, Gandhi was attracted by Nehru's countenance, family background, English education and popularity among the working men. He discovered in Nehru all the qualities to become his successor.

This was not free of politics and mutual interests. The left-wing in the Congress was a menace to Gandhi. It should have to be shielded. The left-wingers were socialists in ideas and believed in armed revolution contra Gandhi's firm faith in non-violent non-cooperation. The British Government was also feeling disturbed and growing violent to suppress the violent revolutionaries. This had made Gandhi's policy of compromise more unworkable. For all these Gandhi was urgently in need of a 'shield'. And to him Nehru was "the best shield of the Congress against left-wing groups and organizations."[17]

Side by side Nehru also realized the truth : "If I can convince Mr. Gandhi, then I know that I can convince the people of India. If not, all my efforts would be in vain. He is the touchstone."[18] So Nehru in his own interests became a 'disciplined' follower of Gandhi.

Running for Power

Motilal Nehru, father of Jawaharlal Nehru, had the wish to see his son settled in top position of the Congress. He approached Gandhi in 1927. Gandhi favoured him with response. It may be recapitulated that Motilal Nehru was a swarajist, who in company with C.R. Das sponsored Swaraj Party that forced Gandhi to retire from Congress in 1924. In 1929 when Nehru was only forty Gandhi nominated him as the Congress President. Consequently, Nehru succeeded his father as the Congress President. The electors however voted for Gandhi (10), Patel (5), Nehru (3). Nehru's own admission : he was elected by "negative backing".[19]

Nehru assumed Presidentship at the Lahore Congress. Subhas Chandra Bose said : "Lahore Congress was a great victory for the Mahatma. Pandit Jawaharlal Nehru, one of the most prominent spokesmen of the Left Wing, was won over by him and the others were excluded from the Working Committee. The Mahatma could henceforward proceed with his own plans without fear of opposition within his Cabinet. . . With a subservient Cabinet, it was possible for him to conclude the pact with Lord Irwin in March, 1931".[20]

Nehru fought for 'complete independence'. It was he who at the Madras session of the Congress in December 1927 moved the resolution of complete independence. Now being the Congress President and under the pressure of Gandhi he changed his stand in favour of Dominion Status. Bose in his letter to Mrs. C.R. Das on 5 November 1929 wrote : "Jawaharal has now given up independence at the instance of the Mahatma." What was the cause for Nehru? It was all for 'party discipline'.

Nehru had the spirit of independence. At times he felt degraded at the bondage of Gandhi. Once he became so desperate that he said : "I am getting more and more certain that there can be no further political cooperation between Bapu (Gandhi) and me. At least not of that kind that has existed. We had better go our different ways."[21] It was not an emotional outburst. It was the exposure of his subconscious mind. His head was looking for the right opportunity to corner the man who had become the barrier in his way to proceed for power independently. Gandhi simply smiled out all this, however wry. He knew Nehru's basic characters. The Delhi Pact (Gandhi-Irwin Pact) antagonized a large section of Congressmen. Gandhi felt that enough. He threatened the Congress in his characteristic undemocratic temper that he would retire from the organization if his settlement with Lord Irwin was repudiated and he also demanded personal obedience to him if it was not approved by the Congress. Nehru was also displeased with the Delhi Pact and he remarked : "Humiliation of the people, and the leaders and invitation to break their pledge is hardly the way to approach peace."[22] Shortly after he repented : "Foolishly I said so in Delhi a few hours after the truce. How Bapu (Gandhi) was pained at my remark."[23] Nehru's confession of foolishness was nothing else than to renew his pledge of loyalty to Gandhi, ofcourse, befooling his own conscience. His principle was befool your own conscience but not the pledge of loyalty to Gandhi. For Gandhi was the man of the people, symbol of unity and to lose Gandhi would mean not only to lose yourself but also "the benefit of collective action and of organization". Possibly that was the major reason why Gandhi declared Nehru as his "heir' and desperately distanced Subhas Chandra Bose from his orbit.

Socialist Nehru

Nehru was a socialist. He was impressed by the 'scientific socialism' of Marx so much and so far that he said : "the communist philosophy of life gave comfort and hope."[24] He wrote to Gandhi : "I function as a revolutionary, meaning thereby a person working for fundamental and revolutionary changes, political and social, for I am convinced that no other change can bring peace or satisfaction to India and the world."[25]

Nehru even pronounced socialism (and not Gandhism) was his : "vital creed which I hold with all head and heart."[26] Gandhi's assessment of Nehru's socialism : "He is a firm believer in socialism, but his ideas on how best the socialist principles can be applied to Indian conditions are still in the melting pot. His communist views need not, therefore, frighten anyone."[27] In short, Nehru's socialism was a 'paper tiger' to Gandhi. To the communists Nehru was a 'timid reformist' and to Gandhi : "a practical statesman who tempered his ideas to suit surroundings."[28]

G.D. Birla, a big industrialist, in his letter to Purusottamdas Thakurdas on April 20, 1936 wrote : "Jawaharlalji seems to be like a typical English democrat who takes defeat in a sporting spirit. He seems to be out for giving expression to his ideology, but he realizes that action is impossible and so does not press for it."[29] To this Gandhi's reaction : "he is sobre in action" and then with lovely spirit embraced Nehru : "Though the gulf between us as to the outlook upon life has undoubtedly widened, we have never been so near each other in hearts as perhaps we are today."[30] Nehru's biographer S. Gopal's remark is also interesting : "He was groping more in the direction of utopian."[31]

Gandhi must have been impressed by the mutation of Nehru. He again nominated him as the Congress President and that was for two consecutive terms, 1936 and 1937. Such was such that Nehru was at that time in Europe while he was 'elected' for the second term. It may be recalled that in 1939 Gandhi refused to nominate Bose for the second term as the President. However, Nehru was growing unrestful with his ideas of socialism and wanted to make the Congress a socialist organization. Gandhi marked it and to stall Nehru he inducted his 'yes men' in the Congress Working Committee. Of 14 members in the Committee not less than 10 were hard-core Gandhiists. They became vocal against Nehru's anti-capitalism and pro-socialism stand. Nehru found himself virtually fettered. He was determined to resign. This far, instantly he tracked back. For his threat of resignation was rebuked by Gandhi who reminded him : "You are in office. . . but you are not in power yet. To put you in office was an attempt to find you in power quicker that you would otherwise have been."[32] Thus Gandhi advised Nehru not to be impatient, be loyal and disciplined, being his 'heir' it was his responsibility to put him in power of India quicker than otherwise had been. Nehru cooled his socialist temper for the quickest opportune time.

The Opportune Time

In the Second World War Gandhi was at the cross-roads. He was sandwitched by war of attrition. Moreover, he was constantly haunted by the spectre of Bose whose entry into India would mean the defeat of his *ahimsa* experiment. This was an unprecedented situation to Gandhi. Nehru came close by his side. He continued to wash the brain of Gandhi with the idea that it was not an imperialist war but a 'holy war' waged by the Allied powers against the Axis powers. The 'holy war' was for 'democracy and freedom' against domination and racism of Nazism and Fascism. So India must fight along with the British for democracy and freedom that would follow in India after the war. But Gandhi was feeling in the voices of the people the voice of Bose. They wanted defeat of the British and freedom at any cost taking advantage of the war opportunity.

The diplomatic non-compromising attitude of the British Empire made the situation more complex to Gandhi. The Empire as a feeler sent Cripps Mission which was summarily dismissed by Gandhi. Nehru was not pleased with Gandhi's attitude. Cripps, who happened to be Nehru's friend, enthused Nehru : "Let me make a final appeal to you. . .The chance which now offers cannot recur. . . Leadership — the sort of leadership you have — can alone accomplish the result. It is the moment for supreme courage of a great leader to face all the risks and difficulties — and I know they are there. . . I know your quality and your capacity and I beg you to use them now."[33]

It was a subtle call of the British Empire to Nehru to throw out from the leadership the Mahatma and exercising all his quality and capacity to wield all power in his hands.

In the meantime, Gandhi was growing pro-Japan. He found no reason to stand against Japan. To him it became clear that Japan was not the enemy of India. Her enmity was with Britain. He, however, said that if Japan acted otherwise she would be confronted with non-cooperation and no obstacles would be placed in the way of the British army on Indian soil. Nehru was not at one with Gandhi. He took it as Gandhi's passive partnership with Japan. He would be the last person to embarrass the British Empire in its war efforts. Incidentally, it was Nehru who in early twenties asked the British to Quit India when they frightened India that she might be attacked by Afghanistan. His answer was let India tackle the Afghans or whoever might be. If not, "we shall not help you even with a pie or a soldier".[34]

Nehru himself was hovering. At times he rose up with his idea of 'guerrilla warfare' and scorched earth policy to resist the entry of Japanese troops into Indian soil. Instantly, Gandhi pulled him down to normal temper. But Nehru did never remain inactive to resist the entry of Japanese troops, that is, the Bose with his INA. He started begging to the Allied powers for aid. He approached Roosevelt, President of the United States, for a joint declaration with China on war aims of the Allies assuring freedom and self-determination to India and also resolving to defend India at all costs from the aggression of Japan. He was convinced that Gandhi's policy of non-cooperation would be ineffective tc resist the Japanese troops. The irony is that Nehru accused Bose for his struggle for liberation of India with the help of enemy of the enemy, while he then himself had taken up the same course and that too was only for protection of India against the invasion of Japan. Bose conditioned with Japan that she would not make any claim, even an inch of the Indian soil, whereas Nehru asked for Dominion Status now and independence after the war. However, Roosevelt was reluctant to intervene.

When Nehru found all the doors of begging were closed for him he became a staunch nationalist : "If India perishes, I must say — selfishly, if you like to call it — it does not do me any good if other nations survive."[35] He had further discovered that both Axis and Allied powers were equal enemies to democracy: "If freedom was to be established in the world not only Fascism and Nazism had to go but imperialism had to be completely liquidated."[36]

Tired for Power

Nehru was arrested on August 9, 1942 along with other Congress leaders, including Gandhi. He had been in prison for long 34 months. He had never been in prison for so long a period at a stretch. He became a changed man while in prison. He was tired of going in-and-out of prison, while age was fast running out. The struggle for freedom would be useless without power in hands during lifetime. He became firm to have a settlement with the British Empire on transfer of power to the hands of Congress, that is, to his hands. Maulana Abul Kalam Azad was then the President of Congress. He was not in the good books of Gandhi. He was replaced by Nehru. Thus, Gandhi prepared the ground for Nehru to come to power of free India. It was his long cherished dream. On 15th January, 1942, possibly that was his last testament, Gandhi said : "I have said some years ago and say now that not Rajaji (Rajagopalachari) but Jawaharlal will be my successor. . . when I am gone he will speak my langauge."[37] Perhaps the future smiled cynically.

Action for Power

With the induction of Lord Mountbatten as the Viceroy of India the political scenario was fast changing. Both the Congress and the British Empire were impatient for transfer of power. The Muslim League was all the time busy measuring how far more and more territories could be snatched out from India for Pakistan. Nehru as the self and supreme representative of the Congress continued durbaring with Mountbatten. Gandhi was cornered both by Mountbatten and Nehru. Nehru, however, kept in touch with Gandhi. Gandhi himself was also not much interested in durbar. Patel and Jinnah did exist but with secondary role. All the threes were in favour of partition of the country. Mountbatten wondered how the Congress which fought all along for united India could be so impatient for division of the nation. Jinnah to whom Pakistan was a mere daydream was also surprised to see that the Congress was going to be the maker of Pakistan.

While all this was going on Gandhi was in Sodepur (Bengal) Ashram. In spite of adverse developments in durbars Gandhi remained firm in his conviction that the British must Quit India for their own interests leaving India undivided. On May 9, 1947, that is, some three months before partition of the country, Gandhi said : "The British are surely going to Quit India and if we have any difference between ourselves let us make it completely our own affair and not approach the British for a settlement." He added : "All ills can be settled between ourselves as between brother and brother."[38] He even asked Mountbatten to transfer power to the Interim Government to be formed by Jinnah to function with reasons without disturbing unity of India and also pleaded with him to act as the judge as a man but not as a British agent.

Neither Mountbatten nor Jinnah was impressed by his proposal. To Jinnah it was a tact to impose the rule of democracy, that is, the rule of Hindu Raj, Hindus being the majority.

Mountbatten was against taking any 'chances of bloodshed'. Gandhi although a man of non-violence was not reluctant to bear with the 'grievous loss of life'. But Nehru was reluctant to back out from the ongoing process of partitioning the country. Lack of patience apart, the Congress was afraid of 'civil war'. It was a plus point to Nehru. He developed the fear psychosis in the mind of Gandhi and at the same time solacing him with assurance of transfer of power peacefully and legitimately that would bring in the long desired peace and unity. To make all this reality Nehru and Mountbatten were working hard to come to some common terms and conditions. The Muslim League's Direct Action taking thousands of lives in Great Calcutta Killings accelerated the process. But confusion was there. Two nation based Pakistan was nothing but a fantastic cry: 'Islam in Danger' in India, to create Islamic State in Pakistan and when the impracticability of partitioning the country on two-nation basis was declared by the British Government the League had to come down to accept 'moth-eaten' Pakistan – one in the North-West and another in the North-East having distance between the two of about thousand miles and bearing different culture and different language. It may be mentioned that Punjab and Bengal, the two most revolutionary provinces, were the worst victims of partition.

The next course of Mountbatten-Nehru plan was to highlight the democratic right. The Hindu and Muslim members of the Assemblies were asked to vote for or against annexation to India or Pakistan. Naturally, the Hindus voted for India and the Muslims for Pakistan. This is called the expression of the people's 'free will' to divide or not to divide the nation.

In partitioning the country the dependence and friendship of Nehru and Mountbatten is accepted by Nehru himself. Thus, on 11 May, 1947 Nehru wrote to Mountbatten : "You were good enough to speak to me frankly and in a very friendly manner last night and to give me an opportunity to see the tentative proposals. I need hardly tell you how much I appreciate your confidence in me or that I am convinced of your earnest desire to help India to achieve her freedom as early as possible. It has been a privilege to get to know you better and I hope that our understanding of each other will be helpful to both and to the wider causes we have at heart."[39] Nehru was the only person who had attained the confidence of understanding of Lord Mountbatten and Sir Stafford Cripps. He was convinced that His Majesty's Government would never betray him; likewise the HMG was also convinced that Gandhi could betray it but never would Nehru.

Nehru then drafted a Congress resolution, amended thereafter by Gandhi. It reads : "There should be no compulsion in making or enforcing a Constitution for India on any unwilling parts. . . The announcement[39a] of February 20, 1947 (see Appendix III), led to an intensification of this Muslim League policy and what used to be riots developed into organized large-scale violent attempts to overcome provincial governments. . . We reiterated that we are against any compulsion over any part of India, and even indicated our acceptance of the principle of a partition of India to avoid conflict."[40] Then, to 'avoid conflict' between Hindus and Muslims and at the 'will' of the people the Congress had accepted the 'principle of partition'!

Earlier on March 8, 1947 the Congress Working Committee had passed the following resolution :

> "The Congress has already expressed its acceptance of the British Cabinet Mission's Scheme of May 16th, 1946 and has further accepted the interpretations put upon it by the British Cabinet on December 6, 1946.
>
> "The Working Committee have frequently stated that there can or should be no compulsion in the making of a Constitution for India. It is the fear of compulsion or coercion that has given rise to distrust and suspicion and conflict. . . it has been made clear that the Constitution framed by the Constituent Assembly will apply only to those areas which accept it. . . Thus there must be no compulsion either way, and the people will themselves decide their future. This peaceful and cooperative method is the only way to make democratic decisions with the maximum of consent."[41]

The Congress, which itself was an organization under the supreme command of Gandhi, time and again declared that partition was the result of the democratic decision of the people. The people were made scapegoats because Gandhiji had laid down two conditions to become a party to partition: not to be taken place through the British agency, and, if the people of the areas concerned desire a division.

On May 17, 1947, Nehru wrote to Mountbatten : "As you know we have stood for a united India and we have worked for it for the greater part of our lives. The partition proposed is not of our seeking. Our part in this proposed partition is only this that if there is to be a partition according to the will of the people, there should also logically be a partition of certain provinces. We have further agreed to certain territorial adjustments because HMG has apparently decided to hand over power to a divided India. Because of our anxiety to have power handed over and because of our belief that the present situation urgently demands this, we are prepared to agree to the proposals made on behalf of HMG"[42]

It may be asked when the nation was heading towards partition why Gandhi did not resort to fast where his creed says: "My religion teaches me that whenever there is great distress which one cannot remove, we must fast and prey." How a man like Gandhi who had ever functioned with dictatorial temper suddenly surrendered to the 'will of the people' knowing partition was a 'sin'? Is it because he wanted to go down the history clean? But history has its own say : Since 1942 Gandhi was in political coma—living dead.

Let Nehru Say

The people also haunt Nehru. During war time why Nehru became an 'internationalist'? He was a 'socialist' and as such he became extremely anti-nazim and anti-fascism. Well. But why did he not condemn Stalin when he hailed Hitler on conclusion of Non-Aggression Pact 1939 : "The friendship of the peoples of Germany and the Soviet Union, cemented by blood, has every reason to be lasting and firm"? Instead, he shed tears for the Soviet Union when it became the prey of Axis powers. Being a revolutionary socialist how could he be afraid of 'civil war' under the organization of the Muslim League. Is it not civil war is a blessing for revolution? The League was an anti-national organization. In spite of that instead of non-cooperation why did he durbar with it? What more, the Direct Action of the Muslim League was to him "similar to those of the Nazis in their early days"[43] Why then he did not rise up against the League as he did against Nazism and Fascism during the war? Is it not a fun to take a hard stand against the League when all was complete? Thus : "All Congress leaders are firmly united in their complete refusal to be dictated to by Jinnah any longer...Both Nehru and Patel said they would face any consequences rather than yield once more to Jinnah."[44]

Nehru was then in search for a new '*guru*' : "a *guru* more sensitive to the complex problems that would assail him there."[45] Who was that '*guru*'? It calls for no guess.

The history rolls on : Impatience for power; innovation of means to crush the image of Netaji; new '*guru*' to dump the image of Mahatmaji; placement of all blames for vivisection of the nation on the shoulders of the people for exercising their 'free will' in favour.

Father of Partition

Mountbatten was the 'pusher and arbitrator'; Jinnah the 'tuner and taker'; Gandhi the 'founder and sinner"; Patel the 'hater and heater' of partition. And Nehru?

The following events may be brought in focal point for searching out that somebody who was the 'Father of Partition'.

1. Gandhi made the Congress, led the nation, left the people in dissertation and vanished in isolation in early 1940s.
2. Pandit Jawaharlal Nehru, the 'uncrowned king of India', was pushed in from position to power by Gandhi to crown

him as the king of India, in his lifetime, which was his long cherished dream, for in Nehru he found the person who would ever speak his language.

3. Nehru stepped in with the ambition to wield power to establish Nehru Raj dismantling the Gandhian structure of Ram Raj.
4. He was waiting for the opportune time to bring an end in his political cooperation with Gandhi to go in own and different way.
5. The Second World War was a golden opportunity to Nehru to capture Gandhi developing the spectre of Netaji and creating fear-psychosis that Hindu-Muslim conflict and 'civil war' would not only make impossible to have transfer of power but also endanger his *ahimsa* creed.
6. Sir Stafford Cripps, although hit hard by Gandhi, but as a diplomat he did not lose hopes in Nehru. He urged Nehru to take up leadership of the Congress.
7. The war-effects forced Britain to Quit India. The Empire empowered Lord Mountbatten to plan out for quick transfer of power to the people of India.
8. Mountbatten picked up Nehru, West-oriented old friend of his and also an avowed partner of the allies, to durbar with him, also secretly, to work out ways and means to give a new colour of 'divide and quit' to 'divide and rule' offering moth-eaten – Pak to the Muslim League.
9. To them Gandhi was a great hurdle. However, he was aged and was at the cross-roads. To remove the hurdle, democratic means was adopted. That is, in this critical situation let the people decide their own future exercising their voting rights. Both Mountbatten and Nehru knew that the situation was such that the people have to vote for partition. This helped to open a narrow path for Gandhi to escape voicing, however low, that the voice of the people was the voice of the truth.
10. Gandhi felt comfort and pronounced that he had won freedom by 'peaceful and legitimate means', which was professed by him.

11. The Western world as well as the United States were happy to visualize a truncated India as that would embroil India and Pakistan in hostility and make them dependent in future on the foreign powers for settlements.
12. To Nehru, a tired person, power today was in consideration and not how today would penetrate into tomorrow as the curse to the future generations.

In conclusion, now let the readers ascertain themselves who had a great hand in making the partition when Gandhi was in isolation, in coma—living dead.

NOTES AND REFERENCES

1. Azad, *India Wins Freedom,* p. 198.
2. Tendulkar, *Mahatma,* Vol. 8, p. 190.
3. *India Wins Freedom,* p. 198.
4. *Ibid.*
5. Larry Collins and Dominique Lapierre, *Freedom at Midnight,* p. 125.
6. Azad, *India Wins Freedom,* p. 202.
7. *Ibid.*, p. 226.
8. *Ibid.*, p. 227.
9. G.A. Natesan in *Reminiscences in Gandhi,* p. 215.
10. *India Wins Freedom*, p. 203.
11. Tendulkar, *Mahatma,* Vol. 5, p. 329.
12. *Freedom at Midnight,* p. 156.
13. *India Wins Freedom,* p. 203.
14. Collected Works, Vol. 84, p. 385.
15. On December, 1, 1944.
16. Tendulkar, *Mahatma*, Vol. 7, pp. 414-415.
17. Sarvepalli Gopal, Jawaharal Nehru, Vol. 1, p. 137, Oxford University Press.
18. Romain Rolland, *Diary,* October, 1937.
19. S. Gopal, *op. cit.,* p. 127.

20. Bose, *The Indian Struggle*, *op. cit.*, pp. 200-201.
21. *Diary* Entry, July 18, 1933.
22. S. Gopal, *op. cit.*, p. 151. Quoted from AICC File G6 (KW) (1), 1931.
23. *Ibid.*, Quoted from Prison Diary, March 4, 1932.
24. Nehru, *Autobiography*, p. 364.
25. Nehru Collected Works, Vol. 6, p. 270. Letter on 13 August, 1934.
26. S. Gopal, *op. cit.*, p. 208.
27. *Ibid.*, p. 180.
28. *Ibid.*, p. 137.
29. *Ibid.*, p. 209.
30. *Ibid.*, Letter to Agatha Harrison, April 30, 1936.
31. *Ibid.*, p. 136.
32. *Ibid.*, p. 215.
33. *Ibid.*, p. 284.
34. Nehru Collected Works, Vol. 1, p. 187.
35. Press Conference, April 12, 1942 : *National Herald*, April 13, 1942.
36. Nehru, *Autobiography*, p. 601.
37. Tendulkar, *op. cit.*, Vol. 6, p. 43.
38. Selected Works of Jawaharlal Nehru, Second Series, Vol. 2, p. 129.
39. *Ibid.*, p. 130.

39a. On 20th February, 1947 the British Prime Minister Attlee stated that power would be handed over to the authorities established by a constitution approved by all the Indian parties.

40. Selected Works, *op. cit.*, Vol. 2, pp. 108-109.
41. *Ibid.*, pp. 63-64.
42. *Ibid.*
43. *Ibid.*, p. 95.
44. Mountbatten Telegram to Attlee, July 2, 1947, in The Transfer of Power, 1942-1947, Vol. II, p. 826.
45. *Freedom at Midnight*, *op. cit.*, p. 87.

Note : Nehru's letter to Mountbatten on 14th May, 1947 : "It is largely because of your personality and our faith in your sincere goodwill for India, that we have proceeded so far, I earnestly trust that we shall see some light soon and put an end to the horrors that are disfiguring India."

Nehru earnestly requested Mountbatten to "continue in this office and help us with your advice and experience". Letter on May 14, 1947.

12

PARTITION
Inevitable or Avoidable

Introduction

Some say, partition of India was inevitable; some others, it was avoidable. The other shades of opinion : 'reality'; 'impatience of the people for freedom'. In the sphere of accusations, some accuse the British, some others the Muslim League, and still some others the Congress. In personal plane Lord Mountbatten accused Jinnah, the 'evil genius' responsible for partition; the Congressman Maulana Abul Kalam Azad instead accused Sardar Vallabhbhai Patel and obliquely Pandit Jawaharlal Nehru. Some intellectuals accused Lord Mountbatten. But it is useless to accuse him, he being the agent of the Empire. It is also useless to accuse the British responsible for division of the country for it was in their interests. They came to India to be civilized by India's resources and not to 'civilize' culturally or materially the Indians. About Jinnah — who was he and how that very Jinnah became the 'evil genius' to the Englishmen and also to Gandhi? The findings will reveal how the 'Congress genius' Jinnah became the 'evil genius'. Maulana Azad knew best both the Congressmen and the Muslims and his conclusion that the Congress was the prime accused could not be said to be motivated. Leaving all this aside, let us take up 'reality' and 'inevitability'. Nehru was the propagator of 'reality' and Gandhi 'inevitability for impatience'. To Nehru the struggle for freedom at a certain stage created such conditions that the reality offered: face civil war or have power dividing the nation peacefully and legitimately. He preferred power, peace, legitimacy. So also Gandhi. But Gandhi pinpointed the impatience of the people : "Everybody is today impatient for freedom. Therefore, there is no other help."[1]

Creation of Conditions

Who had created the 'conditions' or 'reality' for inevitability? Was it God-made or man-made? If it was God-made then it is better to close the discourse for nothing can be discussed in the absence of God for that would be one-sided and unjust. If it is admitted that it was man-made then we may proceed and the discourse would be lively. Taking for granted that it was man-made let us resume and place before who represented 'man' – the people or the leaders? It would be wise to take up the leaders first.

There was initially two forces in India's political scenario: the British and their 'safety valve', the Congress, for peaceful governance of India. Since 1920 Congress meant Gandhi, Gandhi meant loyal movement against the Royalty. His spirit worked for realization of self-salvation, not independence: "non-violent revolution is not a programme of 'seizure of power', but it is a programme of transformation of relationships, ending in a peaceful transfer of power."[2] But by turn of events the Congress began to behave bitterly that annoyed the British Raj. It needed instead of the 'safety valve' a 'favourite wife' and that was the Muslim League. In a sense the Congress was the creation of the Englishmen so also the League was the creation of the Raj. That was the direct action of its 'divide and rule' policy that made the Muslims in general non-cooperative with the nation, cooperative with the British.

Gandhi's now and then campaign, agitation and movement marched forward only to step back whenever he could trace his 'loyalty' was going to face violence. After being backed out he came forward to accuse the people in his smiling style for their coward violence posing themselves as brave non-violent revolutionaries. In December 1947, when partition was complete Gandhi discovered that God had now restored his eyesight : "My eyes have now been opened. I see that what we practised during the fight with the British under the name of non-violence, was not really non-violence. God had purposely sealed my eyes, as He wanted to accomplish His great purpose through me. That purpose being accomplished, He has restored to me my sight."[3] Who had sealed the eyes of Gandhi was known to Gandhi alone but history knows that Gandhi blindfolded the eyes of the people under the name of 'non-violence' in the struggle for freedom.

It cannot be denied that Gandhi's dictatorial temper did not allow any young leader to emerge in democratic line; instead, he appointed his successor in a feudalistic style. Subhas Chandra Bose had to take the course of self-exile under compulsion of Gandhi to whom Bose was intolerable because of his different reasonings. Jinnah was a Congress leader, once worked well for the unity of Hindus and Muslims, had to retire from politics and leaving India settled in London, largely because of his differences with the reasonings of Gandhi and his line of actions. Gandhi might have been relieved then but afterwards he had to greet Jinnah as 'Qaid-e-Azam' and 'salute' Bose as 'Netaji', 'Jai Hind'. History reveals the truth at right time.

Gandhi took up the Khilafat issue as a golden opportunity that would not come in next hundred years. There was success. He was jubilant. But shortly after in 1924 riots broke out in Delhi, Lucknow, Aligarh, Shahjahanpur, Jubbulpur. The Khilafat 'success' revamped in his mind in 'Calcutta Miracle' (1946) but he was so reduced that he said : During Khilafat the Muslims accepted me as their true friend. I have now come to be regarded as so evil and detestable."[4]

Gandhi was an astute politician. He could, if not he did, easily understand the ploys of the Muslims in Khilafat and the gimmicks in the British diplomatic divide and rule policy. He could easily rise up firmly against the communalism of the Muslim and non-secular character of the Hindus as well as the evility of the British in designing partitioning of the country. Instead, he swallowed one after another 'communal awards' to hold high the success of his transformistic revolution by his non-violent means. He took up with all seriousness his jehad against 'untouchables' but that was mostly to counter the jehad of B.R. Ambedkar who was a challenge to sanatan Hinduism. The Muslims in general were Hindu converts from the oppressed classes. After conversion they remained unlettered, poorest of the poor and neglected classes as before save that in Islamism they were not religiously 'untouchables'. This made them extremely sensitive towards their own religion and fantastic about Pan-Islamism. The Muslim League, organized by the feudalist and fundamentalist Muslims oriented by political zealots like M.A. Jinnah, and the leaders of the depressed Hindus like B.R. Ambedkar, in connivance with the British, continuously developed the feelings of distrust and hatred between Hindus and Muslims and between upper and lower castes in Hindus. Gandhi's preaching of 'tolerance' in Hinduism and chanting of *Gita*, *Bible* and *Koran* in prayers were more un-Islamic than 'tolerance' for the Muslim fundamentalists.

Jinnah was not for Pakistan, which was just a cry for him. He was after teaching Gandhi a lesson who became Mahatma by representing the Hindus so also he would be a Mahatma by being the 'Father of Pakistan' by representing the Indian Muslims. Had Gandhi been mindful and determined to unmask the conspiratorial role of the League and British nexus he could have easily entered into the communities of the Muslims taking them as the real social 'untouchables' in politics. Instead, he had left the unlettered, abysmally impoverished Muslims in the hands of the communal Muslims who were acting under the umbrage of the British. In short, as if, freedom of India was the replacement of British Raj by the Hindu Raj and that too led by the elite Hindu classes.

Nehru was a socialist ideologist. He was also the mentor of Gandhi in international, political and ideological affairs. What was his stand on Muslim communalism? His analysis cannot be undermined : "Indian nationalism was dominated by Hindus and had a Hinduised look. So a conflict arose in the Moslem mind;

many accepted that nationalism, trying to influence it in the direction of their choice, many sympathised with it and yet remained aloof, uncertain; and yet many others began to drift in a separate direction for which Iqbal's poetic and philosophic approach had prepared them."[5] Thus distrust grew in the minds of young Muslim generation. What were Nehru's positive suggestions and actions to remove or dilute the growing communal distrust? It would not be inept to say he remained undisclosed. He always looked forward for the word of Gandhi, however otherwise it was in his mind. However, he had the impression that the slogan of Pakistan in Iqbal's philosophy had no impact on the Muslim masses. It played in the mind of Nehru that this stint could be removed by offering a socialist state. He was impressed by the mechanism of the Soviet Union to remove distrust and hegemony in a multinational state. But the Gandhi-wing was against 'socialism', that is, anything else than 'Gandhiism'. So Nehru's tact was to win power first by Gandhian means : "It is clear that any real settlement must be based on the goodwill of the constituent elements and on the desire of all parties to it to cooperate together for a common objective."[6] The crucial point is 'common objective'. But that remained unresolved. And his idea resembles the wishes of the British Cabinet Mission knowing well that the League's Islamic mind for Islamic Pakistan would never reconcile with Hindus 'tolerance' nor with any form of modern democracy.

Netaji Eulogized

Both Gandhi and Nehru held high the image of Netaji for his unique success in consolidating solidarity among all communities. Gandhi hailed this as "trinity of virtues" : "The hypnotism of the Indian National Army has cast its spell upon us. Nataji's name is one to conjure with. His partiotism is second to none...The lesson that Netaji and his army brings to us is one of self-sacrifice, unity irrespective of class and community, and discipline." Possibly being aware that he was going too far in adoring violence he resisted and added : "If our adoration will be wise and discriminating, we will rigidly copy this trinity of virtues, but we will as rigidly abjure violence."[7]

Both Gandhi and Nehru reversed their stand from 'conjure' to 'abjure' and none had the mind to go indepth into the cause of success of unity in the performance of Netaji. It is definitely a fallacy to hold violence was the means of 'hypnotism'. There is nothing 'miracle' or 'magic' in Netaji's unity success. It was the result of logic. Netaji had his 'common object'. It has two phases : Freedom : Democratic Socialism. His call was : 'Victory to India' (*Jai Hind*), to have all powers to the people and let the people decide their future. His personal ideology was 'democratic socialism'. Thus, Netaji and his INA were acting as the transmitter of power to the people and not transformer of the society. It was the possession of the people who were to decide the system of the society according to their free will irrespective of class and communities, certainly for the welfare and interests of all as a world model. Be that as it may, it is now transparent that non-violence as the means resulted in national disunity, caused partition and ceaseless flow of blood and distrust between the two pieces of India.

Impatience

1. British Empire

The British Empire organized conditions for 'war of attrition' in the process of its will to transfer the power to the common will of all the Indian parties. The warring parties were the Muslim League and the Congress and the organizer of the war itself. The results of the war of attrition depend on the life of patience. Whoever, would feel impatient earlier would lose more than the others.

The British Empire was most impatient otherwise how the British Prime Minister Clement Attlee could pronounce transfer of power by any means on or before June 1948, knowing that he was becoming the first British Minister to preside over the liquidation of the Empire? Was it a show to pressurize the Muslims and the Congress to come to civil war? No, for in that case the British administration would have collapsed more rapidly. Was that the policy of the Labour Party in power whose outlook was anti-colonialism? No. If so, then when the Prime Minister Winston Churchill said that he would not become the King's first minister in order to preside over the liquidation of the British Empire how the Labour Party stood up by his side and stressed that the British people must keep the Empire together after the war. Then how to account for such great volte-face?

Causes : Inward and Outward Contradictions

Inward

An Empire generally falls because of inner contradictions and outer conflicts. The British Empire was no exception. The miracle of imperialist war is that defeat is destined for both the warring forces. The conquered is the prey to war efforts, the conqueror to war effects. That is, the efforts of both end in defeats of both.

The British economy was in severe crisis. The economy was trade-oriented. The 'invisible' exports were a potential source of earnings of the country. The international infrastructures were affected by war affecting imports and exports and the war necessity forced the poor resource stock to be used for production of arms and ammunitions and food and clothing for war supply, creating thereby severe shortage of consumer goods for general consumption. For affording its war efforts Britain had to beg to the United States. The United States proclaimed on September 4, 1939 its neutrality in the war. This was followed by the New Neutrality Act, November 4, 1939. The Act permitted 'cash and carry' sales of arms to belligerents. On September 3, 1940 the United States gave Britain 50 destroyers in exchange of military bases in West Indies and Newfoundland. Then on March 11, 1941 Land-Lease Act permitted the President to supply materials to Britain and the Soviet Union. Then for post-war rehabilitation the Marshall Plan was introduced on June 5, 1947 to provide aid to the European countries to rebuild their economies and preserve their freedom. The European Recovery Programme had begun on April 3, 1948.

This short history shows the depth of indebtedness of Britain to the United States and consequently, the extent of social unrest in post-war Britain. The people were almost at the stage of starvation. The country had to pay for food imports more than its dollar imports. The Government's 'Battle Orders' were issued on August 21, 1947 (power was transferred to India an August 15, 1947) to the British farmers to step up output to 100 million tons within four years. The balance of payments becoming so unfavourable that on August 27, 1947 the British Government announced new restrictions on food imports, foreign travel, petrol and other things to improve the situation. The United States sanctioned $ 3,750 million worth of goods from the United States annually. The United Kingdom had to meet most of its deficit by withdrawing from American loans. The foreign economic relations of the United Kingdom were also at a low ebb. Its import debts to India, Ceylon and Egypt amounted to Rs. 3,000 million. It had to dispose of £1,200 million of its foreign investments to adjust the debts.

The Indian economy was virtually a handkerchief of the British economy. India had also to face supply crisis in consumer goods and affiliation. The supply of Indian currency rose from Rs. 179 crore in 1939 (August) to Rs. 356 crore in 1942 (January), further to Rs. 1,034 in 1944 (January) and Rs. 1,152 crore in 1945 (June). (From 1942 to 1943 the Indian currency circulation in Burma was not considered). Incidentally, the war opened an opportunity to the United States to become the world's supreme power, which it did not fail to seize.

Outside : In India

INA Trial : A Penance

Gandhi did his best as a loyal subject of the British Empire to protect the Empire from the assault of violence in his non-violent movements. He had also safeguarded himself and the British Government from the left-wingers in the Congress organization declaring Nehru as his successor reducing his left feelings into a disciplined Congressman. A time came when Gandhi-Nehru, in word and deed, stood unitedly by the side of the British Empire which was in severe war trouble. Their common aim was to have transfer of power to the hands of the Congress peacefully and legitimately. Nonetheless, the British were apprehending upsurge of the people any time under the command of the Indian army. For Netaji was still living and working in the minds of the people of India.

The members of the Indian National Army and the Indian prisoners of war returned home. The British Government decided to court-martial certain INA officers for making war against the King-Emperor. The Congress favoured the decision. But shortly after feeling the pulse of the people pulled back and set up a defence committee for the accused INA officers.

The INA trial took place at the Red Fort in New Delhi in November 1945. Nehru donned himself as the barrister after some thirty years in profession in the Court in defence of the accused. Bhulabhai Desai, also a renowned Congressman, acted as the senior lawyer. The communists also came forward and started collecting donations for sharing the expenditure in defence of the accused officers.

Bhulabhai Desai highlighted that there was no ideological link between the INA and the Japanese Axis force. Its primary concern was to win India's freedom. He also placed that it was the right of every Indian, if he thought fit, to disclaim his allegiance to the British Crown and join an army of liberation for gaining freedom of motherland.

Nehru's voice : "It became a trial of strength between the will of the Indian people and the will of those who hold power in India and it was the will of the people that triumphed in the end."[8] Unwittingly perhaps Nehru had voiced the voice of the people that the "will of Netaji" was the "will of the people". His transformation is a wonder. On April 22, 1942 in a press conference Nehru branded INA as "a dummy force under

Japanese control". It may now be his lip service only.[8a] And it was only to move with time which was his basic character. He had observed the people were greeting each other with '*Jai Hindi*'. Even the Muslim League stood by the INA officials, not to speak of the communists, the great betrayers of Netaji.

Gandhi's reactions were well measured : "Though I have nothing in common with any defence by force of arms, I am never blind to the valour and patriotism often displayed by persons in arms. . . India adores these men who are on the trial".[9] His characteristic style of balancing his 'idea' with the given conditions is well expressed in his draft resolution which was adopted by the Congress Working Committee on December 7, 1945 : "Whilst the Congress must feel proud of the sacrifice, discipline, patriotism, bravery and the spirit of unity displayed by the Azad Hind Fouj. . . and whilst it is right and proper for the Congress to defend the members of that body, now undergoing trial, and to aid its sufferers, the Congressmen must not forget that this support and sympathy do not mean that the Congress has in any way deviated from its policy of attaining independence by peaceful and legitimate means."[10] Thus he warned the Congressmen not to be swayed by the practical vision of Netaji to win freedom at any cost but to struggle on to win freedom only by peaceful and legitimate means, that is, by means of *ahimsa* and 'truth'.

Navy Mutiny

The INA Trial was a bombshell to the British Empire : "threatening to trumble down the whole edifice of the Indian Army."[11] Another jolt was felt in mid January 1946 when the British authorities were feeling the rebellious temper in the British units of the Royal Air Force stations in India and the Middle East over delays in repatriation and demobilization. The Royal Indian Air Force also became insubordinate and declared its sympathy with the INA. However, they were non-violent in character.

The violent situation arose with the Navy Mutiny. On February 18, 1946 in Bombay, which was the principal naval base of India, a number of ratings refused to eat or attend parade. Next day three thousand Indian sailors mutinied on board their ships and in barracks ashore. They removed their white officers, attacked the British soldiers in the streets of Bombay and roamed the city in lorries with slogans and the flags of the Congress and the Muslim League. The Indian troops seen rounded them up and the mutineers were confined to their barracks. The next day they tried to break out and the troops on guard fired. The British had to resort to aircrafts. The mutineers who were in ships trained their guns on the city and threatened to bombard.[11a] The Bombay mutiny spread over the Naval bases in Calcutta, Madras and Karachi. The mutiny could not reach the final stage. Sardar Vallabhbhai Patel, the Home Minister, came forward to mediate. He gave some positive assurances following which the mutiny was withdrawn. However, Patel simply deceived the mutineers.

Gandhi was furious. For it was for the first time in his political life that the Indian soldiers dared to take up arms in their own hands defying the Gandhian creed of non-violent non-cooperation. And that too when the transfer of power was undergoing finalization. He attacked the mutineers lavishly, never as before. He condemned the mutiny as "thoughtless orgy of violence". He became so much nationalist that he did not hesitate to say : "Inasmuch as a single person is compelled to shout '*Jai Hind*' or any other popular slogan, a nail is driven into the coffin of *swaraj*."[12] The phraseology of "compelled to shout '*Jai Hindi*'" was Gandhi's own creation. All was spontaneous with rebellious character. Then to eulogize his non-violent creed as the means to attain *swaraj* he raised his voice : "Let it not be said that India of the Congress spoke to the world of winning *swaraj* through non-violent action and belied her word in action and that, too, at the critical period in her life."[13] The 'critical period' may be in the sense that Gandhi was overpowered by the declaration of the British Empire of its intention to 'quit' India in favour of the non-violent action of the Congress. Then he condemned 'unity' for the purpose of violent action : "A combination between the Hindus and the Muslims and others for the purpose of violent action is unholy and it will lead to and probably is a preparation for mutual violence — bad for India and the world."[14] Thus, the 'unity' ushered in by Netaji was 'unholy', what was 'holy' was Khilafat unity, which was not of the "preparation for mutual violence". Perhaps the future smiled, however dry and wry. History cannot deny that non-violent unity of Gandhiji was ever accompanied with 'mutual violence'.

It may now be summed up that the British economy was in severe crisis, there was distressful unrest in the breast of the people of India, evidence of insubordination in Indian army and navy and expression of moral bankruptcy in the administration. So the Empire was heavily impatient to transfer power to Indians as early as possible.

It may be asked why not instantly? The answer is simple. The British Empire wanted to transfer power peacefully through settlement between the two warring communities, the Hindus and the Muslims. It did not like to go down the history as the betrayer. This is all secondary. The disunity between these two communities was irreversible under its rule because it was the effect of its 'divide and rule' policy, well organized and skilfully materialized. Its end policy was to break up the solidarity of the multinationality in India for good and at the same time to make the two Indians obliged to the British Crown. The offer of Commonwealth was an indication of that.

Through mediations the Empire finally asked the people of India to opt either for 'transfer of power peacefuly and leigtimately' or for 'civil war'. It announced the deadline June 1948.

2. *Muslim League*

In the war of attrition the Muslim League did never lose patience. For there was no cause as such. It was the League which was the promoter of civil war by 'direct action', being believer in 'sword-force' and was so prepared to opt for 'civil war', unless its demand for Pakistan was accepted through settlement. Even if the British had betrayed the Muslims at the last moment they had nothing to lose. They would remain in India as the Indian Muslims. Pakistan was their desired 'homeland', the 'motherland' was India. The truth that cannot be effaced. The League was patiently observing the movements of the Congress to act on time.

3. People

Gandhi made the people responsible for partition of the country. The people were impatient for freedom. If so, who was responsible for that? Gandhi was the leader, the people were his blind followers. He was Mahatma to them — a rare image for a politician. They were imbued with the feelings of Mhatmaji's *ahimsa* creed. In return he assured them to have freedom within a year, that is, in 1921. When they were betrayed Gandhi accused the people for it on the pretext that they did not abide by the conditions set by him. In another round Gandhi asked the British Government to grant Dominon Status by the end of 1929, if not, he would launch mass civil diobedience movement. The people again stirred up with the spirit of self-sacrifice. But that too ended in farce. In 1934 Gandhi being baffled retired from the Congress leadership. In 1942 Gandhi briefed the people with the *mantra* 'Do or Die' to force the British to Quit India by non-violent means. This also ended in farce and Gandhi refused to accept any responsibility of its failure. Subhas Chandra Bose by then became a 'spectre' to him as the probable destroyer of his *ahimsa* creed and to his successor Nehru as the possible successor of the people. The Congress begged the British Government not to leave India leaving her in the hands of Bose and the INA. For that it was prepared to accept vivisection of India. The people of India were not foolish. They understood how the Congress leaders, the communal Muslims and the anti-national communists were betraying the 'golden opportunity' of war. Instead, they were the victims of Bengal Famine (1943) and the Great Calcutta Killings (1946).

Thus, from 1921 the people were virtually betrayed by the leaders by their false promises. If in the circumstances they became impatient for freedom at any cost was it their fault? Yet such was the nature of their impatience and obedience to the leadership of Mahatmaji that there was no people's upsurge against their leaders nor against the British Government. To conclude, for the 'impatience' of the people, if at all, the leaders and not the people were responsible. They were simply betrayed decade after decade, without any voice of protest from their side.

4. Congress

The Congress had no reason to get impatient. For it was within its knowledge that so long as the British would exist in India the unity would be impossible. Gandhi's gospel was once 'quit first, unity after'. But he did not pursue his mass non-cooperation movement unto the last. His mind was at the negative stage. He was hopeful of British transfer of power because of conversion of their hearts. But the course was not of conversion but compulsion under war efforts. Gandhi might be ignorant of the nature of compulsion of the Empire but what about Nehru who had scholastic outlook? It was not unknown to him that for their own interests the British would be forced to Quit India today or tomorrow. Could he not understand the inner meaning of the statement of Lord Mountbatten : "unless I act quickly, I will find the beginning of a civil war on my hands."[15] Was that civil war in India or in Britain? If not on both soils. Yet why he was feeling too much tired of prisons? He was a Marx-oriented socialist then why he was afraid of civil war? Is it not an opportunity for social revolution? What had made him convinced that the transfer of power would be peaceful and legitimate? And how could he assume that partition of India would resolve all Hindu-Muslim problems and make possible friendly existence of the two Indias? Sardar Patel, however, marched more forward to say that Pakistan would not exist. In short, why Nehru did not take a firm stand knowing the fall of the British empire was imminent : No compromise with partition; India must remain undivided, come what may? Further, if Gandhi himself could shun the bondage of "trained to look to the British power for everything" and retain patience, partition might not be the reality.

Thus, in the war of attrition the Congress being tired most surrendered to the 'third force' to go down the history as the winner of *swaraj* 'peacefully and legitimately'— the historic victory of Gandhian means of *ahimsa* and truth!

Who Won Freedom

Who won freedom — Mahatmaji or Netaji? The means of non-violent revolution or of violent revolution? The most competent authority to give the verdict is Clement Attlee, the first minister of the King-Emperor who presided over the liquidation of the British Empire.

When Phani Bhusan Chakravarty was the Governor of West Bengal, Lord Attlee came to India (in 1955) and spent two days at the Raj Bhavan. At that time Governor Chakravarty asked Lord Attlee what had made the British to leave India so hurriedly in 1947 when the political situation of India was peaceful. Lord Attlee had given a number of reasons, of which the most important one was the growing feelings of insubordination among the Indian army and navy. The cause of it was the Netaji and his Azad Hind Fouj. Governor Chakravarty proceeded to know the impact of Gandhi's line of actions. The reply was "m-i-ni-mal".

But that does not mean the 'minimal' had no significance in India's freedom struggle. Netaji himself a number of times had addressed Gandhi as the 'father of the nation' with open heart for his contributions to rouse the patriotic feelings among the masses. This far and no farther. His line of actions commands that at the last stage non-violent active resistance will develop into an armed revolution. Then and then only will come the end of the British rule in India. The last stage was the phenomenon of the INA trial and Navy Mutiny that brought an end of the British rule in India and stunned Gandhi, a man professed by the idea of non-violence.

Dr. Ramesh Chandra Mazumdar, noted historian, had brought to the focal point the heroic contributions of Adolf Hitler. It is he who has revolutionized the world history and brought an end of the colonial imperialism. Dr. Mazumdar has named Gandhi, Bose and Hitler as 'Trinity' of India's independence. This is a considerable thesis.

NOTES AND REFERENCES

1. Tendulkar, *op. cit.,* Vol. 7, p. 415.
2. *Ibid.,* p. 29.
3. *Ibid.,* Vol. 8, p. 231.
4. *Ibid.,* Vol. 6, p. 193.
5. Nehru, *Discovery of India, op. cit.,* p. 351.
6. *Ibid.,* p. 530.
7. Collected Works, *op. cit.,* Vol. 83, p. 135.
8. Tendulkar, Vol. 7, p. 18.

8a. The change of Nehru was only an appearance. At heart he remained as before. He was reluctant to recruit the INA soldiers in Indian Army and display photos of Netaji at prominent places in Unit Lines, Canteens, Quarters Guard or Recreation Rooms. (Letter issued by Major General Staff, M. 155211.1, 11th February, 1949, H.Q. Bombay Sub-area, Colaba, Bombay).

9. Tendulkar, Vol. 7, p. 18.
10. *Ibid.,* p. 23.
11. Tuker in While Memory Serves, London, 1950, p. 43.

11a. See The Last Years of British India, Michael Edwardes, The New English Library, 1967, p. 125.

12. Tendulkar, Vol. 7, p. 68.
13. *Ibid.*
14. *Ibid.,* p. 69.
15. *Freedom at Midnight,* Larry Collins *et al, op. cit.,* p. 82.

13

WHY EXPERIMENT FAILED

Effects of Dualism

Gandhi being hurdled in South Africa in experimenting with his discovery of *satyagraha* left for India, possessed with the idea that it could be experimented effectively in the soil of his motherland. Soon he became a Congressman not to serve the Congress but to instrumentalize it for the purpose of experimentation with *satyagraha*. The Congress was at that time the only national party which had heart to heart approach to the people. So it was the best bridge to Gandhi to arrive at the doors of the people. Side by side he converted himself by all-round simplicity into an *Avatar* to the masses. But that does not mean that he aspired to be a 'saint'. To him it is too sacred a word. He claimed to be a humble searcher after 'truth'. He like a scientist aspired to experiment with the problems of day-to-day life as a means to realize truth. In short, his ambition was to free the world from aggravation for salvation. *Ahimsa* was not his discovery, it was the gift of *Rishis* and saints. Their parameter was only to preach to make men grands. Gandhi stepped forward to convert the devils into grands. For to him : "The religion of non-violence is not meant merely for the *Rishis* and saints. It is meant for the common people as well. Non-violence is law of our species, as violence is the law of the brute. The dignity of man requires obedience to a higher law — to the strength of the spirit." This spirit induced him to take up the noble idea : "I want India to recognize that she has a soul that cannot perish and that can rise triumphant above very physical weakness and defy the physical combination of a whole world."[1]

Gandhi was fully aware that the object of the people of India was freedom and not non-violence — freedom at any cost But he himself was firm in his conviction that freedom would be the result of non-violence. It would come to the hands of the people only when they all would be purified with the spirit of non-violence, and the nation as a whole would became an army of sacrificial disciplined non-violent soldiers. Herein lies the inner conflict with him and the people. The people urged independence at any cost while Gandhi set the vital condition, 'purification with the idea of non-violence', which was the stipulation of *Rishis* and saints, not of the nation professed by the idea of freedom as birth right.

Thus, there had been 'unity of opposites' between the people and Gandhi. Both had the urge to use each other for self-interest. The people's interest was to have the servicing image of Gandhi and Gandhi's interest was to use the mass strength of the people — the real strength behind his experiment. This 'unity of opposites' could not take the form of synthesis because of the resolute ideas of both. Had Gandhi followed the vow of 'Do or Die' unto the last without any precondition of compromise save that of complete independence then the people would have followed him blindfold as his disciplined non-violent followers and the nation could have attained freedom making Gandhi to go down the history as the 'liberator of India' with the noble means of 'non-violence'.

Instead, Gandhi played with dualism. In that he sometimes acted as an astute politician and immediately after as a social scientist experimenting with the creed of *ahimsa* as the means of conversion of the devils into grands. And when the devils became more devils taking advantage of the weakness of *ahimsa* and the people could no further bear with the excesses of devilry and resorted to the path of violence Gandhi at once, and sometimes on assumption, pulled back and bowed to come to terms with the devils. This continued to distance the people form his fold. Even his left-and-right-handers began to distance themselves from his camp. Gandhi's intolerance of other's ideology and means of realization distanced himself, mostly from the young generation. In addition, his too much patronization of religion, particularly Hinduism, helped to rouse communalism and separatism.

Even in his inner self he had been suffering from dualism. Thus, when he was caught up with his 'inner voice' he felt the warmth of *ahimsa* so much so that it "will transcend even my love for India herself." And then when found entrapped in failures of his *ahimsa* means he used to flare up with violence : "I would rather see India freed by violence than enchained like a slave to her foreign oppressors."[2] Of course he did not fail to display his reluctance : "Even if I was assured that we could have independence by means of violence, I shall refuse to have it. It won't be real independence."[3] And it was so much so that a number of times he himself came forward to stand against the violent operations of the revolutionists in the interest of the existence of the British Raj. As a result of this duality in thoughts and deeds he could neither win *swaraj* nor could he be a claimant of nothing succeeds like success. In other words, he could neither be a greater genius than Newton nor a greater warrior than Wellington, only he felt weary of his failure to teach the warring world the usefulness of non-violence as the means of salvation. Rather he proved by his deeds that the religion of non-violence is meant for the *Rishis* and saints and not for the worldly common people.

To sum up, Gandhi was possibly the only religious political leader who had ventured to revolutionize the world history by scientific experimentation with non-violence as the sole means of conversion. But all that ended in incessant flow of blood, hatred and distrust, and developed the sense of separatism that resulted in division of India. Dualism worked behind all this. Its basic features are as follows :

1. To Gandhi : "Man as animal is violent, but as spirit is non-violent. The moment he awakes to the spirit within, he cannot

remain violent."[4] Thus, man is basically animal and as such by nature violent. That is, until he becomes a spiritual being he remains violent by nature. One's conversion from animality to spirituality is a self-drawn or evolutionary process, none can accelerate the process by one's own will. Gandhi's endeavour was to impose his idea framed in political freedom from above.

2. Further, "mankind has steadily progressed towards *ahimsa*... Nothing in this world is static, everything is kinetic."[5]

   To repeat, Gandhi did not follow this law of history. He wanted to be the maker of new law of history, thereby a new world history. It is a character of defying the reality.

3. Further, "truth, harmony, brotherhood, justice — all are attributes of *ahimsa*."[6]

   But these attributes are non-visible as yet in 'human civilization'. What is visible is the force of sword, not 'soul'. Non-violence lies in violence and until 'animality' is dried out the emergence of the 'soul-force' through synthesis is an impossibility. To be precise, so long as man exists in matter animality in him will exist. What best could be expected is sublimation of animality balancing materialism with spiritualism.

Thus, Gandhi's major lapses are :

(i) He himself was 'impure' in his realization of 'truth'. What he had attained by his experience and experiment was more theoretical and intuitive than reality.

(ii) In spite of his self-impurity he fielded himself to convert the people of different faiths into the faith on *ahimsa*. And he allured them that 'freedom' would be within a year by means of *ahimsa* — and only by means of *ahimsa*. All others were marked as 'doomed to be failure'. Thus, he had played with the lives of the people and the future of the nation by way of 'experiment''.

(iii) The social impact of transitional conflict between patience for 'purification' and impatience for freedom was seemingly underrated by Gandhi. The conflict had subtly incurred devastating effect on the experimentalist as well as on the society.

(iv) Gandhi was so much in possession of an idea that to him : "If such a man cannot get an organization, he become an organization".[7] The result was neither he could be an organization nor did he allow the Congress to become a democratic organization.

Gandhi's experiment was an adventure at the irredeemable cost of the nation. His own confession is that "he, like a scientist, is making experiments about some of 'the external verities' of life, but cannot even claim to be a scientist because he can show no tangible proof of scientific accuracy in his methods or such tangible results of his experiments as modern science demands."[8]

The duality of Gandhi is well expressed by Romain Rolland in a few words : "The moral value of such an action is incomparable, but as a political move it was disconcerting."[9]

However, Gandhi is a man possessed by idea, has shown nobility and enough confidence in darkness in his adventurism which has aptly made him 'Mahatma'— a cross curiosity to the intellectuals then, now and ever.

NOTES AND REFERENCES

1. Romain Rolland, Mahatma Gandhi, Publications, Division, GOI, 1976, New Delhi, p. 35.
2. *Ibid,* p. 32.
3. M.K. Gandhi, Edited by V.B. Kher, Vol. VI, p. 68.
4. Tendulkar, *op. cit.,* Vol. 5, p. 316.
5. *Ibid.*
6. *Ibid.*
7. Collected Works, *op. cit.,* Vol. 76, p. 450.
8. *Young India,* May 12, 1920.
9. Romain Rolland, *op. cit.,* p. 102.

14

NEW SOCIAL SYSTEM
A Utopia

The Idea

Gandhi had his own social idea for free India. The idea was the outcome of Gandhi's humble following of Tolstoy, Ruskin, Thoreau, Emerson and others, who were philanthropists. Gandhi's idea was expressed in his book '*Hind Swaraj*' ('Indian Home Rule'), which was written when he was only forty. He prepared the manuscript running into 261 pages only within nine days. He wrote about fifty pages with the left hand because his right hand was exhausted. He was engaged with the manuscript day and night and that too while on board during his return to South Africa from London in 1899. Such hasty product without any touch of the revolutionary evolution of society did not satisfy Gandhi's political '*guru*', Gokhale, to whom it was crude and hastily conceived and prophesised that Gandhi himself would destroy the book after spending a year in India. But Gandhi was a man for creation, not destruction, which was beyond his faith in *ahimsa* and truth. The '*Hind Swaraj*' was eternal to him.

Hind Swaraj : Basic Features

1. There is no impassable barrier between East and West.
2. There is no such thing as Western or European civilization,

but there is a modern civilization which is purely material.

3. The people of Europe, before they were touched by modern civilization, had much in common with the people of the East and even today the Europeans who are not touched by modern civilization are far better able to mix with Indians than the offspring of that civilization.

4. It is not the British people who are ruling India, but it is modern civilization, through its railways, telegraph, telephone and almost every invention, which has been claimed to be a triumph of civilization.

5. Bombay, Calcutta, and other chief cities of India are the real plague-spots.

6. If British rule was replaced tomorrow by Indian rule based on modern methods, India would be no better.

7. East and West can really meet when the West has thrown overboard modern civilization, almost in its entirety. They can also seemingly meet when East has also adopted modern civilization, for that meeting would be an armed truce.

8. It is impertinence for any man or any body of men to begin or to contemplate reform of the whole world. To attempt to do so by means of highly artificial, and speeding locomotion, is to attempt the impossible.

9. Increase of material comforts, it may be generally laid down, does not in any way whatsoever conduce to moral growth.

10 Medical science is concentrated essence of black magic. Quackery is infinitely preferable to what passes for high medical skill as such.

11. Hospitals are the instruments that the devil has been using for his own purpose in order to keep his hold on his kingdom.

12. The railways, telegraphs, hospitals, lawyers, doctors and such like have all to go, and the so-called upper classes have to learn to live consciously and religiously and

deliberately the simple life of a peasant knowing it to be a life giving true happiness.

13. India should wear no machine-made clothing whether it comes out of European mills or Indian mills.
14. England can help India to do this and then she will have justified her hold on India.
15. There was true wisdom in the sages of old having so regulated society as to limit the material conditions of the people; the rude plough of perhaps five thousand years ago is the plough of the husbandman today.[1]

Concept of State

Gandhi conceived State as *Ram Rajya. Ram Rajya* is 'Kingdom of God on Earth :

> "It can be religiously translated as Kingdom of God on Earth; politically translated, it is perfect democracy in which inequalities based on possession and non-possession, colour, race or creed or sex vanish; in it land and State belong to the people, justice is prompt, perfect and cheap and, therefore, there is freedom of worship speech and the Press — all this because of the reign of self-imposed law of moral restraint.
>
> "Such a State must be based on truth and non-violence and must consist of prosperous, happy and self-contained villages and village communities. It is a dream that may never be realized. I find happiness in living in that dreamland, ever tying to realize it in the quickest way."[1a]

Thus, Gandhi's own admission is that his State had no science behind — it was a 'dreamland' where he found happiness to live in a small way. It is mentionable in this context that according to Gettele the ancient Hindu States were not theocratic. Religion did not dominate Hindu politics. It was restricted to principles of moral guidance for ruler and ruled both. The State had the democratic character in that the ruler was the authority of the State but as a person he was subject to law as was every other individual.

Violence was devil to Gandhi. He was against any other form of State than a non-violent one. For that the State should have least possible power and only such power that could not be used for violence. State is a soulless machine, it cannot be converted into grand : "the State is a soulless machine, the State can never be weaned from violence to which it owes its very existence.[2] The violent State "will be caught in the coils of violence itself and fail to develop non-violence at any time."[3]

The violent feelings of State can develop out of its will to forcibly convert the capitalist system into socialist system, private property into national property and to impose the will of the State over the will of the people. And all this would be possible when power would concentrate in the hands of the State. To thwart all this Gandhi conceived Trusteeship to replace capitalism, Village *Swaraj* to make the villages free from market-war, and Panchayat Raj to constitute village-based governments of the people.

Thus, the three pillars of Gandhi's conceptual State and society are : Trusteeship; Village *Swaraj*; Panchayat Raj. Before we take them up it needs to be answered about defence and law and order of the village *swaraj*. To defend the villages from foreign aggressions Gandhi advocated soul-force, the practical means of which was passive resistance. He was confident that a non-violent State had enough power to counter the combined world arm forces. He philosophized this taking in Rama's reply to Vibhishana when the latter wondered how it would be possible for Rama to fight with Ravana who was well equipped militarily: "my dear friend, there is no enemy who can conquer the man who takes his stand on the chariot of *dharma.* He who is powerful like this is a warrior who can conquer even that great and invincible enemy — the world."[4]

In practice, Gandhi asked for organizing non-violent army having "immovable faith in God, willing and perfect obedience to the chief of the non-violent army and perfect inward and outward cooperation between the units of the army."[5]

Is it that Gandhi was speaking all this from his 'dreamland'? To Gandhi, not so : "Reasons suggest no flaw in the theoretical conception of it (non-violent State). Whether human nature will respond to what has been called an exactions call is another question. . . I passionately believe in the possibility of attainment through the perfection of the non-violent technique whose hidden resources no one has fathomed. We have only found a foothold."[6] When compressed, he did not hesitate to say : 'better to be crushed than to be vanquished'." But reality demands neither to be crushed nor to be vanquished, only reordering the unordered.

About law and order Gandhi had no objection to police force. Its ranks would be composed of believers in non-violence. They would be servants not masters of the people. Through mutual cooperation with the people they would exactly deal with the ever-increasing disturbances. They would have some kinds of arms, but that would be rarely used, if at all, and their work would be confined primarily to robbers and dacoits.

Thus, Gandhi's conceptual non-violent State is an 'ordered anarchy' which governs the least and a true democratic State: "a nation that runs its affairs smoothly and effectively without much State interference is truly democratic. Where such a condition is absent, the form of Government is democratic only in name."[7] He had fear psychosis about concentration of power in the hands of the State : "I look upon an increase of the power of the State with the greatest fear...it does the greatest harm to mankind by destroying individuality, which lies in the root of all progress."[8]

Trusteeship

The Trusteeship Formula was drafted by Prof. Dantwala and after some amendments finalized by Gandhi.

1. Trusteeship provides a means of transforming the present capitalist order of society into an egalitarian one. It gives no quarter to capitalism, but gives the present owning class

a chance of reforming itself. It is based on the faith that human nature is never beyond redemption.

2. It does not recognise any right of private ownership of property, except so far as it may be permitted by society for its own welfare.
3. It does not exclude legislative regulation of the ownership and use of wealth.
4. Thus under the state-regulated trusteeship an individual will not be free to hold or use his wealth for selfish satisfaction or in disregard of the interest of society.
5. It is proposed to fix a decent minimum living wage, even so a limit should be fixed for the maximum income that could be allowed to any person in society. The difference between such minimum and maximum incomes should be reasonable and equitable and variable from time to time so much so that the tendency would be towards obliteration of the difference.
6. The character of production will be determined by social necessity and not by personal whim or greed.

   To develop further :

7. The 'superfluous' portion of income of one will remain as the property of the possessor who will act as the public trustee of the property to be used for the welfare of the people.
8. The trustee has the right to nominate his successor but the choice must be finalized by the State to put checks both on the State and the individual.

A Glimpse

Gandhi's trusteeship is a discovery of means of salvation of the capitalists through dispossessions of possessions without compromising with the individual's right to possess and dispossess. This economic philosophy he had discovered in *Gita* : "I understand the *Gita* teaching of non-possession to mean that those who desired salvation should act like the trustee who, having control over great possessions, regards not an iota of them as his own. It became clear to me as daylight that non-possession and equitability pre-supposed a change of heart, a change of attitude."[9]

His philosophical logic is : "Everything belonged to God and was from God. Therefore, it was for His people as a whole, not for a particular individual. When an individual had more than his proportionate portion he became a trustee of that portion for God's people."[10]

There was in it practical philosophy as well. The doctrine of trusteeship was conceived to minimize the violene inherent in capitalism. Gandhi had no ill feelings against the capitalist class. He wanted to protect it just only converting a capitalist into trustee of his 'superfluous' property for his own salvation. Trusteeship was a vital instrument in his hands to answer to the issue of class conflict : "Trusteeship is my answer to the issue of class conflict."[11] He was horrified at the class struggle in Marxism and Russian Revolution followed by totalitarianism. This was further followed by the rise of nazism and fascism and Second World War that rocked the entire *ahimsa dharma.* Under the circumstances he was possessed by the idea of trusteeship. He pleaded with : "I want them (privileged classes) to outgrow their greed and sense of possession, and to come down in spite of their wealth to the level of those who earn their bread by labour. The labourer has to realize the wealthy man is less owner of his own, *viz.*, the power to work."[12] He had cautioned the capitalist class : "As for the present owners of wealth, they would have to make their choice between class-war and voluntary converting themselves into trustees of their wealth."[13] Simultaneously, he addressed the communists of India : "I must warn you that I do not bear any ill to the capitalists, I can think of doing them no harm. But I want, by means of suffering, to awaken them to their sense of duty. I want to melt their hearts and get them to render justice to their less fortunate brothers. They are human beings and my appeal to them will not go in vain."[14]

Hovering

Gandhi's trusteeship rests on man-making by conversion, persuasion and alluring to salvation. Objectively his mind was working to revolt against the modern civilization in favour of ancient Indian civilization. To him to rediscover men in ancient civilization was not so easy task, however 'miracle' must happen.

In an interview with Nirmal Kumar Bose Gandhi said : "Love and exclusive possession can never go together. Theoretically when there is perfect love there must be perfect non-possession... But that is true in theory only. Men will remain imperfect... So that perfection in love or non-possession will remain an unattainable ideal as long as we are alive, but towards which we must ceaselessly strive."[15]

To quote Acharya Kripalani :

> "Gandhi was rather disillusioned in the end and held that his capitalist friends could never become the trustees of the people. . . The capitalists went to him for their own purposes mostly. . . but Gandhiji could not turn the heart of even one capitalist. They remained what they were."[16]

There is nothing unusual in it. Trusteeship is an expansion of Gandhi's objects of experiments with *ahimsa* as the means of conversion, where conversion itself is a utopian idea. According to Gandhi's own definition 'body is a possession' and 'it calls for other possessions'. But why? For man does not fear God, fears Death, that is the non-cooperation of body which is deprived of 'calls for other possessions'. In order to gain cooperation of body possession is the most covetable means.

Even if it was a reality it would cause insurmountable crisis in growth and development, for trusteeship is neither state ownership nor entrepreneurship; it was the ownership of a class of persons spirited with 'detachment' to give up one possession after another.

Village Swaraj

Gandhi formulated village *swaraj* to offer India a 'complete republic'. Thus, "My idea of village *swaraj* is that it is a complete republic, independent of its neighbours for its own vital wants, and yet interdependent for many others in which dependence is a necessity. Thus, every villager's first concern will be to grow its own food crops and cotton for its cloth."[17] Elsewhere he said : "The essence of what I have said is that man should rest content with what are his real needs and become self-sufficent."[18] Gandhi's imagination was to organize a 'village civilization' contra 'city civilization'. That is, 'handicrafts' contra 'industrialization' : "The village civilization and the city civilization are totally different things. One depends on machinery and industrialization and the other on handicrafts. We have given preference to the latter."[19]

Gandhi was not hopeful about the probability of village *swaraj*. In his conscience however he left it for the future to determine whether it was a social science or utopia. He wrote "To model such a village may be the work of a lifetime. Any lover of true democracy and village life can take up a village, treat it as his world and sole work, and he will find good results."[20] His village-oriented hand-spinning mind was against the modern trend of urbanization. His idea worked in terms of conversion of seven lakh villages of India into village republics in an oceanic circle for which every individual should always be ready to perish for the village. He said : "I may be taunted with the retort that this is all utopian." Yet he insisted : "Let India live for this true picture, though never realizable in its completeness."[21] He hit the national sentiment : "If the village perishes India will perish too. It will no more be India."[22]

Panchayat Raj

Gandhi revamped the India's constitutional concept of village republics which functioned for the longest period in India as well as in different European countries before the industrial revolution. Gandhi opined that the village republic would be governed by Panchayat, consisting of five persons to be elected annually by the villagers possessing prescribed qualifications. The Panchayat would be the legislature, judiciary and executive combined to operate for its year of office. Gandhi described this: "The Government of the village will be conducted by Panchayat of five persons, annually elected by the adult villagers, male or female, possessing minimum prescribed qualifications. This will have all the authority and jurisdiction required. Since there will be no system of punishment in the accepted sense, this Panchayat will be the the legislature, judiciary and executive combined to operate for its year of office. Any village can become such a republic today without much interference even from the present Government whose sole effective connection with the village is the exaction of the village revenue."[23] The village republic would provide complete independence to each and every villager : "Here there is perfect democracy based upon individual freedom. The individual is the architect of his own government. The law of non-violence rules him and his government."[24] Thus, the village republic is a partyless democracy, that is, free from 'partiocracy', the prime source of democratic anarchy and corruption.

The village republic was not a solitary unit. It presupposed formation of federal village republics. It would be an 'oceanic circle' whose centre would be the individual. Gandhi's elucidation: "In this structure composed of innumerable villages, there will be ever widening, never ascending, circles. Life will not be a pyramid with the apex sustained by the bottom. But, it will be an oceanic circle, whose centre will be the individual always ready to perish for the village, the latter ready to perish for the circle of the villages, till at last the whole becomes one life composed of individuals, never aggressive in their arrogance, but ever humble, sharing the majesty of the oceanic circle of which they are integral units."[25] This elucidation is a decent combination of Gandhian philosophy and Indian Constitution. Gandhi's conceptual federation of village republics would consist of seven lakh Panchayat Governments, self-contained individually within the parameter of gross regional disparity. How far such federation in India could be cohesive and purposive can easily be guessed.

Gandhi had another purpose behind the Panchayat Raj. The Panchayat being a small unit with a small area elected by the people of that area must have enough strength to convert the devils into grands. Gandhi wrote : "When the Panchayat Raj is established, public opinion will do, what violence can never do. The present power of the *zamindars*, the capitalists and the rajas can hold sway, only so long as the common people do not realize their own strength. If the people non-cooperate with the evil of *zamindars* and capitalism, it must die of inanition. In Panchayat Raj only the Panchayat will be obeyed and the Panchayat can only work through the law of their making."[26]

Gandhi's approach to capitalists was kindly and humanitarian as well as rational. The capitalist as man and capitalist as exploiter are two different beings. The 'man' is convertible and if the 'man' can be converted into 'trustee' the labour of exploitation would automatically vanish. Gandhi was friendly with the capitalists, zamindars, and maharajas for he found no wrong in them as men. They were not the enemies of the people. The people were their own enemies. For no person could amass wealth without the cooperation, willing or forced, of the people concerned. As such he advised the people not to cooperate with the exploiters. He was further kindly to the exploiters because they were the victims of the social system. What was to be destroyed was not the exploiters but the evil system. And there came in the role of panchayats to build up Village Raj.

The Village Raj was the modern model of *Rama Rajya* of Gandhi. In that rajya industrialism would have no place to exploit the villages, actively or passively, by creating competition and marketing problems. The villages would not be allowed to be exploited and drained by the cities. Man and machine are inseparable. But in *Rama Rajya* machine would not be allowed to rule over man. Machine would not be allowed to produce what the villages could produce without difficulty. Production would be labour-intensive, not capital-intensive in order to avoid employment problem. High-tech economy would remain confined to key industries without affecting equitable distribution of national income. *Rama Rajya* was for peace, not for aggression and bore no ambition to build up empire on the ruins of other nations. The imperialist wars were the market wars between aggressive developed capitalist countries. *Rama Rajya* was against war, that is, industrialism. Gandhi visualized : "if India becomes industrialized, we shall need a Nadir-shah to find out other worlds to exploit."[27]

Gandhi's modern model of *Rama Rajya* may be a utopia but the truth underlying it demands further revelations for experimentation.

Economic Outlook of Gandhi

Gandhi was a man of ethics. Modern civilization based on matter and machine was unethical to him. He had divided civilization distinctly into modern civilization and village civilization. He was averse to open entry of machines and machine civilization into the villages as that would spoil the soil and pollute the souls of villagers. Even for urban areas he was not happy with large-scale modern industrialization. Ethical reasons apart, it would pollute nature and the machine-made mass products would force out the village industrial products from village markets through competition. This would cause the death of village civilization. This called for protection against invasion of modern civilization and hence he had developed the ideas of Village *Swaraj* and Panchayat Raj and out of that the federation of village republics governed by the panchayats. The federation would be the people's raj, fully democratic in character and non-violent in policy and principle. Commodity exchange, market war, unemployment and social unrest would wipe out. The productive capacity would be labour-intensive, distribution would be need-based and the 'surplus' would be the property of trustees for public welfare.

During his lifetime Gandhi had to face severe criticisms about his social and economic ideas. Subhas Chandra Bose in his Presidential address at the 51th Session of the Congress on February 19, 1938 said : "However, much we may dislike modern industrialism and condemn the evils which follow in its train, we cannot go back to the pre-industrial era, even if we desire to do so. It is well, therefore, that we should reconcile ourselves to industrialization and devise means to minimize its evils."[27] Nehru did not remain silent. He also reminded Gandhi that independence of India would not be possible : "Unless she is a technically advanced country. . . From the economic or political point of view isolated India may well be a kind of vacuum which increases the acquisitive tendencies of others and thus creates conflicts."[28] Nehru, however, analysed Gandhi's outlook with his socialist tools. Thus, "This fact of increasing mass poverty influenced Gandhi powerfully. It is true, I think, that there is a fundamental difference between his outlook on life generally and what might be called the modern outlook. He is not enamoured of ever-increasing standards of living and the growth of luxury at the cost of spiritual and moral values. . . He reacted. . . looked back with yearning to the days of the old autonomous and more-or-less self-contained village community where there had been an automatic balance between production, distribution, and consumption, where political or economic power was spread out and not concentrated as it is today; where a kind of simple democracy prevailed; where the gulf between the rich and the poor was not so marked; where the evils of great cities were absent and people lived in contact with the life-giving soil and breathed the pure air of the open spaces."[29]

All this is the substance of dreamland of the socialists. Even the capitalists dream like that a new world by promoting Welfare State through greater and wider redistribution of national income and market expansion through understanding in globalization and liberalization. In that respect the capitalists are also socialists. All this was sham to Gandhi. To Gandhi modern civilization was devoid of spiritual and moral values. It was aggressive in character. Its object was to destruct the village civilization. Gandhi's model of Village Swaraj and Panchayat Raj was framed to passively resist the aggression of the modern civilization. The model may or may not be a reality but to Gandhi it was the 'truth'.

Marxism Contra Gandhism

Gandhi in his interviews said that he was a socialist, a non-violent communist. But Marxism and Gandhiism are two opposite poles. The profile is as under :

1. Marxism is dialectical materialism.

   Gandhiism is dialectical spiritualism.

2. Marxism holds economics commands politics.

   Gandhiism holds religion commands politics.

3. Marxism says revolutionary consciousness of the working men grows from within.

   Gandhiism says revolutionary consciousness of all classes grows from without.

4. Marxism asserts a revolutionary soul needs a democratic body for its revolutionary manifestations.

   Gandhiism asserts a revolutionary soul needs a democratic non-violent revolutionary body for its revolutionary manifestations.

5. Marxism discloses all forms of antagonism and exploitation and enthuses the working men to abolish them.

   Gandhiism discloses 'truth' in 'means and end' and enthuses all classes of people to follow the means of *ahimsa* for freedom and salvation.

6. Marxism highlights 'class struggle'

   Gandhiism highlights 'class cooperation', renounces 'class struggle'.

7. Marxism dissolves 'advanced class' or 'great man' as an abstraction from metaphysics.

   Gandhiism absorbs 'advanced class' or 'great man' as the natural behaviour of the Almighty.

In short, Marx was a determinist; Gandhi a relativist; Marx

was a materialist; Gandhi a spiritualist; Marx was a glass struggler; Gandhi a class cooperator : Marx was for classless society; Gandhi for class-exist society.

Communist Society

Engels has given an outline of communist new social order :

First of all it will inaugurate a 'democratic constitution' to repose political power to the proletariat. Having the power the society will be transformed one with the following growing features : Restriction of private ownership : Gradual expropriation of landed properties, factory owners, railway and shipping magnates; Confiscation of the property of all emigrants and rebels against the majority of the people, Putting as end to competition among the workers themselves to compel the factory owners, as long as they still exist, to pay same high wages as those paid by the State; Equal liability to work for all until the abolition of private ownership is completed and formation of industrial armies, especially for agriculture; Increase the number of national factories etc. and development of agriculture; Education of all children which will be production-oriented; Concentration of all means of transport in the hands of the nation; Centralization of credit and banking systems in the hands of the State.

"Finally, when all capital, all production, and all exchange are concentrated in the hands of the nation, private ownership will automatically have ceased to exist, money will have become superfluous, and production will have so increased and men will have so changed that the last forms of the old social relations will also be able to fall away."[30]

Indubitably, the 'final' phase of communist society resembles Gandhi's *Rama Rajya* — both are symbols of utopia.

NOTES AND REFERENCES

1. Tendulkar, *Mahatma*, Vol. 1, p. 107.

"As to franchise, he swore by the franchise of all adult, male and female, above the age of twenty-one or even eighteen. He would bar old men like himself. They were of no use as voters." *Harijan*, March 2, 1947.

1a. Collected Works, Vol. 80, p. 300.

2. Tendulkar, *op. cit.*, Vol. 5, p. 11.

3. *Ibid.*

4. *Economic and Political Life and Relations* by M.R. Gandhi, compiled by V.B. Kher, Vol. 1, p. 59.

5. *Harijan*, May 12, 1946.

6. *Ibid.*, April 5, 1942.

7. *Ibid.*, January 11, 1936.

8. *Modern Review*, October 1935.

9. Gandhi, *Autobiography, op. cit.*, pp. 305-306.

10. *Harijan*, June 3, 1939.

11. Collected Works, Vol. 76, p. 467.

12. *Harijan*, June 3, 1939.

13. Collected Works, Vol. 83, p. 27.

14. *Young India*, March 26, 1931.

15. Tendulkar, *Mahatma*, Vol. 4, p. 11.

16. Gandhian Outlook and Technique, Ministry of Education, GOI, 1953, pp. 116-117.

17. Collected Works, Vol. 76, p. 308.

18. Tendulkar, *Mahatma*, Vol. 7, p. 15.

19. Nirmal Kumar Bose, Selections from Gandhi, Sec. 366.

20. *Harijan*, July 26, 1942.

21. Collected Works, Vol. 85, p. 33.

22. *Harijan*, August 29, 1936.

23. *Ibid.*, July 26, 1942.

24. *Ibid.*

25. Tendulkar, *Mahatma*, Vol. 7, p. 169.

26. *Ibid.*, p. 405.

27. *Harijan*, November 3, 1935.

28. Tendulkar, *Mahatma*, Vol. 7, p. 16.

29. Nehru, *Discovery of India, op. cit.*, p. 404.
30. Karl Marx and Frederick Engels, Selected Works, Vol. 1, pp. 90-91, Progress Publishers, Moscow.

15

SUMMARY AND CONCLUSION

Summary

M.K. Gandhi was born in a religious family having deep faith in Hinduism with wide sense of tolerance towards other religions. He was a humble being, not highly educated nor had he any ambition. He left for South Africa to labour for bread. But there came a surprising turn in his life. He was a victim of barbaric racism in South Africa like many other Indians who were living there. Individual protest did not pay off. His inner spirit rose up against this social injustice. His inner voice prompted him to resort to the means of non-violence preparing himself to get killed but not to kill the devil for his deed. It was a practical means as well, for he had no other means save that two bare hands and open head and mind. Besides, his Godly spirit at heart must one day win the devilish spirit of the devil which was just working outside. Inside the devil had also the Godly spirit for all are children of God. Gandhi also realized that was the only means to realize 'truth'.

Thus, Gandhi became a changed man. He organized some associations to experiment with his discovery of non-violence as both redress and realization of truth. He attained considerable success but his mind was walking towards his home where he would have greater scope for experimenting with his philosophy. Finally, he came back to India not to become a politician but as an experimentalist.

India was at that time under the British domination. The people were striving for freedom. The Congress was then the only national organization working for freedom. But it was staggering for want of dynamic leadership with new means in hands. Gandhi observed all this maintaining distance for a year. Then at the right time he entered into the Congress politics to seize the helm of the organization to remake it in his own way for his own cause — freedom as redress and truth for realization. Redress was his policy and truth was his principle. That is, the policy was the means and the principle was the end.

India by nature is a religious country and the people were then fighting for freedom preferably to win without killing the devils. Gandhi offered them freedom without bloodshed. He simplified the matter from practical field. He addressed the people that they were deprived of food and arms. It would be absurd to rise up with arms in hands and that too against the mighty British power. Gandhi further addressed that the rulers were ruling India by the Indians. If the Indians could unitedly rise up to non-cooperate with the rulers then the entire edifice of the British Raj must collapse. Non-cooperation might induce the Government to take up arms to force the people to cooperate. But that would not be productive if the people could resort to the means of active non-violence. For only violence provokes violence. The non-cooperation should be non-violent. The people should march forward bravely with sacrificing spirit to resist non-violently. That is, the movement should be non-violent non-cooperation. This would help convert the devils into grands for the devil is a man, man is born grand, becomes devil under circumstances.

Gandhi was not a preacher. He was a practical idealist. He demonstrated his idea in practice. The All-India *Hartal*, Khilafat Agitation, March to Dandi are some landmarks in history. The people roused up and Gandhi became both Mahatma and political hero. Even the militant revolutionists could not disown the heroism of Gandhi. The British Government was not sitting idle. It had in its hands a number of loopholes in Gandhian policy and principle. The policy was dependent on Hindu-Muslim unity, which was an impossibility. For the Muslims were such a community that they could not totally get themselves absorbed in Indian culture. They were too much conscious of their religious identity. The overwhelming number of Indian Muslims were the Hindu converts from the oppressed classes. By tradition they were too much averse to Hindu trust. Further, once India was under the Muslim domination which made the Hindus apathetic to the Muslims. This background was enough for the British diplomats to develop more distrust and hatred between these two communities. The Muslims were extremely backward in all aspects. The British Government took advantage of that. The Government came forward with assurance of awards for them as rewards for their faithful cooperation with the Government.

Gandhi's principle was not to cooperate but to compromise with the devil, but never to compromise with violence. He was steadfast in his principle that the violence of devil should be resisted by active non-violence of braves. But the people are by nature violent and what the Government had to do was to rouse that passion by violence and that was to hit at the principle of Gandhi's adherence to non-violence. The strategy was to foil the forward march of Gandhi against the Raj for *swaraj*. Gandhi had nothing to be displeased with for that had helped him to retract whenever he had traced darkness ahead. The blame then automatically came down on the shoulders of the people who were blamed for their disobedience to the creed of non-violence of braves. The Government was aware of the unswerving loyalty of Gandhi to the British Empire. He was such a man that he would never consider the distress of the Empire an opportunity for the Indians to kick the Raj out. His cooperation at the time of distress was his faith. His object was to have freedom peacefully and legitimately, that is, as redress and truth. That would be the victory of his experiment of conversion by means of non-violence and also realization of liberty and truth. Hence Gandhi was no problem to the British Government. So also not the Muslim League, which was its 'favourite wife'. The League was possessed by the fear psychosis of Hindu Raj. On the other side, the Government was ever prepared to raise sword-force to crush Gandhi's soul-force in winning independence against the will of the Empire. But Gandhiji's image was unbreakable to the people of India. In spite of forward to backward march, fasting and penance, retirement and resumption, confession of Himalayan blunders he remained Mahatma and hero as ever. The only way open to the Government was to create such circumstances at such time that Gandhi would feel himself isolated from the people and politics.

The time and opportunity arrived. The Second World War broke out. Unilaterally the British Government declared India belligerent. War means violence, violence means war against Gandhi. But the war was a global phenomenon. Gandhi was crippled. He was in dilemma.

In the meantime, Subhas Chandra Bose being expelled from the Congress left for Germany. There he joined the Axis powers to fight for freedom with the aid of the enemies of common enemy — the British Empire. The German troops were then heading towards the other European states. London was heavily bombed. The Empire was rocked. India was restless for freedom. The Empire sent Sir Stafford Cripps with some proposals indicating also that partition was heading on. All this was dismissed by Gandhi as 'post-dated cheque'. Nehru was displeased. He was looking for some compromise with the ruling power. Gandhi was feeling the hot temper of the people for freedom. He approached repeatedly to the Government to come to some terms for the present. But the Government was firm not to grant anything now, all after the war. Frustrated Gandhi was looking for a way out. Suddenly sparked off his 'inner voice': 'Do or Die', 'Quit India'. The movement was launched in 1942 but had faced a tragic end.

The Japanese troops were marching towards India. Bose was then in Japan. There he reorganized the Indian National Army and declared a provisional government for free India and raised the slogan : 'To Delhi, To Delhi'. This horrified Gandhi. If Bose could enter into India he must have to leave for Himalayas leaving aside for good his lifelong dream of realization of truth in *ahimsa* means. Nehru was also being haunted by the spectre of Bose. For the entry of Bose in India would mean his exit from power politics.

The war began to take a turn in favour of the Allied powers. This helped the British Empire to take upper hands in negotiations about transfer of power to whom, how and when. The transfer of power was unavoidable to the Empire. For the British economy was ravaged by the war-effects, the Indian economy and politics were in turmoil, and what most there was open insubordination among the Indian army and navy that had gone to the stage of revolt. Thus, there was enough indications that the colonial era was at its end.

The British Empire delegated a Cabinet Mission. Its hands were full of concrete and coercive proposals, even it was equipped with a 'basic form' of constitution. The transfer of power by June 1948 was declared. The Muslim League took up arms in hands. It declared 'direct action' against the Hindus to initiate civil war to pressurize the Congress and the Empire to yield to its demand of Pakistan. Lord Mountbatten entered into the scenario. He hurriedly settled up all the floating troubles in a very diplomatic manner. He forced the Muslim League to remain satisfied with a moth-eaten Pakistan and durbared with Nehru to work out how to isolate Gandhi within the scenario. The twos found out the means to convey to Mahatmaji that 'civil war' would be against the non-violent creed of the Congress. So let the people decide whether they wanted partition or civil war. Partition would not be a 'sin' if it was the effect of the free will of the people. Gandhiji with tears in eyes was 'convinced' that the will of the people was the will of God. His only mission was to free India peacefully and legitimately. So he agreed to partition however submissively. Then he declared that the Congress had won freedom by means of non-violence — which was his creed, the creed of the Congress.

Gandhi was not a politician nor a saint. He was a socio-religious experimentalist — a science unknown in history. The purpose of the experiment was to create a new world over the head of the determining nature of the history itself. The creation would be some sort of imposition of the will of invisible force. The consequences revealed the unrealistic and unscientific character of the experiment. The freedom was won not by any non-violent means. It was the result of war and violence all over the world. The British India was ruled by the Indians. Gandhi's non-violent non-cooperation was a logical means to topple the rule of British Raj in India. But that required unification of all the divided forces and true adoption of the pledge 'Do or Die', 'March to Delhi' until freedom was achieved. But Gandhi was a half-way man : Neither a politician nor a saint; neither he could adhere to non-violence nor to violence. He was at bottom ever at the cross-roads.

Conclusion

There is poverty in the philosophy of Gandhi. In practice, he was the dictator in Congress politics, the creator of dynasty in Indian democracy, the inductor of religion in politics, the barrier of entry into national politics of the young intellectual revolutionaries and so on and so forth. And above all, he was the founder of partition. In theory, he was acting as a duello in dualism.

But when reviewed from the point of the experimental character of his philosophy what Gandhi had done was only to safeguard his means in search of eternal truth. He adopted the means of non-violence to project his creed distancing the devils through non-cooperation. This simple call of Gandhi's non-violent non-cooperation awoke the masses to become conscious and active for struggle for freedom. Miracle had happened! Partition.

There is plenty in Gandhian philosophy. His village *swaraj,* panchayat raj, and trusteeship are all to caution the civilized world which is marching forward with high-tech swords in hands to challenge the law of nature. His village civilization is not a challenge to modern civilization. It is only an indication that 'grand' lies in village civilization, 'devil' in modern civilization. The epoch of conversion is ahead.

APPENDICES

APPENDIX I

CRIPPS PROPOSALS

The terms of the proposals made by Sir Stafford Cripps March 1942 were as follows :

(a) Immediately upon the cessation of hostilities, steps shall be taken to set up in India, in the manner described hereafter, an elected body charged with the task of framing a new Constitution for India.

(b) Provision shall be made, as set out below, for the participation of the Indian States in the Constitution-making body.

(c) His Majesty's Government undertake to accept and implement forthwith the Constitution so framed subject only to :

(1) The right of any Province of British India that is not prepared to accept the new Constitution to retain its present constitutional position, provision being made for its subsequent accession if it so decides. With such non-acceding provinces, should they so desire, His Majesty's Government will be prepared to agree upon a new Constitution giving them the same full status as the Indian Union, and arrived at by a procedure analogous to that herein laid down.

(2) the signing of a treaty which shall be negotiated between His Majesty's Government and the Constitution-making body. This treaty will cover all necessary matters arising out of the complete transfer of responsibility from British to Indian hands; it will

make provision, in accordance with the undertakings given by His Majesty's Government, for the protection of racial and religious minorities; but will not impose any restriction on the power of the Indian Union to decide in the future its relationships to the other member states of the British Commonwealth.

(3) Whether or not an Indian State elects to adhere to the Constitution, it will be necessary to negotiate a revision of its treaty arrangements, so far as this may be required in the new situation.

(d) The Constitution-making body shall be composed as follows, unless the leaders of Indian opinion in the principal communities agree upon some other form before the end of hostilities :

Immediately upon the result being known of the provincial elections which will be necessary at the end of hostilities, the entire membership of the Lower Houses of Provincial Legislatures shall, as a single electoral college, proceed to the election of the Constitution-making body by the system of proportional representation. This new body shall be in number about one-tenth of the number of the electoral college.

Indian states shall be invited to appoint representatives in the same proportion to their total population as in the case of the representatives of British India as a whole, and with the same powers as the British Indian members.

(e) During the critical period which now faces India until the new Constitution can be framed, His Majesty's Government must inevitably bear the responsibility for and retain control and direction of the defence of India as part of their world war effort, but the task of organizing to the full the military, moral, material resources of India must be the responsibility of the Government of India with the cooperation of the people of India. His Majesty's Government desire and invite the immediate and effective participation of the leaders of the principal sections of the Indian people in the councils of their country, of the Commonwealth and of the United Nations. Thus they will be enabled to give their active and constructive help in the discharge of a task which is vital and essential for the future freedom of India.

'QUIT INDIA' RESOLUTION

Resolution of the All-India Congress Committee, Bombay, 8th August, 1942.

The All-India Congress Committee has given the most careful consideration to the reference made to it by the Working Committee in their resolution dated 14th July, 1942 and to subsequent events, including the development of the war situation, the utterances of responsible spokesmen of the British Government, and the comments and criticisms made in India and abroad. The Committee approves of and endorses that resolution and is of the opinion that events subsequent to it have given it further justification, and have made it clear that the immediate ending of British rule in India is an urgent necessity both for the sake of India and for the success of the cause of the United Nations. The continuation of that rule is degrading and enfeebling India and making her progressively less capable of defending herself and of contributing to the cause of world freedom.

The Committee has viewed with dismay the deterioration of the situation of the Russian and Chinese fronts and conveys to the Russian and Chinese people its high appreciation of their heroism in defence of their freedom. This increasing peril makes it incumbent on all those who strive for freedom and who sympathize with the victims of aggression to examine the foundations of the policy so far pursued by the Allied Nations which has led to repeated and disastrous failure. It is not adhering to such aims and policies and methods that failure can be converted into success, for past experience has shown that failure is inherent in them. These policies have been based not on freedom so much as on the domination of subject and colonial countries and the continuation of the imperialist tradition and method. The possession of empire, instead of adding to the strength of the ruling power, has become a burden and a curse. India, the classic land of modern imperialism, has become the crux of the question, for by the freedom of India will Britain and United Nations be judged, and the people of Asia and Africa be filled with hope and enthusiasm.

The ending of British rule in this country is thus a vital and immediate issue on which depends the future of the war and the success of freedom and democracy. A free India will assure this success by throwing all her great resources in struggle for freedom and against the aggression of Nazism, Fascism and Imperialism. This will not only affect materially the fortunes of the war, but will bring all subject and oppressed humanity on the side of the United Nations, and give these nations, whose ally India would be, the moral and spiritual leadership of the world. India in bondage will continue to be the symbol of the British Imperialism and the taint of that imperialism will affect the fortunes of all the United Nations.

The peril of today, therefore, necessitates the independence of India and the ending of British domination. No future promises or guarantees can affect the present situation or meet that peril. They cannot produce the needed psychological effect on the mind of the masses. Only the glow of freedom now can release that energy and enthusiasm of millions of people which will immediately transform the nature of the war.

The All-India Congress Committee, therefore, repeats with all emphasis the demand for the withdrawal of the British power from India. On the declaration of India's independence, a provisional Government will be formed and free India will become an ally of the United Nations, sharing with them in the trials and tribulations of the joint enterprise of the struggle for freedom. The provisional Government can jointly be formed by the cooperation of the principal parties and groups in the country. It will thus be composite Government representative of all important sections of the people of India. Its primary function must be to defend India and resist aggression with all the armed as well as the non-violent forces at its command, together with its Allied powers, and to promote the well-being and progress of the workers in the fields and factories and elsewhere, to whom essentially all power and authority must belong. The provisional Government will evolve a scheme for a Constituent Assembly which will prepare a Constitution for the Government of India acceptable to all. This Constitution, according to the Congress view, should be a federal one, with the largest measure of autonomy for the federating units and with the residuary powers vesting in these units. The future relations between India and the Allied Nations will be adjusted by representatives mutual advantage for their cooperation in the common task of resisting aggression. Freedom will enable India to resist aggression effectively with the people's united will and strength behind it.

The freedom of India must be a symbol of and prelude to the freedom of all other Asiatic nations under foreign domination. Burma, Malaya, Indo-China, the Dutch Indies, Iran, and Iraq must also attain their complete freedom. It must be clearly understood that such of these countries as are under Japanese control now must not subsequently be placed under the rule of control of any colonial power.

While the All–India Congress Committee must primarily be concerned with the independence and defence of India in this hour of danger, the Committee is of the opinion that the future peace, security and ordered progress of the world demand a world federation of free nations, and on no other basis can the problems of the modern world would be solved. Such a world federation would ensure freedom of its constituent nations, the prevention of aggression and exploitation by one nation over another, the protection of national minorities, the advancement of all backward areas and peoples, and the pooling of the world's resources for the common good of all. On the establishment of such a world federation, disarmament would be practiceable in all countries, national armies, navies and air forces would no longer be necessary, and a World Federal Defence Force would keep the world peace and prevent aggression.

An independent India would gladly join such a world federation and cooperation on equal basis with other nations in the solution of international problems.

Such federation should be open to all nations who agree with its fundamental principles. In view of the war, however, the federation must inevitably, to begin with, be confined to the United Nations. Such a step taken now will have most powerful effect on the war, on the peoples of the Axis countries, and on the peace to come.

The Committee regretfully realizes, however, that despite the tragic and overwhelming lessons of the war and the perils that overhang the world, the Governments of few countries are yet prepared to take this inevitable step towards world federation. The reaction of the British Government and the misguided criticism of the foreign Press also make it clear that even the obvious demand for India's independence is resisted; though this has been made essentially to meet the present peril and to enable India to defend herself and help China and Russia in their hour of need. The Committee is anxious not to embarrass in any way the defence of China and Russia, whose freedom is precious and must be preserved, or to jeopardize the defence capacity of the United Nations. But the peril grows both to India and these nations, and inaction and submission to a foreign administration at this stage is not only degrading India and reducing her capacity to defend herself and resist aggression, but is no answer to the growing peril and is no service to the peoples of the United Nations. The earnest appeal of the Working Committee to Great Britain and the United Nations has so far met with no response, and the criticisms made in many foreign quarters have shown an ignorance of India's and the world's need, and sometimes even hostility to India's freedom, which is significant of a mentality of domination and racial superiority which cannot be tolerated by a proud people conscious of their strength and of the justice of their cause.

The All-India Congress Committee would yet again, at this last moment, in the interest of world freedom, renew this appeal to Britain and the United Nations. But the Committee feels that it is no longer justified in holding the nation back from endeavouring to assert its will against an imperialist and authoritarian Government which dominates over it and prevents it from functioning in its own interest and in the interest of humanity. The Committee resolves, therefore, to sanction, for the vindication of India's inalienable right to freedom and independence, the starting of a mass struggle on non-violent lines on the widest possible scale, so that the country might utilize all the non-violent strength it has gathered during the last twenty-two years of peaceful struggle. Such a struggle must inevitable be under the leadership of Gandhiji and the Committee requests him to take the lead and guide the nation in the steps to be taken.

The Committee appeals to the people of India to face the dangers and hardships that will fall to their lot with courage and endurance and to hold together under the leadership of Gandhi, and carry out his instructions as disciplined soldiers of Indian freedom. They must remember that non-violence is the basis of this movement. A time may come when it may not be possible to issue instructions or for instructions to reach our people, and when no Congress Committees can function. When this happens, every man and woman who is participating in this movement must function for himself or herself within the four corners of the general instructions issued. Every Indian who desires freedom and strives for it must be his own guide urging him on along the hard road where there is no resting place and which leads ultimately to independence and deliverance of India.

Lastly, while the All-India Congress Committee has stated its own view of the future governance under free India, the All-India Congress Committee wishes to make it quite clear to all concerned that by embarking on a mass struggle it has no intention of gaining power for the Congress. The power, when it comes, will belong to the whole of India.

APPENDIX III

BRITISH GOVERNMENT'S STATEMENT OF 3 JUNE

1. On February 20th, 1947, His Majesty's Government announced their intention of transferring power in British India to Indian hands by June 1948. His Majesty's Government hoped that it would be possible for the major parties to cooperate in the working out of the Cabinet Mission's Plan of May 16th, 1946, and evolve for India a Constitution acceptable to all concerned. This hope has not been fulfilled.
2. The majority of the representatives of the Provinces of Madras, Bombay, the United Provinces, Bihar, Central Provinces, and Berar, Assam, Orissa and the North-West Frontier Provinces, and the representatives of Delhi, Ajmer-Merwara and Coorg have already made progress in the task of evolving a new Constitution. On the other hand, the Muslim League Party, including in it a majority of the representatives of Bengal, the Punjab and Sind as also the representative of British Baluchistan, has decided not to participate in the Constituent Assembly.
3. It has always been the desire of His Majesty's Government that power should be transferred in accordance with the wishes of the Indian people themselves. This task would have been greatly facilitated if there had been agreement, the task of devising a method by which the wishes of the Indian people can be ascertained has developed upon His Majesty's Government. After full consultation with political leaders in India, His Majesty's Government have decided to adopt for this purpose the plan set out below. His Majesty's Government wish to make it clear that they have no intention

of attempting to frame any ultimate Constitution for India, this is a matter for the Indians themselves nor is there anything in this plan to preclude negotiations between communities for a united India.

4. It is not the intention of His Majesty's Government to interrupt the work of the existing Constituent Assembly. Now that provision is made for certain provinces specified below, His Majesty's Government trust that, as a consequence of this announcement, the Muslim League representatives of those provinces, a majority of whose representatives are already participating in it, will now take their due share in its labour. At the same time it is clear that any Constitution framed by this Assembly cannot apply to those parts of the country which are unwilling to accept it. His Majesty's Government are satisfied that the procedure outlined below embodies the best method of ascertaining the wishes of the people of such areas on the issue whether their Constitution is to be framed,

   (a) in the existing Constituent Assembly; or
   (b) in a new and separate Constituent Assembly consisting of the representatives of those areas which decide not to participate in the existing Constituent Assembly.

When this has been done, it will be possible to determine the authority or authorities to whom power should be transferred.

5. The Provincial Legislative Assemblies of Bengal and the Punjab (excluding the European members) will, therefore, each be asked to meet in two parts one representing the Muslim majority districts and the other the rest of the province. For the purpose of determining the population of districts the 1941 census figures will be taken as authoritative. The Muslim majority districts in these two provinces are set out in the Appendix to this announcement.

6. The members of the two parts of each Legislative Assembly sitting separately will be empowered to vote whether or not the province should be partitioned. If a simple majority of

either part decides in favour of partition, division will take place and arrangement will be made accordingly.

7. Before the question as to partition is decided, it is desirable that the representatives of each part should know in advance which Constituent Assembly the province as a whole would join in the event of the two parts subsequently deciding to remain united. Therefore, if any member of either Legislative Assembly so demands, there shall be held a meeting of all members of the Legislative Assembly (other than Europeans) at which a decision will be taken on the issue as to which Constituent Assembly the province as a whole would join if it were decided by the two parts to remain united.
8. In the event of partition being decided upon, each part of the Legislative Assembly will, on behalf of the areas they represent, decide which of the alternatives in paragraph 4 above to adopt.
9. For the immediate purpose of deciding on the issue of partition, the members of the Legislative Assemblies of Bengal and the Punjab will sit in two parts according to Muslim majority districts (as laid down in the Appendix) and non-Muslim districts. This is only a preliminary step of a purely temporary nature as it is evident that for the purposes of final partition of these provinces a detailed investigation of boundary questions will be needed ; and as soon as decision involving partition has been taken for either provinces a boundary commission will be set up by the Governor-General, the membership and terms of reference of which will be settled in consultation with those concerned. It will be instructed to demarcate the boundaries of the two parts of the Punjab on the basis of ascertaining the contiguous majority areas of Muslims and non-Muslims. It will also be instructed to take into account other factors. Similar instructions will be given to the Bengal Boundary Commission. Until the report of a boundary commission has been put into effect, the provisional boundaries indicated in the Appendix will be used.
10. The Legislative Assembly of Sind (excluding the European

members) will at a special meeting also take its own decision on the alternatives to paragraph 4 above.

11. The position of the North-West Frontier Province is exceptional. Two of the three representatives of the province are already participating in the existing Constituent Assembly. But it is clear, in view of its geographical situation and other considerations, that if the whole or any part of the Punjab decided not to join the existing Constituent Assembly, it will be necessary to give the North-West Frontier Province an opportunity to reconsider its position. Accordingly, in such an event a referendum will be made to the electors of the present Legislative Assembly in the North-West Frontier Province to choose which of the alternatives mentioned in paragraph 4 above they wish to adopt. The referendum will be held under the aegis of the Governor-General in consultation with the provincial Government.
12. British Baluchistan has elected a member, but he has not taken his seat in the existing Constituent Assembly. In view of its geographical situation, this province will also be given an opportunity to reconsider its position and to choose which of the alternatives in paragraph 4 above to adopt. His Excellency the Governor-General is examining how this can most appropriately be done.
13. Though Assam is predominantly a non-Muslim province, the district of Sylhet which is contiguous to Bengal is predominantly Muslim. There has been a demand that in the event of the partition of Bengal, Sylhet should be amalgamated with the Muslim part of Bengal. Accordingly, if it is decided that Bengal should be partitioned, a referendum will be held in Sylhet District under the aegis of the Governor-General and in consultation with the Assam Provincial Government to decide whether the district of Sylhet should continue to form part of Assam Province or should be amalgamated with new province of Eastern Bengal, a boundary commission with terms of reference similar to those for the Punjab and Bengal will be set up to demarcate the Muslim majority areas of Sylhet District and contiguous

Muslim majority areas of adjoining districts, which will then be transferred to East Bengal. The rest of Assam Province will in any case continue to participate in the proceedings of the existing Constituent Assembly.

14. If it is decided that Bengal and the Punjab should be partitioned, it will be necessary to hold fresh elections to choose their representatives on the scale of one for every million of population according to the principle contained in the Cabinet Mission's Plan of May 16, 1946. Similar election will also have to be held for Sylhet in the event of it being decided that this district should form part of East Bengal. The number of representatives to which each area would be entitled is as follows :

Province	*General*	*Muslims*	*Sikhs*	*Total*
Sylhet District	1	2	nil	3
West Bengal	15	4	nil	19
East Bengal	12	29	nil	41
West Punjab	3	12	2	17
East Punjab	6	4	2	12

15. In accordance with the mandates given to them, the representatives of the various areas will either join the existing Constituent Assembly or form the new Constituent Assembly.

16. Negotiations will have to be initiated as soon as possible on the administrative consequences of any partition that may have been decided upon :

(a) Between the representatives and the respective successor authorities about all subjects now dealt with by the Central Government including defence, finance and communications.

(b) Between different successor authorities and His Majesty's Government for treaties in regard to matters arising out of the transfer of power.

(c) In the case of provinces that may be partitioned, as to the administration of all provincial subjects, such as the division of assets and liabilities, the police and other services, the high courts provincial institutions etc.

17. Agreements with tribes of the North-West Frontier of India will have to be negotiated by the appropriate successor authority.
18. His Majesty's Government wish to make it clear that the decisions announced above relate to British India and that their policy towards Indian States contained in the Cabinet Mission's memorandum of 12th May, 1946 remains unchanged.
19. In order that the successor authorities may have time to prepare themselves to take over power, it is important that all the above processes should be completed as quickly as possible. To avoid delay, the different provinces or parts of provinces will proceed independently as far as practicable with the conditions of this plan. The existing Constituent Assembly and the new Constituent Assembly (if formed) will proceed to frame Constitutions for their respective territories; they will, of course, be free to frame their own rules.
20. The major political parties have repeatedly emphasized their desire that there should be the earliest possible transfer of power to India. With this desire His Majesty's Government are in full sympathy and they are willing to anticipate the date of June 1948, for the handing over of power by the setting up of an Independent Indian Government or Governments at an even earlier date. Accordingly, as the most expeditious, and indeed the only practicable way of meeting this desire, His Majesty's Government propose to introduce legislation during current session for the transfer of power this year on a Dominion Status basis to one or two successor authorities according to the decisions taken as a result of this announcement. This will be without prejudice to the right of the Indian Constituent Assemblies to decide in due course whether or not the part of India in respect of which they have authority will remain within the British Commonwealth.

His Excellency of the Governor-General will from time to time make such further announcements as may be necessary in regard to procedure or any other matters for carrying out the above arrangements.

The Muslim majority districts of the Punjab and Bengal according to 1941 (census):

1. THE PUNJAB

LAHORE DIVISION – Gujranwala, Gurdaspur, Lahore, Shikupura, Sialkot.

RAWALPINDI DIVISION – Attock, Gujarat, Jhelum, Mianwali, Rawalpindi, Shahpur.

MULTAN DIVISION – Dera Ghazi Khan, Jhang, Lyallpur, Montgomery, Multan, Muzaffargarh.

CHITTAGONG DIVISION – Chittagong, Noakhali, Tipperah.

DACCA DIVISION – Bakerganj, Dacca, Faridpur Mymensingh.

PRESIDENCY DIVISION – Jessore, Murshidabad, Nadia.

RAJSHAHI DIVISION – Bogra, Dinajpur, Malda, Pabna, Rajshahi, Rangpur.

BIBLIOGRAPHY

Ahluwala, B.K. and Shashi Ahluwala, *Sardar Patel : Rebel and Ruler*, AKBE Group, New Delhi, 1981

Ayer, S.A., *Selected Speeches of Subhas Chandra Bose*, Publications Division, Information and Broadcasting, GOI, 1962

Bharathi, K.S., *The Social Philosophy of Mahatma Gandhi*, Concept Publishing Company, New Delhi, 1991

Bose, Nirmal Kumar, *Selections from Gandhi*, Navjivan Publishing House, Ahmedabad, 1948

– –, *Studies in Gandhism*, Navjivan Publishing House, Ahmedabad, 1972

– –, *My Days with Gandhi*, Nishana, Calcutta, 1953

Bose, Sisir (Ed.) *Netaji and India's Freedom*, Netaji Research Bureau, Calcutta, 1975

Bose, Subhas C., *The Indian Struggle, 1920-1934*, Wishart & Company Ltd, London, 1935

Chakravarty, Sibdas, *Bipin Chandra Pal*, Chalantika Prakashan, Calcutta

Chopra, P.N. (Ed.) *Quit India Movement*, British Secret Documents, Internet, New Delhi, 1986

Collins, Larry and Dominique Lapierre, *Mountbatten and the Partition of India*, Vikas Publishing House Pvt. Ltd., New Delhi 1982

– –, *Freedom at Midnight*, Vikas Publishing House Pvt. Ltd., New Delhi

Edwards, Michael, *Last Years of British India*, The New English Library, 1967

Fischer Louis (Ed.), *The Essential Gandhi*, George Allen and Unwin Ltd., London, 1963

– –, *A Week with Gandhi*, George Allen and Unwin Ltd., London

Gandhi Outlook and Technique, Ministry of Education, GOI, 1953

Gandhi, M.K., *Hind Swaraj*, Navjivan Publishing House, Ahmedabad, 1946

– –, *Speeches and Writings of Mahatma Gandhi*, G.A. Natesan & Company, Madras, 1934

– –, *An Autobiography*, Navjivan Publishing House, Ahmedabad, 1927

– –, *Gandhi's Correspondence with the Government*, Navjivan Publishing House, 1945

Gopal, Sarvepalli, *Jawaharlal Nehru*, Oxford University Press, New Delhi

Gupta, Shanti Swarup, *Economic Philosophy of Mahatma Gandhi*, Concept Publishing Company, New Delhi, 1994

Makers of Modern India, ICHR, New Delhi

Marx and Frederick Engels, *Selected Works*, Progress Publishers, Moscow.

Mosoley, Leonard, *The Last Days of the British Raj*, Jaico Publishing House, Bombay, 1961

Nanda, B.R., *Gokhale,* Oxford Press, Delhi, 1977

– –, *Mahatma Gandhi*, Beacon Press, Boston, 1958

Netaji Collected Works, Netaji Research Bureau, Calcutta

Nehru, J.L., *Selected Works*, Sangam Books, Delhi

– –, *Collection of Speeches*, Publication Division, GOI, New Delhi

– –, *An Autobiography*, Oxford University Press, New Delhi, 1989

– –, *Discovery of India*, Teen Murti House, New Delhi, 1956

Pyarelal, *Mahatma Gandhi: The Last Phase*, Navjivan Publishing House, Ahmedabad, 1965

– –, *Towards New Horizons*, Navjivan Publishing House, Ahmedabad, 1959

Rath, Radhanath and S.B. Chatterjee (Ed.), *Rash Behari Basu*,

RBBS Samiti, Calcutta

Rolland, Roman, *Diary*, December 1921 in Roman Rolland and Gandhian Philosophy, Publication Division, Ministry of Information and Broadcasting, GOI, New Delhi, 1976

– –, *Roman Rolland and Gandhi Correspondence*, Publication Division, Ministry of Information and Broadcasting, GOI, New Delhi, 1976

– –, *Mahatma Gandhi*, Publication Division, Ministry of Information and Broadcasting, GOI, New Delhi, 1965

Selections from Swami Vivekananda, Advaita Ashram, Calcutta, 1981

Shriman Narayan, Gandhian Plan of Economic Development in India, Padma Publication, Bombay, 1944

Tendulkar, D.G., *Gandhi, His Life and Works, Keshav Bhikaji Dhawale*, Bombay, 1944

– –, *Mahatma*, Life of Mohanchand Karamchand Gandhi, GOI, 1969.

– –, *The Collected Works of Mahatma Gandhi*, Publication Division, Ministry of Information and Broadcasting, GOI, New Delhi, 1965

Wolpert, Stanley, *Nehru: A Tryst with Destiny*, Oxford University Press, Delhi.

INDEX